INTIMATE PLAY

Creating Romance
in Everyday Life

WILLIAM BETCHER, M.D., Ph.D.

PENGUIN BOOKS

To Martha, with love

PENGUIN BOOKS
Published by the Penguin Group
Viking Penguin Inc., 40 West 23rd Street,
New York, New York 10010, U.S.A.
Penguin Books Ltd, 27 Wrights Lane,
London W8 5TZ, England
Penguin Books Australia Ltd, Ringwood,
Victoria, Australia
Penguin Books Canada Ltd, 2801 John Street,
Markham, Ontario, Canada L3R 1B4
Penguin Books (N.Z.) Ltd, 182–190 Wairau Road,
Auckland 10, New Zealand

Penguin Books Ltd, Registered Offices:
Harmondsworth, Middlesex, England

First published in the United States of America by
Viking Penguin Inc. 1987

Published in Penguin Books 1988
Copyright © William Betcher, 1987
All rights reserved

Pages 375 and 376 constitute an extension of this copyright page.

LIBRARY OF CONGRESS CATALOGING-IN-PUBLICATION DATA
Betcher, William.
Intimate play.

Bibliography: p.
1. Marriage. 2. Interpersonal relations.
3. Intimacy (Psychology) I. Title.
HQ734.B618   1988   646.7′8   87-25767
ISBN 0-451-82183-1

Printed in the United States of America by
Offset Paperback Mfrs., Inc., Dallas, Pennsylvania
Set in Times Roman

ACKNOWLEDGMENTS

I am grateful to many people who made important contributions to this book. Dr. Joseph Glenmullen was the first to see the value of writing a book of this nature and made important editorial and content suggestions. He also helped edit some of the couple interviews such that they would be succinct and readable. I am especially grateful also to Dr. Jeane Whitehouse and Dr. Rick Michael, who offered many insights into adult play. I feel fortunate indeed to count these three clinicians as my colleagues and dear friends.

The writing of this book really began when I was a graduate student in clinical psychology at Boston University. Dr. Frances Grossman was my first reader for my Ph.D. dissertation on intimate play and helped me focus my thinking in its early stages, and she has continued to be a generous and thoughtful mentor. Dr. George Goethals and Dr. Stuart Pizer have also been important mentors; it is to them that I owe my introduction to British object relations theory. I would also like to thank Dr. Helen Schwartzman and Dr. Lawrence Hartmann for sharing with me some of their thoughts about adult play, and Mr. Roger Rosenblatt of *Time* magazine for helping me to locate some of the famous love letters that appear in the book. Ms. Lorna Forbes and Dr. Carolynn Maltas gave generously of their time to read the final manuscript and made some valuable suggestions.

This book owes much to the efforts of my agent, Ms.

Gail Hochman, of Brandt and Brandt, who believed in this book from the beginning. She has been everything a literary agent should be—a conscientious, intelligent, and constructive critic, a champion of quality, and a friend. My editor at Viking Penguin, Mr. Daniel Frank, has also been a delight to work with. In addition to making many valuable editorial suggestions, he has always supported me in trying to write the kind of book I believe in.

I am indebted to McLean Hospital for providing an atmosphere conducive to independent inquiry; in particular, I would like to thank Dr. Phillip Isenberg, Director of Residency Training, for making it possible for me to complete this book during the course of my internship and residency.

I also owe a debt of gratitude to my patients, my friends, and to the couples who have participated in my research—their willingness to share intimate parts of their lives is a precious gift; I can only hope this book is worthy of them.

Last, I would like to thank my wife, Dr. Martha Markowitz, for her loving care and patience, and for helping to inspire this book.

CONTENTS

Playing
for Keeps

No one needs to be told how to be happy when falling in love. It's something that comes naturally, and one of the blessings of finding that peculiar human chemistry with another person is that you have an enormously freeing sense of being okay, just as you are. Even if you wanted to direct the course of love, it's generally impossible. As one of my friends once put it, it's like trying to steer a runaway truck from the back seat.

But *staying* in love is a lot more difficult. Many would argue that the best you can hope for over time is a quiet kind of loving that is full of care and tenderness but with few fireworks, and that, at worst, love ends in disenchantment. Even couples who feel that they're doing well together tend to feel anxious about their future. Divorce statistics pose a grim challenge to romantic notions of "till death us do part." Part of the problem is that what worked for our parents (or what they thought worked for them) doesn't necessarily work for us, and when you look around for couples who seem to be making it and whom you could emulate, there aren't many good models available. Should we then resign ourselves to the fleeting nature of happiness in our love relationships and, as William Blake so beautifully expressed it, "kiss the joy as it flies"?

I believe in romantic pragmatism, which I would characterize as an outlook born of an equal mixture of hope and experience. Yes, it's very hard to stay intimate with another person for many years and continue to recapture the feeling

1

of wanting to be with each other, of passionately loving the other and choosing him. The romantic in me says that it is possible. The pragmatist reminds me that it takes work, indeed, everything you and your partner have, not the least of which is your sense of play.

Most couples engage in some form of spontaneous play, and I'm not referring to relatively formalized, public forms of recreation, such as tennis and bowling and board games, but rather to joking around, fantasies, rituals, mock fighting, and the private nicknames people invent for each other—types of activity that I call intimate play.

Jean has a tendency to be bossy, a trait she picked up from her father, Harold. She just can't help telling people how to do things at times. When Jean's old boyfriends would confront her about her bossiness, she would get defensive and argumentative, even though deep down she knew it was true. One of the first things she noticed in her relationship with John, to whom she is now married, was that he handled the situation quite differently.

She can still remember the first time she tried to tell him how to go about something: John was helping her cook a meal. He was standing near her at the kitchen counter, peeling the carrots. Jean decided that he was doing the job all wrong and started to tell him how he should do it. John turned to her and leaned back against the counter with a sort of whimsical, knowing look on his face and said, "Yes, Harold." He drew the words out and said them in an exaggerated, joking kind of way. Jean thought this lighthearted reference to the origin of her bossiness was very funny. Instead of getting defensive, she picked up on the joke and began to imitate her father all the more—putting on his accent and pretending to look out over a pair of eyeglasses as her father often did. After they had a good laugh over the incident, the two went back to their work, with Jean providing no more comments on how John should do his share.

Since then, John's expression, "Yes, Harold," has become a signal to Jean that she is tending to become bossy, a characteristic that has greatly decreased since it has been addressed in a non-threatening way.

Richard and Laura are both lawyers. Their jobs are demanding and, while exciting, require long hours and hard work. When they get home after a long day in court and at the office, letters still have to be drafted and cases have to be read. Even on weekends they find it hard to avoid meeting associates or potential clients. As a result, Richard and Laura began taking "special vacations," which have evolved into an annual event.

The vacation is treated like an illicit affair. They tell no one where they are going and always go out of state, where they will not know anyone. They dress up in the evenings, eat out at expensive restaurants, indulge each other in romantic play, and enjoy a lot of creative sex. They keep to themselves and rebuff attempts by other vacationing couples to get to know them. These vacations are so out of the ordinary for them that at the end of each one they jokingly say to one another, "Well, back to your husband," and "Back to your wife." Throughout the year Richard and Laura plan the next vacation elaborately and refer to it with a secretive, illicit air.

Michael and Ann are avid skiers. Much of their free time is spent cross-country skiing, and on weekends they often make the trip north to go downhill skiing. Neither one can remember when they first used their shared nickname, but they are sure it must *have occurred while on a ski trip. They spend a lot of time in their cabin wrapped up in blankets sitting in front of a warm fire. They often wrap themselves together in one big blanket and talk or just watch the fire. At some point one of them began using the expression "snug as a bug in a rug" for the warm feeling of closeness they had on these occasions.*

From this expression came their shared nickname, "Bug." For Michael and Ann, "Bug" now represents the feeling of a private, special world they share whenever they are alone. In fact, they've become so used to calling one another "Bug" that when they are alone and one of them calls the other by his or her own name, it is a sign that something is wrong.

Each of these stories is an example of intimate play, a spontaneous, unique way of relating that each couple creates in accord with its own needs. Equally as important as the specific play activity is the playful attitude with which the activity is approached. Such play tends to be extremely private, and while a particular type may recur over and over as a theme in a relationship, intimate play is always charged with improvisation and creativity. The give-and-take flexibility of Jean and John, the fanciful adventure of Richard and Laura's "illicit affair," and the special, idiosyncratic meanings of Michael's and Ann's nicknames are all characteristic of intimate play. In all these instances the couples discover and share private selves that few, if any, people outside the relationship will ever know. In each case, an underlying care and respect characterize the relationship.

I became interested in intimate play while doing psychotherapy with couples who were struggling to make their relationships work. I had been taught to understand marriage from three perspectives. From psychoanalytic theory I knew that couples relate to each other as if they were significant people from their pasts, and that a therapist needed to help couples become aware of how they unwittingly concealed these unconscious motivations. From behavioral therapists I came to appreciate how behavior that causes trouble in an intimate relationship is learned and is rigidly maintained because it continues to be rewarded. According to the behavioral model, it doesn't matter if a therapist or a couple believes in the unconscious so long as the precise sequence of how partners relate can be described. Put most simply, psychoanalysts are primarily interested in the *why* of behavior and in gut reactions, while behaviorists hone in on what they see couples do—the *how* and the *when*. I had also learned about the family systems model, which, like the behaviorists' theory, prefers to stay in the here and now, but focuses on how couples "talk" to each other in verbal and nonverbal ways. Except for a handful of family therapists, these theories say very little about play.

Watching what seemed to characterize couples who were able to weather crises and improve their relationships, I realized the critical importance of flexibility, a shared sense of humor, and the wisdom embodied in the saying that "we cannot love anybody at whom we never laugh." When I thought about the relationships that had been most special in my own life, I again was struck by the fact that they were full of "intimate play." In talking with friends, I found that they, too, especially cherished this kind of play and that for reasons that were not yet clear to me playfulness seemed to typify healthy, intimate relationships in general. Couples frequently cited their spontaneous play as the aspect that they would miss most if their relationship ended, because it constituted a unique manner of relatedness that could never be the same with anyone else. As one woman told me:

"It is the one clear sign of our feeling of closeness and trust in each other that we feel free to be silly

together. It reaffirms a closeness and sensibility to one another that would be hard to express in any other way—it makes me aware of how relaxed I feel with him and he with me."

It is also clear that some couples use play in destructive ways; for instance, by ridiculing their mates or using humor to avoid difficult issues. In fact, adult play has acquired an unwholesome reputation because of its association with manipulative game playing, as popularized in Eric Berne's *Games People Play.* Play has also become tainted because psychoanalytic theorists have branded it as regression; in their view, couples act childlike because they can't hack it as adults. The value of healthy play has perhaps been overlooked because it has been assumed that *all* play is associated with immaturity and the avoidance of intimacy. In general, play after childhood has been given little attention by psychologists and psychiatrists, who have concentrated more on why relationships *don't* work. If you view play as childish, you may have difficulty believing that it is a good thing and an important part of your relationship, in spite of your own experience. In actual fact, mature individuals do not give up playful ways of relating as they grow older; rather, they continue to elaborate and transform them creatively in accord with their own needs and the needs of their relationship. Rather than analyze couples' individual neuroses, my approach in my research and in this book is to see what playful couples can teach us about emotional health and loving.

There are other reasons why play has previously received less attention from marital researchers and therapists than it deserves. First, since it is by definition very private, intimate play tends not to be discussed beyond the couple and has been relatively inaccessible to psychotherapists, who normally have access to many areas of private life. As one training analyst confided to me, "There are some things you don't even tell your analyst." I had to interview a number of couples repeatedly and in great detail as well as use anonymous questionnaires in order to circumvent this reticence. Even so, people were often shy. As one put it,

> "I wish I could be really specific, but I just can't expose myself that much. When I first saw this questionnaire I became suddenly aware of the play that we do engage in and became very self-conscious about it for a while, as though someone were watching me! It is so personal that writing down some of the things we say and the way we say them would be humiliating. Sorry."

Second, even people who play a lot may not be aware of it. Like dreams, play is often rich in irrational ideas and images and quickly slips into the unconscious. During my research I very often found that couples had engaged in some play that they had thought of telling me about but in the time between interviews they had *forgotten* what it was!

My experience in researching intimate play over the last eight years is that it is too elusive for statistics to be meaningful. Certain kinds of play can be quantified, such as how many times couples play tennis or board games: the more conventional and rulebound the play, the easier it is to identify. Intimate play, however, is characterized more by an attitude than by a specific activity—you can be playful building a house, and you can also turn sexual foreplay into routinized work. My definition of play includes fantasy, the play of the imagination, and states of mind in which two people are relaxed enough to let go and see what happens. You would do better to think of intimate play as "playfulness" rather than to categorize it in terms of the activities that you may be accustomed to regard as play.

If so diffuse a concept as intimate play cannot be formally studied, how can you prove its value? Marital research is faced with a similar problem, because the ultimate test of the efficacy of marital therapy or a "successful" marriage doesn't lie in its ability to be measured statistically: one person's marital satisfaction would be another's justification for divorce. What I have to offer is more in the way of concepts than facts. Much of what I have learned about intimate play came by way of a small number of couples whom I have studied in depth and by indirect means such as anonymous questionnaires. I have not studied "gay" relationships, but I expect that much of this book applies as well to same-sexed couples.*

Each of the chapters will show how playfulness can improve the quality of a couple's relationship and will provide illustrations drawn from couples studied in research and from couples in psychotherapy. In Chapter 1 I touch on the other sources of support for the theory of intimate play. These ideas will not be as immediately applicable to your relationship as the material in other chapters, but you will be much more apt to experiment with play in your relationship if you understand the theory behind the technique.

I've found that it's impossible to write a book about something as personal as intimate play without bringing myself into the telling. My ideas about play are shaped not just by my professional training but by my own history and psychological make-up. For instance, as children my best friend and I were continually creating new ways to play with each other, such as a tackle football game played on our knees in my parents' apartment in New York City. My friend had an ancient Wollensak tape recorder, and we made up ghost stories and taped "interviews" with famous monsters such as Frankenstein ("How do you feel about your mother?") and created parodies of quiz programs. In later years we'd go to Central Park and play wiffle ball,

*For a more in-depth theoretical discussion of the concept of intimate play, please see R. William Betcher, "Intimate Play and Marital Adaptation," *Psychiatry,* Vol. 44, February 1981, pp. 13-33.

our rival teams made up of colorful fantasy characters such as Juan Dominguez, the Dominican screwball artist, and Rocky Sampson, the fabled slugger. As an adult my play continues:

> *I'm playing left field in a pickup softball game. There's a spaciousness to left field, a sense of wide open freedom, yet of being close enough to hear and see everything that's going on. I pound my glove as the hitter steps in. He connects—the ball is rising quickly on a steep arc down the left field line. He's really kissed this one, but I think I have a chance, and I'm on my horse, legs pumping as I track the ball against the sky. I'm closing now but the ball's still alive, barely descending now. It's right above me, huge, as I reach up. I extend backhand as far as I can, my final lunge making me lose sight of it at the last instant. Then a beautiful "thwap" as the ball enters the webbing.*

I've replayed that scene many times in my mind since it happened—my friend and I joke about our mutual tendency to have "highlight films" of great sports plays we've made that we can fantasize about while driving to work or sitting in boring staff meetings. I love to fantasize. In this example it's sports hype that I use as an escape, but my fantasy life is also something that I've learned to share in my intimate relationships. For reasons of privacy I, like all the other people described in this book, have my identity disguised, but some of the vignettes come from my own life. For me, loving and playing are intimately related. This book is about both and also about marriage. It celebrates an ideal of what intimacy can be and the opportunity for its realization.

Like many people who went to college during the sixties, I am nostalgic for those times' erratic idealism and social experimentation. I remember joking years ago that I might eventually wind up as an aging hippie—the kind I saw at peace marches, with love beads and an oversized peace symbol around their necks. But my commemoration of that time of my life has taken another form. It's not a delapidated Volvo or a pair of old bluejeans with an embroidered mandala that's worth preserving from those times but the spirit of discovery, and a reverence for freedom and intimacy.

Learning to Play

Prior to the second presidential debate in 1984 President Reagan was considered vulnerable on the issue of his advanced age. During the debate he quipped, "I will not make age an issue in this campaign. I am not going to exploit, for political purposes, my opponent's youth and inexperience." This response stood the concern about his own age on its head and effectively defused the whole issue. A similar coup was scored by Walter Mondale during the Democratic presidential debates when he attacked the substance of Hart's "new ideas" by echoing the hamburger commercial slogan "Where's the beef?" Humor, like other forms of play, has impact and can be used to sidestep issues, to manipulate another person, or to gain the upper hand in a struggle of wills, just as it can be used to foster good feelings in a relationship. The purpose of this book is to make clear how intimate play can serve as a defense or to promote personal growth in your relationships.

There is a fundamental paradox in attempting to teach people how to play, similar to the irony inherent in sexual enrichment guides: how can you self-consciously try to be more spontaneous? I have always been dubious about the value of self-help guides that offer global prescriptions; I don't believe that any one pattern, no matter how well tailored, can fit everyone. Further, emotional growth requires a relationship, whether with a therapist or with a partner in a fortuitous friendship or love relationship. We all learn best through experience and with loving assistance. No book can help you work through the subtle and tenacious resistances to change that yield slowly only to skillful psychotherapy. But sometimes it helps to be reminded about what you already know, or to be given a new perspective about what you thought you already knew. In the English language we have a dearth of words for describing play, and just as the Eskimos have many words for "snow" and none for "time," the types of words we have can determine our experience. My hope is to help you recognize different types of intimate play so that you can see an important facet of your relationship more clearly. I don't believe you can really teach people how to play, just as you can't teach sexual responsiveness. But you can learn to minimize the obstacles to healthy play and to foster conditions most conductive to its occurrence.

The sequence of chapters is chronological and problem-centered, consistent with the natural arc of a couple's relationship. This book is meant for couples who basically are doing all right but who either want to hold onto the joy or think they can do better. My hope for you is not simply to adjust smoothly and handle the tasks of adult development, but to grow in accord with your own self-chosen goals. This is a kind of relationship more often wished for than encountered. It requires nothing less than the courage to face all the difficulties of an intimate relationship and to explore the hidden corners of your emotional lives. I trust that you will find that your psychological universe is not flat—you need never reach the end of exploring or drop off the edge into some emotional abyss. You will not be alone: intimate play invites collaboration.

The examples of play and exercises for couples contained in this book are not intended as models but as ideas to try out en route to defining your own style of play. You may find that some of the examples make you uncomfortable and others may seem silly. Such reactions are understandable because the specific forms of play and the issues people play about are different for each couple. For example, one couple may do a lot of play about money problems, while another couple would not because they either feel too sensitive about money or because they have no problems in this area. That is, play tends to emerge around aspects of people's lives where *moderate* tensions exist. Further, play styles are so individualized that, just as with dreams, play may only feel right and make sense to the person involved. My sense is that even with those examples that feel foreign to you, they may help you reflect on the play that you already do. The best play is the kind that emerges out of the unique way you and your partner relate to each other.

Years ago I was fortunate to have a wise photography teacher whose first assignment was to have her students photograph light, with the one requirement being that we not leave our homes. "If you can't see it there," she said, "you won't see it anywhere." I hope you will approach this book similarly, as a dynamic aid to be incorporated into your daily life, rather than as merely something to tack onto your relationship, like a new addition to the house or an extra vacation. Intimate play is the play of everyday life. The secret is only to recognize it.

CHAPTER ONE

Steps toward
a Theory of
Intimate Play

The ancient Greeks personified love in two ways; as Aphrodite, a surpassingly beautiful and lusty goddess; and as Eros, a mischievous boy with golden wings whose arrows could turn Stoic philosophers into dirty old men. While Eros's playfulness at times provokes more sober deities, who grumble about his irresponsibility, his magic is as powerful as it is capricious. What intrigues me, however, is that Grecian mythology should associate playfulness so closely with the phenomenon of human love. Thus it is clear that intimate play was celebrated in antiquity, and to appreciate the importance of play in marriage is to rediscover old truths rather than invent them anew. Evolution has lessons to teach us about play, and so do human children; we also need to follow the twists and turns of a modern mythology—psychoanalytic theory—as the heirs of Freud have come to see play as a friendly ally of maturity.[1]

Animal Play

You will not find animals engaging in intimate play— true, young primates playfully mount each other and thrust, practicing sexual behaviors that they will perform as adults, but animal courtship is generally not playful at all: an amorous animal relentlessly pursues his goal without any funny business. Yet the ways that animals play when not involved in fornication or finding their next dinner can still teach us something about the more complex human forms of play.

Young domestic cats will delight indefinitely in a paper bag or a piece of string and will endlessly pounce, wrestle, or chase each other. Ravens will hang upside down from their perches, play balancing games on branches, and slide down polished surfaces; badgers and mongooses somersault, otters spend hours playing with a rubber ball, and dolphins surf, waiting, like beachbums, outside of breakers to catch the best waves in toward shore. It is not only domesticated animals or wild animals in captivity that play, as Konrad Lorenz makes clear in his poetic description of jackdaws playing in high winds:

> At first sight, you . . . think that the storm is play-ing with the birds, like a cat with a mouse, but soon you see, with astonishment, that it is the fury of the elements that here plays the role of the mouse and that the jackdaws are treating the storm exactly as the cat its unfortunate victim. Nearly, but only nearly, do they give the storm its head, let it throw them high, high into the heavens, till they seem to fall upwards, then, with a casual flap of a wing, they turn them-selves over, open their pinions for a fraction of a second from below against the wind, and dive—with an acceleration far greater than that of a falling stone —into the depths below. Another tiny jerk of the wing and they return to their normal position and, on close-reefed sails, shoot away with breathless speed into the teeth of the gale . . . playfully and without effort. . . .[2]

There is always the danger of anthropomorphism in de-scribing animal play. How indeed can animals be said to play at all since they clearly do not "work," in our usual sense of the term? The very real pitfalls of too readily drawing parallels to human characteristics from animal be havior are exemplified by one nineteenth-century observer who, upon seeing bacteria under his microscope jump and spin about, concluded that this constituted a playful dance. Similarly, for a long time it was believed that some species of fish played since it appeared that they jumped over stones for no intrinsic reason. It turned out that this "play" is really a means for such fish to scrape off parasites. My own tendency to anthropomorphize my cat was pointed out once by a friend who is a naturalist. I had always been endeared to Tuna by her affectionately greeting me by rub-bing up against my leg. My friend pointed out that cats have scent glands at the sides of their eyes and tip of their tail and when rubbing up against things are leaving their scent. His reassurance that "She probably does love you, anyway" didn't entirely assuage my feelings. But we also shouldn't require exact equivalence between animal and human behaviors before we admit to any kinship. Any owner of a dog will tell you that his pet's direct invitation to play is unmistakable. Our responsiveness to such whimsy is proof of our playful cousinage.

There is also a definite relationship between how much any species plays and the sophistication of its brain. Dino-saurs, for instance, played less than primates. Although no one has as yet advanced a theory that dinosaurs became extinct because they had a terrible sense of humor or a seven-day work week, the implication is that play may be exceedingly adaptive. One may ask if it actually does chimpanzees any good, for instance, when they chase each other for what appears to be no reason:

During a serious chase, the pursuer rarely takes his eyes off the pursued animal. His fur is erect and bristling, his lips are pursed and protrude in the ag-gressive manner. His movements are rapid and economical; if he catches the animal he is pursuing, the sequence of events will be snatch, grab, pull-towards-mouth and bite, at whatever portion of the offender is most readily available. . . .

A play-chase, on the other hand, takes place at an altogether different tempo. The initiator may approach another animal by walking or trotting towards him with a highly characteristic bounce to the gait; the head bobs up and down, his gaze may not be directed at the animal he approaches, he is often wearing the playface, and soft guttural exhalations may be audible. (The playface is a special expression indicating playful intent in which only the lower teeth show. It appears to occur most often at the beginning of a playful interaction, the point at which it is most necessary to avoid being misunderstood.) As he reaches the animal he is approaching and gains his attention he turns around and makes off at a slow lolloping pace in the opposite direction, looking back over his shoulder to see if the other animal is following. . . . A play-chase may occur in one direction only, or pursuer and pursued may switch roles several times in the course of a few minutes. . . . If a play-chase ends in direct contact (not by any means inevitable), play-wrestling may occur, different from the grab-pull-bite sequence of the serious fight both in intensity and in the order of this particular sequence. Pulling alone may occur, or a great deal of biting of each other's fingers or toes, or of the area between the neck and the shoulder.[3]

Far from being irrelevant activity, such play may enable animals to become adept at complex behaviors by practicing their component parts. More intriguing is the probability that in play animals experiment with new behavioral sequences. It is possibly a counterpart to the reassortment of chromosomes and random mutation during sexual reproduction, by which genetic variability is assured and adaptive evolutionary serendipity occurs. (A technological parallel might be the maneuvers that a new aircraft is put through in order to generate information about its performance and characteristics—while inefficient in terms of fuel and time, such "playing around" in the long run helps improve design.) In addition to a flexibility of behavior, animal play also involves a flexibility of attention that enables the creature to take in a maximal amount of information about its environment. More highly developed animals seek out mild degrees of novelty—curiosity may occasionally kill the cat, but in the evolutionary scheme it has enabled curious species to prevail.

As dinosaurs have give way to apes, survival has been increasingly geared away from fixed patterns toward a flexible relationship with the environment that requires considerable learning and not just genetics. Instead of reacting automatically to a stimulus in the environment, such as the way a bull charges a red flag, the later developing animals rely on a less focused, playful attentiveness to a wide range of stimulation. Here then may lie the explanation of why playfulness increases with evolutionary level. Play is inherently creative and helps develop a flexible behavioral repertoire. *Could it be, then, that the play of intimate couples is an equivalent evolutionary process, that it provides a safe, adaptive means by which adults can experiment with creative, flexible ways of relating?*

Primate play, like intimate play, is helpful in relationships: young monkeys learn how to get along with their peers through play: they practice grooming, sexual behavior, and test the limits of hierarchical dominance. Primate play also serves to help control aggression, as described earlier in the play-chase of chimpanzees. In play, serious predatory behavior is practiced and aggressive behavior toward peers permitted, but they are kept within safe bounds. As the psychologist Jerome Bruner points out, every species must develop a system of mutuality.[4] Our structured games, such as boxing and tennis, may similarly channel strife toward coexistence. It's completely compatible with a close friendship to want to figuratively whip the ass of your squash partner, and sports have been a highly ritualized way, particularly for males, to sublimate aggression and feel "safe" to make physical contact. Similarly, as we will see demonstrated by couples in later chapters, *intimate play fosters mature relationships in which tenderness, passion, and muted hostility can coexist*. There is also a lesson for us in that animals do not play when predators are in the vicinity. Primate play occurs only in an atmosphere of familiarity, when basic survival needs are satisfied, and in situations in which the possible consequences of trying out new behaviors are minimized. *Adult intimate play may provide similar cumulative contributions toward a secure relationship that can freely allow experimentation*.

In the example of the play-chase of chimpanzees, reference was made to the playface, one of the ritualized signals by which a message indicating "I'm just kidding," is communicated. "Mouthing" instead of biting is another such signal. The anthropologist Gregory Bateson was intrigued by such communications. If an animal was able to communicate directly with us, he might say, "Although it looks like I'm biting you, keep cool. I'm doing it nicely so that you know I don't want to bite and that I don't want to fight." Play signals, in other words, establish a frame around behaviors, clearly designating them as "pretend." I mention Bateson's observations because in animal play we see once again the foreshadowing of functions served by intimate play: *play constitutes a special form of communication and allows for the simultaneous expression of apparently mutually contradictory messages*. In the next example, for instance, a couple pairs a serious message with an intimate way of communicating it, so that a creative shift in their thinking occurs.

After their landlord doubled their rent, Richard and Eliza had struggled for months about whether to stay in their apartment or buy a condominium.

*"Richard is very anxious about buying anything,"
says Eliza, "but with so many of our friends having
bought their own places and property values going
out of sight, I felt that we were being left behind.
One evening, while we were going over our finances
for what seemed like the tenth time, I realized I was
fed up with the whole thing. After our last heated
argument, I just wasn't up for another fight. Then
Richard leaned over toward me and whispered in my
ear something about mortgage rates. I then whispered something back in his ear. It was so incongru-
ous, having a serious discussion about buying
property while whispering like lovers or little kids,
that we both had to laugh. We went on like this for a
while and for the first time in a long while made
some movement toward a decision."*

Children's Play

We take for granted that children play. It is the child who
does not play who worries us, leading parents to run for the
thermometer of a psychiatrist. But what are children doing
when they play, and is their play similar at all to that of
animals or to adult intimate play? I find it striking that
despite the vast differences in cognitive equipment between
children and other primates there is still so much in common. For example, almost identical patterns of play fighting and chasing occur in children as ethologists have
described in rhesus monkeys. Further, as with animals,
children's play is closely associated with social interaction:
the first stage of peer social contact is the simultaneous
exploration of common objects, and peer interaction continues to characterize children's play thereafter. In fact,
children will often create imaginary playmates when no
real ones are available.

There are enough theories of children's play to satisfy

anyone's philosophic inclinations. Psychoanalysts see play as a compulsion to repeat upsetting events and as a safe way of partially satisfying instinctual cravings; existentialists see the creative upsurge of human freedom, and ethologists stress the child's need to explore his environment and to seek stimulation. In fact, as Piaget suggested, all theories of play are probably correct since play can serve all purposes. But, recognizing that in making comparisons between children's and adults' play we are dealing in metaphors and not in statistical fact, certain observations may serve as stepping stones toward a theory of intimate play.

Practice, Practice, Practice

Little girls and boys often look as if they are practicing to be adults, as Mark Twain described in *Tom Sawyer:*

> He was eating an apple, and giving a long, melodious whoop, at intervals, followed by a deep-toned ding-dong-dong, ding-dong-dong, for he was personating a steamboat. As he drew near, he slackened speed, took the middle of the street, leaned far over to starboard and rounded to ponderously and with laborious pomp and circumstance—for he was personating the *Big Missouri,* and considered himself to be drawing nine feet of water. He was boat and captain and engine-bells combined, so he had to imagine himself standing on his own hurricane-deck giving the orders and executing them:
> "Stop the stabboard! Ting-a-ling-ling! Stop the labboard! Come ahead on the stabboard! Stop her! Let your outside turn over slow! Ting-a-ling-ling! Chow-ow-ow! Get out that head-line! *Lively* now! Come—out with your spring-line—what're you about there! Take a turn round that stump with the bight of it! Stand by that stage, now—let her go!

Done with the engines, sir! Ting-a-ling-ling! *Sh't!
sh't! sh't!*" (trying the gauge-cocks).

In Mark Twain's time, boys played at being steamboat captains, now both boys and girls might instead imagine they are astronauts. The roles chosen are culturally mediated, but the anticipation of some kind of adult activity is a consistent theme. Here children's and adults' play part company, for although some adults look as if they could use some remedial help, theoretically at least they don't need to pretend to be doctors, mothers, fathers, and firemen. Nevertheless, in intimate play, future possibilities in a relationship are anticipated and enacted. *Adult play may be a form of rehearsal in which the stakes of failure are lessened because all moves are tentative and awkwardness is understood.*

Mark Twain's steamboat captain also teaches us that while children's play may indeed involve elements of practice, it usually encompasses much more than that. The child is not methodically imitating an adult; he is using his creative imagination.

The Pleasure Principle

The extent of our ignorance about the nature of play is revealed in the fact that we don't entirely know *why* play is fun. The most simple truth is that children and adults (and perhaps animals as well) play because it is fun. Much of the joy of play is that you don't have to be productive, make sense, or in fact be doing anything at all. That is, play is pleasurable because, as with many dreams, it often involves wish fulfillment. Adults, just as children, are not bound by reality in their play. You can, at least in fantasy, be and do anything you desire. Children go through developmental stages in how they go about having fun, starting with solitary activity and moving on to parallel play, in which they are side by side but not interacting. Finally, children do truly play jointly with other kids. What concerns me is that so many adults go about having fun in a solitary or parallel fashion. On a recent vacation I met a couple in which the husband had spent every day playing golf while his wife took the kids to the beach (solitary play). He then rented a wind-sail for the afternoon, which he sailed around the bay while his wife read a novel on shore (parallel play). The wife commented to me that she had spent less time with her husband on this vacation than she usually did at home.

Another common leisure pattern that is averse to mutual intimate play is jogging. Runners will leave their spouses at home while they ecstatically mellow out on the endorphins spewed into their bloodstream. They return spent, too tired to make love, and with their relationship not at all enriched by this solitary form of fun, which can best be called aerobic masturbation. Their willingness to endure painful orthopedic insults likewise merits the name self-abuse.

The message is that for many people it's a lot easier to have fun by yourself than it is to have fun in a way that brings you and your partner closer together. We all need to have our own world of play apart from our partners—one of you may like to play tennis, the other prefers to do crossword puzzles. But your relationship will stay healthier if your play is sometimes intimate.

Beyond the Pleasure Principle

Freud was a very keen observer of behavior and the strength of his theoretical contributions lies in their being based on carefully detailed clinical description, as in this famous case, from *Beyond the Pleasure Principle,* written in 1919. Here Freud describes a game invented and played by a one-and-a-half-year-old boy:

At the same time, he was greatly attached to his mother, who had not only fed him herself but had also looked after him without any outside help. This good little boy, however, had an occasional disturbing habit of taking any small objects he could get hold of and throwing them away from him into a corner, under the bed, and so on, so that hunting for his toys and picking them up was often quite a business. As he did this he gave vent to a loud, long-drawn-out "o-o-o-o," accompanied by an expression of interest and satisfaction. His mother and the writer of the present account were agreed in thinking that this was not a mere interjection but represented the German word *fort* [gone]. I eventually realized that it was a game and that the only use he made of any of his toys was to play "gone" with them. One day I made an observation which confirmed my view. The child had a wooden reel with a piece of string tied round it. It never occurred to him to pull it along the floor behind him, for instance, and play at its being a carriage. What he did was to hold the reel by the string and very skillfully throw it over the edge of his curtained cot, so that it disappeared into it, at the same time uttering his expressive "o-o-o-o." He then pulled the reel out of the cot again by the string and hailed its reappearance with a joyful *da* [there]. This, then, was the complete game—disappearance and return. As a rule one only witnessed its first act, which was repeated untiringly as a game in itself, though there is no doubt that the greater pleasure was attached to the second act.

The interpretation of the game then became obvious. It was related to the child's great cultural achievement—the instinctual renunciation . . . which he had made in allowing his mother to go away without protesting. He compensated himself for this, as it

were, by himself staging the disappearance and return of the objects within his reach.[5]

Thus children's play is sometimes an active attempt to
master some distressing event in which the child had essentially played a passive role (that is, the one who is acted
upon, rather than the one acting). In Freud's case the
child's game of making his toy appear and disappear repeated his loss of mother in such a way that he felt he
could magically control the experience. Freud saw in this a
fundamental law of psychic life—we are sometimes motivated not just by hedonism but by a compulsion to repeat
painful experiences. Simply put, we live by the old adage
"If at first you don't succeed, try, try again." Both in children and in adults, play is especially suited to such re-
working of old problems. Just as in sleep the doors to our
unconscious are left unlocked, so, too, in play is there
greater flexibility and access to fantasy. Our emotional
lives are never putty that we can mold at will, yet in
dreams and play some shifts along our fault lines can
occur. But context is terribly important. As we have seen,
animals play only under conditions of physical safety, and
the child will feel free to play only when he trusts that he is
psychologically safe. Much of the magic of childplay therapy consists simply of this: of an adult's establishing the
secure conditions under which play can take place. *Adult
intimate relationships pose similar opportunities for integration of painful experiences from the past if partners are
able to give each other leeway to play.*

In Remembrance of Play Past

While as adults we may forget how to play or we may
allow ourselves to suppress our playful sides out of some
sense that maturity requires such a sacrifice, playful ways
of relating may simply lie dormant and can be reactivated
in our current love relationship. As a child I shared a bed-

room with my older brother. The room was a bit small, especially so since our feelings for each other included wishes to destroy, pulverize, and mutilate. We would stay up late into the night, exchanging humorous, insulting names, such as Freeloader and Pluck-a-duck. It was one of the more benign outlets for our intense rivalry and also provided some of our rare moments of intimacy. In my adult love relationships, I found myself using the same kinds of nicknames. Similarly, one of the husbands that I interviewed during my research recalled cherished childhood antecedents to his playful "goosing" of his partner— his grandfather had engaged in very similar coarse joking and innocent touching with him.

The playful ways we related as children can enhance our ways of reaching out as adults. Our intimate past may indeed be prologue, with play a tangible link between old and new cherished relationships.

Beyond Freud's Dualities

Sigmund Freud believed that emotional health is a precarious achievement gained by walking a middle road of compromise between instinctual gratification, and the restraints imposed by civilization and internalized in the form of the superego. This delicate balance is highly vulnerable to disruption by the slithering desires of the "id," which cares not a whit for high ideals or whether it will be respected in the morning—pleasure is its only goal and damn the consequences. But, distinct from pterodactyls, coelacanths, and saber-toothed tigers, man also has an ego, which reins in the id's constant grab for gratification in order that there be opportunity for composing symphonies, erecting office buildings, and reading the Sunday *New York Times*. Freud compared the ego's relation to the id as being like a man on horseback, who struggles to control the superior strength of the horse. Fortunately, the puny ego has a Draconian ally to control the id—the superego—but it, too, cannot be allowed too free a hand. Like a politician faced with the problem of urban unrest, the ego wants neither too permissive nor too repressive a state, for the id, like revolutions, cannot be stamped out. In Freud's elegant terms, "The wish unfulfilled breeds pestilence."

Freud's conception of mental processes was similarly dualistic, with irrational, more primitive modes of thought, such as those apparent in dreams ("primary process"), coexisting with the later developing, rational "secondary" processes. The essence of Freud's therapeutic contribution, still the cornerstone of analysis, is the technique of free association, by which the patient says whatever comes to mind, without censorship or deliberate design. In a sense the ego and its cohort of propriety and reason is invited to have tea while Pandora's box is cautiously opened to reveal our inner demons. Because the balance of psychic forces is thus voluntarily and temporarily tipped toward developmentally more primitive functioning, Freud termed this "regression." But his followers realized that Mozart could never have composed symphonies nor Blake written poems without "regression." Such free form, playful states, in which we are enriched by greater access to fantasy and irrational thinking came to be described as *adaptive* regression.

Still, the concept of regression, which was born from clinical observation of very disturbed people, may obscure as many subtleties as it reveals when applied to healthy play. It makes too much of adult play's roots in childhood and insinuates that there's something backward and immature about it. I have often wished that I could have met Freud and shared some good cigars over a fireside chat. But I find it difficult to imagine *playing* with him—love and work were what he considered to be the two main spheres of adaptation, and there is little mention in his writings of just having a good time. Although there is a less dour, Calvinist cast to our thinking in this era of hot tubs, Club Med, and the four-day week, I think we are still prone to associating play with mere escape and qualifying it as something lesser than more "serious" pursuits.

Play cannot be categorized as either primary or secondary process thinking, nor can it be subsumed under love or work. In play we can become totally absorbed; does this mean we are serious or nonserious while playing? In play we fantasize and pretend, allowing our imaginations to shape what surrounds us; is this process "inner" or "outer," and is an activity "real" or "unreal" when what we pretend on one occasion becomes enacted "for real" the next? I believe that no one really knows the answers to these questions, for in its very essence play cannot be understood through our accustomed dualities.

The Theory of Intimate Play

The British psychoanalyst D. W. Winnicott has aptly called play an intermediate realm of experience that "is always on the theoretical line between the subjective and that which is objectively perceived."[6] To Winnicott play is vital to adults because we are always struggling to relate our inner and outer realities, a task that by definition can never be complete. Play provides a psychological haven in which inner and outer realities can merge, and creative integrations be conceived. It must always remain a chimera, because we need chimera just as much as we need self-evident truths.

Couples need chimeras even more than individuals, because they are constantly trying to reconcile *two* sets of inner and outer realities. I am not suggesting you practice duplicity or self-deceit but that you learn to tolerate ambiguity, to explore personal meanings, and provide for each other the leeway to experiment. Play does not just mean flexibility but a state of being that allows for the coexistence of many and even contradictory realities. In any relationship that involves commitment, two people are simultaneously relating in dynamic ways on many levels, only some of which are conscious. Inevitably, tensions arise, not only because we are two separate individuals with different needs, but also because each of us struggles with our own emotional contradictions. We wish to be independent, yet we yearn for closeness; we seek a reassuring sense of sameness and security, but we also want to keep the spark of romance alive. At each stage of the relationship a variety of dualities must be reconciled, and play can help couples to invent creative solutions. In each case, successful coping requires a balancing act, a blending of the two psychological forces or needs rather than rigid opting for either extreme. Intimate play is ideally suited to the holding together of apparently mutually exclusive alternatives. It embodies the flexibility and humor that couples must cultivate in order to reconcile conflicting needs.

Our behavior is ruled in far greater degree than we would like to think by our early hopes and fears. But adult play is not just a reawakening of childhood ways of relating, nor is intimate play characterized solely by a compulsion to repeat or a nostalgic attempt to reconnect with the past. Play can be backward-looking, but *new* patterns and meanings are also created. The psychiatrist Harry Stack Sullivan wrote that throughout our lives opportunities for new integrations and adaptations present themselves. Playing together with a loving partner is one such opportunity.

Freud's emphasis of the id—our Neanderthal craving for sex and aggression—obscures a more fundamental motivation: to sustain a nurturing *relationship*. We need human contact, we need to huddle together emotionally, just as our ancestors in their caves needed to huddle together physically. Similarly, couples playing together may at times be releasing frustrations or commencing a seduction, but as this book will show, playing may also serve quite sophisticated noninstinctual ends, helping to bend your relationship to the purpose of emotional growth. One of the things that people seek in a long-term relationship is someone with whom they can feel free to express normally suppressed behavior. What is most important to us is not that our instincts be discharged, but that we have *someone who can accept* these hidden parts of ourselves. The British marital theorist H. V. Dicks describes this best:

> Marriage is the nearest adult equivalent to the original parent-child relationship. Thus its success must revolve round the freedom to regress. The freedom to bring into the adult relation the deepest elements of infantile object-relations is a condition of growth. To be able to regress to mutual child-like dependence, in flexible role exchanges, without censure or loss of dignity, in the security of knowing that the partner accepts because he or she can projectively identify with, or tolerate as a good parent this "little needy ego" when it peeps out—this is the promise people seek when they search for the one person who will be unconditionally loving, permissive and strong—who will enable one to fuse all part-object relations into a meaningful whole and be enhanced by it.[7]

Intimate play is one of the ways that couples bring into the relationship the deepest parts of themselves: through playing with another you learn how to approach your partner's most intimate self. Playing is a reconnoitering of the unknown borders of your two psyches, whose contours can become reassuringly familiar only through the experience of mutual vulnerability and nonjudgmental responsiveness.

Intimate play requires a risk—there is always the possibility that in revealing an ordinarily suppressed part of yourself, your partner will not be accepting. In any self-disclosure that winds up licensing you to be more fully yourself with another person, your recognition of the risk of vulnerability may make you fearful of the outcome. Taking a risk is the price of having a truly intimate relationship, and while sometimes you may feel awkward or have your feelings bruised, more often both you and your partner will feel more alive.

I believe that more and more people are seeking relationships involving serious commitments. They don't want to be an "I," but a "we." You, too, may find yourself returning to more traditional values, but you are probably looking for something more exciting than mere security. Human beings are not solely driven to reduce tension; they also are attracted to risk-taking and mild fear. I am reminded of the movie *Casanova 70* in which Marcello Mastroianni plays a man who must endanger his life in order to feel sexual passion. This leads him into a series of comic, adrenaline-pumping escapades, until finally it appears that he has settled down to domestic bliss. In the final scene, as his wife waits in bed expectantly, Mastroianni washes up next door in the bathroom. Having readied himself, he opens up the window and begins to navigate the narrow ledge connecting the two rooms, with the street many stories below.

We all need excitement and novelty in our love relationships. Intimate play is a way of keeping that spark alive.

CHAPTER TWO

Starting a Relationship: Romantic Play

Love is a word very much like play, in that its promiscuous relationships—from "I love my Volvo" to "Love it or leave it" to "Love is a secondhand emotion"—have robbed it of its individuality; like the prostitute, love can always accommodate, but it can no longer react. To be sure, we still venerate her much-abused charms, but the word has lost the power to inform. Love is like the generalist, who can tell us less and less about more and more until he says nothing about everything. In 1786, in Mozart's *The Marriage of Figaro,* Cherubino wonders, *"Che cosa è amor?"* ("What is this thing called love?") As of 1956 Frankie Lymon and the Teenagers were still asking a similar existential question:

> Oo-wah, oo-wah, oo-wah, oo-wah,
> Why do fools fall in love?
> Why do birds sing so gay
> And lovers await the break of day?
> Why do they fall in love?
> Why does the rain fall from above?
> Why do fools fall in love?
> Why do they fall in love?

I will start, then, with the beginning of a relationship, when you first feel attracted to someone, and see how romantic love prepares the way for more mature love. Couples play a lot when getting to know each other, and it may

31

be that this other overworked word can help us understand a few things about the early steps toward intimacy.

Love Magic

Anthropologists investigating so-called primitive cultures described a curious type of courtship, which they called love magic. For example, the would-be suitor (almost always the male) might throw pebbles at the girl or put oily material in her hair or something on her shoulder. Among the Southwestern Apache Indians, the male flashed a mirror at his intended, while the African Azande tried to manipulate the dreams of his beloved. In central India, the Baiga's love potions were made most powerful by adding some dust from the woman's right footprint. These practices are highly ritualized and involve belief in some inchoate powers, which the rituals are able to tap, but they are also communicative acts:

> It is generally necessary for a go-between to put the charm on a girl's shoulder or in her food, and though it is often said that she mustn't know about it, this rule is rarely followed in practice. When a girl knows what is being done, it not only kindles her passion, but it proves the importance of the intrigue. It is not an easy thing to make a love charm, and no one would do it unless he meant business.[8]

When the woman knows of the man's intentions, the "magic" can be understood in psychological terms as hypnotic suggestion. In fact, Sigmund Freud wrote of being in love as having many similarities to a hypnotic state. One benefit over a more direct approach ("Let's make some manna on the savannah") is that, if rejected, the suitor may be less embarrassed. The same function is served in Western industrialized cultures by play. We banter with each other, with the only goal seemingly to entertain ourselves and make each other laugh. But however inane the content, we are checking each other out: am I interested in you, are you interested in me?

Play also facilitates early attraction, for the same reason that a public speaker begins his talk with a couple of jokes —it sets his audience at ease. Only when playful interaction has established a relaxed atmosphere and there seems to be a reasonable chance of success do we make a direct appeal. Another advantage of the playful approach and also analogous to love magic is that it's a way of gaining the attention of the person in whom you're interested. Being creative in your seduction establishes that you're not "just like all the others" and it can make the other person want to get to know you better. The lovelorn Baiga tribesman went to great lengths to impress his woman:

> On a Wednesday, at sunset, dig up the corpse of a young virgin boy and remove the skull. Take it away and wash it in twenty-one streams. Then find a cow which has a calf of the same colour as herself. Milk the cow into the skull, and mix into the milk fresh oil of ramtilla, cow's butter, the blood of a black chicken, and twenty-one grains of rice. Cook it over a slow fire. Go with it to a pipal tree and throw the mixture over the tree. Wherever the grains stick to the tree, gather them carefully and mix them into the food of the girl you desire.[9]

Such intense ritualism has been replaced in Western culture by more flexible and personally elaborated forms of courtship, a good thing considering the rarity of pipal trees and ramtilla, not to speak of the sporadic availability of virgin boys' skulls. Besides, love magic can sometimes backfire, as in this modern tale of woe:

> I took my trouble down to Madame Roue,
> You know that gypsy with the gold tattoo.

She's got a pad on 36th and Vine,
Selling little bottles of Love Potion #9.
I told her that I was a flop with chicks,
I've been this way since 1956.
She looked at her palm and made a magic sign,
She said what you need is Love Potion #9.
She bent down and turned around and gave me a
    wink,
She said I'm goin' to mix it up right here in the sink.
It smelled like turpentine and looked like India ink.
I held my nose, I closed my eyes, I took a drink.
I didn't know it was a day or night,
I thought o' kissing everything in sight,
But when I kissed a cop at 34th and Vine,
He broke my little bottle of Love Potion #9.

If you've had a problem starting a relationship since
1956, you might also consider a different type of magic:
play.

> Not long after beginning to date, Tom decided to
> create a special evening for his new girlfriend. An
> invitation written in beautiful calligraphy arrived for
> her during the week stating that "an admirer" would
> call for her Saturday night, swore her to tell no one,
> and suggested she prepare to be swept off her feet.
> That Saturday night, a horse-drawn carriage (rented
> for the occasion) pulled up at her door, bearing a
> message with familiar calligraphy that announced
> that she would be taken to a place where her "secret
> admirer" was waiting. After a short ride she came to
> a candle-lit restaurant, where her elegantly attired
> boyfriend greeted her.

Such creative touches speak more eloquently than more
direct but prosaic declarations, which leave little to the
imagination.

There is no telling how or when people "fall in love." These feelings may or may not be reciprocated, are known to happen "at first sight" or after long acquaintance, despite gross maltreatment by the person with whom you have been smitten, or which may never occur even though the tenderest of feelings and mutual respect have been established. As Phyllis McGinley put it, "Love is an archer with a low IQ." It's strange that falling in love can be as apt to happen if you know the other person well or not really at all, and it's particularly odd since love is such a damnedly powerful thing. Romantic love is not something that you choose to do or arrange at your convenience. It is said to "strike" you like a thunderbolt, you "fall head over heels" in love and give up control, you are "snowed" and "swept off your feet." Like being pregnant, there's no such thing as being a little bit in love.

Much of the available psychological theory interprets falling in love as due to deficiency. To Freud, the beloved becomes a substitute for the unattained ideal self. Theodor Reik, one of Freud's disciples, remarked that love is based on dissatisfaction with oneself, and cited Plato's *Symposium* as confirmation. In the *Symposium,* Socrates points out that love is the child of Poverty and Plenty. Reik saw love as similarly Janus-headed—a combination of jealousy of the qualities of the beloved and passionate admiration. In addition to love being based on feelings of personal inadequacy, psychoanalysts tells us that love is an attempt to recapture the bliss of union with Mother; that is, in love we face toward our past. If you're in love, however, you're probably enjoying yourself too much to care.

Ultimately, however, love is partly an illusion: we idealize our lovers only to find that their feet are mired in clay as deep as ours. As one cynic concluded, "It doesn't much signify whom one marries, for one is sure to find next morning that it was someone else." My real worry is that such distortions of reality are ultimately harmful, because such love is not for a real person. To the extent that they

fail to fulfill our dreams of our ideal self or of our ideal
parent they will become unacceptable, and we will reject
them in order to hold onto the fantasy that somewhere,
sometime, the perfect lover can be found. The Don Juan
moves on from one relationship to another, perfecting
skills of seduction but never staying around to experience
inner growth.

People in love can appear possessed. In the thirteenth
century the troubadour Ulrich von Lichtenstein would turn
pale in the presence of his beloved princess and was overcome with emotion at the moment that she touched the
flowers which he had secretly placed before her. Ulrich
was so infatuated that he snatched a basin of water in
which his lady had washed herself in order to drink from it
when he was alone.

If Ulrich were alive in the fifties, he probably would
sing it like this:

> She's Venus in Blue Jeans, Mona Lisa with a pony
> tail;
> She's a walkin', talkin' work of art,
> She's the girl who stole my heart.
> My Venus in Blue Jeans is the Cinderella I adore;
> She's my very special angel, too
> A fairy tale come true.
> They say there's seven wonders in the world,
> But what they say is out of date
> There's more than seven wonders in the world.
> I just met number eight.
> My Venus in Blue Jeans
> Is everything I hoped she'd be;
> A teenage goddess from above
> And she belongs to me.

We are too scientifically sophisticated to talk in terms of
magic, but the man or woman in love is under a spell every

bit as powerful as any witchcraft wrought with footprint dust or amulets. In our daily lives we do not depend so much on witchcraft to explain and influence our world, but love is one type of magic that has endured and remains socially sanctioned. Despite the perils of love, it must fulfill some adaptive function. Love is a necessary "illusion," because the alternatives to idealization—cynicism and realism—are not sufficient to make a marriage. The cynic rejects all illusion but thereby becomes incapable of trust. He is always fearful that he will be taken in and lose control. The realist is less handicapped but still limited. Because he believes in only what is tangible and can be proved, he never experiences the realms that only leaps of faith and self-abandonment can reveal.

In these days an "incurable romantic" has come to mean someone with syphilis, gonorrhea, and AIDS. But I, for one, am willing to embrace romanticism, with all its pitfalls; not as an endpoint, though, but as a good beginning. George Bernard Shaw may have been right when he said "to fall in love with a particular woman is to overappreciate the difference between one woman and another," but through this "illusion" much psychological growth becomes possible. Romance at its extreme hinders true love but in its healthier forms contributes to intimacy, especially when aided by a spirit of play. We should not forget Socrates' metaphor that love is the child of Plenty as well as of Poverty.

In the examples that follow many different types of romantic play will be illustrated. In addition to acquainting you with some romantic play that may be fun to experiment with at any stage of a couple's life together, my intent is to show how play can help couples lay the groundwork for a sound relationship, by helping you deal with five key aspects of a beginning relationship.

Sharing Your Inner Selves

Richard and Debra found that early in their relationship a lot of their sharing and opening up took place in long discussions in which they would sit up talking late into the night. Debra described how the talking had both a personal and philosophical tone, reminding her of the "bull" sessions that she had gotten into when a college student. Although both of them had been out of college for several years and had full-time jobs, their late-night talks had the same flavor of earnest spontaneity that they recalled from college days. There also was an unspoken sense of rebellion, of "doing something they shouldn't be doing," because they would be tired for much of the next day at work. However, their fatigue the following day seemed to be an integral part of the experience, a reminder all day of the sweet intimacies of their "all-nighter."

When you hit it off with someone, you often have a sense of *déjà vu*, of harking back to earlier intimate relationships. This is not so much nostalgia for Mom, but echoes of times spent with "best friends." These relationships were intimate but not sexual and may have taken place far back in childhood or more recently. The moral is that the pathways to adult intimacy with a person of the opposite sex may lead you through such earlier playful friendships. Love is very much like the fun you had playing with someone you really liked.

At the start of a relationship, terrific centripetal forces draw two people toward each other, but as with a weight tethered at the end of a whirling string, these forces are balanced by others that pull away. Intimacy beckons but it also threatens, and each of you must reconcile with your-

self and your partner how rapidly you can become intimate. What is most important is not how fast you reveal
yourselves but that each of you makes a commitment in
word and deed to *try* to be emotionally open. At times it
will be very tempting to avoid being fully honest from fear
that the real you, if known, would shatter the delicious
illusion. But real intimacy either deepens or fades—you
can't stand pat at the same level of intimacy for very long.

The poet Ferlinghetti once wrote, "Woman is a wonderful invention of man, and man a wonderful invention of
woman." These lines speak eloquently of the power of two
people's imaginations to create something precious between them. The experience of fantasy is just as important
to adults as to children.

> During the period that Gina and Cole were most
> intensely sharing details about their lives, such as
> their feelings about their respective parents and their
> past love relationships, they spontaneously devel-
> oped a fantasy of "If you only knew me then." It first
> started when Gina was describing the time in sixth
> grade when she wore braces and the other kids
> teased her about her Donald Duck decals and she
> said to Cole, "God, if you only knew me then, you'd
> never have fallen in love with me." Cole gallantly
> demurred, insisting that he would have defended her,
> and the two of them spun out a fantasy of what it
> would have been like.
> Cole was a couple of years older than she and thus
> the fantasy involved Cole as an eighth-grader, with
> Gina's classmates being wowed that an "older kid"
> would take an interest in goofy Gina. Thereafter,
> when one of them would describe an earlier period in
> his life, they would similarly imagine together what it
> would have been like to have known each other then.
> One time while visiting New York City, where Gina

grew up, they walked by her old grade school and Gina pointed out on the playground some of the places that had already become familiar to Cole through their fantasy.

Cole and Gina's fantasy was a creative way for them to get to know about each other's pasts. But it also represents far more than that. When we share something about our past, particularly something with painful associations, we are not merely passing on information but are making use of the relationship to try to integrate parts of ourselves. For example, though a mature woman, Gina still had moments of painful self-consciousness and insecurity similar to those as a sixth-grader. By allowing Cole into her inner life she gained an ally who could support her in a way that she had so much needed as a kid. Their fantasy play contributed to the growth of their relationship also because it was *collaborative*. There was a spontaneous interplay of their inner worlds as each brought in elements from their own memories and imaginations to build a joint fantasy that they could both enjoy.

Sharing pasts can be especially important for older people who are starting a new relationship:

Both Bill and Carol were widowers when they began their relationship in their fifties. Opening up and sharing with each other was complicated by many old memories and their both having spent years living alone. They both were rusty at talking about themselves.

Each of them had many framed old pictures, which they called "the mantlepiece photographs," although, in fact, they were placed in various locations around their respective homes. The photographs provided a comfortable way into their former lives. They would pick one up and tell the story of when it was taken and who were the people in it. As they

realized that they could be accepting of each other's
past, they became more spontaneous. At times, be-
fore the actual details about the photograph were
shared, the partner would try to imagine who the
people were or what was going on at the time. Some-
times this would be done tongue-in-cheek but when
discussed more seriously they each intuitively picked
up on some subtleties about the relationships that the
photos had captured. Whenever new batches sur-
faced, such as during a closet cleanup when Carol's
high school and college yearbooks were unearthed,
they eagerly pored over the pictures together.

The use of photographs illustrates another point about
how couples can best share their inner lives—by using
their imaginations and making use of whatever props are at
hand as windows into each other. In the case of Bill and
Carol they integrated their pasts into their present relationship through collaborative play. One other couple came
upon the idea of adapting the school activity of Show and
Tell:

Soon after beginning to date, Sharon, who was a
second-grade teacher, suggested that they each pick
something that was important to them to show each
other and talk about its history and why they liked it.
Jim was a little hesitant initially, but after Sharon
went first he got into it, and every so often they
would play the game. Most of the time they would
pick a beloved object, rich in memories, such as
Jim's old baseball glove or Sharon's silver candle-
sticks that her grandmother had owned. But once or
twice they also went on a field trip to visit a place
that had special meaning to one of them.

The arts also provides a good vehicle for sharing inner
lives. Good art enables us to touch the artist's unique per-

sonal experience and get in touch with our own feelings. Couples who especially enjoy poetry often find that reading their favorite poems helps them feel deeply connected, and similarly lovers of music can use their beloved pieces as stepping stones toward greater intimacy. A joint visit to an art gallery can bring you together as well, if both of you talk about what the pictures evoke in you. In all of these examples, while ostensibly facing outward toward inanimate objects, you can find ways into each other's deepest feelings. The mode chosen matters to some extent: for example, watching TV or a movie can lead into stimulating discussion, but it more often leads to solitary rather than collaborative fantasy. Most important is your willingness to project yourselves fully into the object and share what you see about yourselves. Learning about each other is like peeling the successive layers of an onion, in that there are always more levels to uncover. Play provides alternative ways for you and your partner to reveal yourselves to each other, and the relaxed spirit of playfulness can help you feel safe to share.

Boundaries

Soon after beginning a relationship partners start to define themselves as a couple. I mean this more in a psychological than a literal sense, in terms of a sense of "we-ness" rather than engagement rings. Early intimacy is a fragile thing and must be protected from outside interference. People reveal their true selves to another only in the safety of knowing that their secrets will be kept in strict confidence and that their time together will not be lightly usurped by other commitments.

The Western tradition of romanticism is rooted in the struggle of lovers to assert the priority of their feelings for each other over the claims of society. In early Rome Plutarch lamented that love based on personal attraction rather than on traditional social values of who should marry whom would destroy the culture. Similarly, St. Augustine, after indulging his own amorous whims in his youth, argued that love based on sacrament and duty must take precedence over romantic notions. In large measure the church saw choice based on personal feelings as a threat because it might lead to intermarriage and dilution of the faith. In the Middle Ages, royalty and nobles married to make political alliances and augment familial wealth, and sentiment could not be permitted to override parental judgment.

Not to be totally denied, however, in the thirteenth century romanticism found expression in the tradition of courtly love. These ideas essentially legitimized love based on sentiment *outside* of marriage—the troubadours' songs glorified burning (but somehow chaste) passion for another man's wife, who was idealized beyond all reason. The important thing was not to consummate this passion but to worship at a distance. To the troubadours such love was its own reward, and elaborate rituals were devised as tests of character: Ulrich von Lichtenstein, piqued that his lady doubted his utter devotion, sent her the present of his little finger. Pierre Vidal, who became infatuated with Loba de Penautier (*loba* means "she-wolf") dressed up in a wolf-skin to pay her a visit; unfortunately for Pierre, some shepherds thought he was a real wolf and let their dogs loose on him. Doubtless, there were other, less neurotic, troubadours who scored in lonely castles with ladies whose husbands were riding off to Canterbury or to the Crusades. Courtly love reflects the limits that society would tolerate. Romantic love was thus provided with the gilded cage of propriety.

In the nineteenth century the poetry of the English Romanticists glorified spontaneous love and open rebellion against society's wishes. The Victorians' prudish and conservative bent again put a damper on the abandonment of self to feeling. But America's insistence on the rights of the individual has been a natural setting for romantic love. In fact, despite this culture's dedication to materialism, the priority of sentiment over pecuniary gain in male-female relationships is now the social norm. Yet, while parents' authority to determine appropriate mates and dates has been severely curtailed, younger couples still experience conflicts between their own choices and their wish to please their parents:

> When Audrey began her relationship with Richard while they were in high school, her parents did not approve because he was from a different religious background. During English class, Audrey had read Shakespeare's Romeo and Juliet, and it became one of her favorite pieces of literature. One of her ways of coping with her parents' disapproval was by identifying with this fabled pair of lovers. Thus, when her parents were giving her a particularly bad time, she would call Richard and whisper into the phone, "O Richard! Richard! wherefore art thou Richard?" In turn, Richard would always end their talk by saying, "Good night, good night! parting is such sweet sorrow," in a reassuring way that acknowledged the stress of her parents' pressure.

Richard and Audrey gained through their playful fantasy a powerful ally against the forces that sought to pull them apart. Romantic lovers very often feel a kinship with lovers from times past. This legitimizes their own very private and powerful experiences, while still enabling them to feel it remains a secret known only to the two of them. Their experience feels at once universal while remaining unique. It is timeless. Thus, in fantasy Richard and Audrey's relationship assumed the same larger-than-life quality as their literary counterparts. But intense absorption in a fantasy, such that the reality is lost, ceases to be play. Identification must be a fluid process, allowing room for both to express their own individuality and to articulate their personal vision of love.

Older couples must set limits on outside interference as well, even though the problems they face may not have to do with parents:

> *Jerry and Ann had known each other for a couple of years through working at the same insurance company. They hesitated to date each other for a long time for fear of gossipy colleagues. Finally, however, they took the plunge and went out for dinner. Part seriously and part for fun, they used a fictitious name for the table reservation and during dinner developed a fantasy about their new secret identities, whispering in conspiratorial tones. They maintained these secret identities for a few months until they felt secure in their new relationship. At that time, they also abandoned their efforts to hide their relationship from their colleagues.*

A couple's boundaries need not be defined in relation to external disapproval, nor is fantasy the only playful approach. Many of the examples of romantic play described in this chapter make partners more intimate and this too contributes to a feeling of "we-ness." One such type of romantic play is the exchange of personal tokens, such as a ring, a lock of hair, or an article of clothing. Couples may dress in the same kinds of clothes or color of clothing, drink from the same cup, or find out their blood types in the hope that they are identical or could allow donating blood to each other if an emergency arose. These acts are similar to "rites of incorporation" described in many societies by anthropologists. Their function is to unite two together in an earthy kind of way and give a sense of psychologically being one. Kuan Tao-Sheng, wife of the famous Chinese painter Chao Mang-Fu, wrote a poem that is beautifully expressive of this experience:

Take a lump of clay,
Wet it, pat it,
Make a statue of you
And a statue of me
Then shatter them, clatter them,
Add some water,
And break them and mold them
Into a statue of you
And a statue of me.
Then in mine, there are bits of you
And in you there are bits of me.
Nothing ever shall keep us apart.[10]

If done in a playful manner, such rituals of fusion can affirm togetherness without suppressing autonomy. But if you like the color blue and your true love likes only shades of pink and red, there will be a price paid down the line if one of you gives up a preference for the sake of we-ness. Merging with your partner will soon make you feel claustrophobic unless you can recognize your differences.

Another type of romantic intimacy involves playing with the crossing of boundaries. In the healthiest relationships, couples zealously protect the privacy of their intimacies, including the playful ones. To a limited extent some couples also enjoy what T. S. Eliot called "private words addressed to you in public." One example is the creative Valentine's Day messages that lovers place in newspapers:

Boris,
I love you madly, dollink!
You're the only one for me,
Bublitchka.

                    Love,
                    Natasha

Carl,
Be my Footsie wootsie

Or I'll break your Armsie warmsie
                              —Sheila

Sarge,
Roses are red, violets are blue,
If you're not my Valentine,
It's meatloaf and okra for you.
                              —Kitten

These same messages could have been delivered privately, but instead their lovers chose to let hundreds of thousands of readers of a major metropolitan newspaper share their Valentine banter. There's a delicious sense of flirting with exposure, while still preserving anonymity, by the use of first names or nicknames. The next couple illustrates another way of playing with boundaries:

Amy met John while she was working as a costume designer for a local repertory company. She loved her work and often brought costumes home to model or just to look at in the familiar surroundings of her apartment.

When she first met John she would sometimes ask him to model male costumes for her inspection. This became quite playful at times—they would often talk about their fantasies as they were triggered by the various outfits. One Saturday afternoon they decided, on a whim, to go outside in some Victorian clothes they were wearing. Feeling a little self-conscious at first, they went out shopping. They had a wonderful time, seeing themselves as quite apart from everyone else, laughing at others who seemed a bit perplexed by their clothing. After finishing their shopping, they strolled down to the business district, acting as if they did this sort of thing every day.

As with the Valentine messages placed in the newspaper, this couple is giving the outside world a peek at their intimate play. There is a hint of exhibitionism triggered by the awareness of other people looking at them, which only heightens a sense of the twosome's being unique. Costumes are a wonderful aid to fantasy, as I will illustrate in other chapters. But this couple also points out the way in which play emerges directly from something already present in our lives. We don't need to be costume designers or even wear costumes—we need only be playful about who we are.

Caretaking

Gifts are a tangible expression of love, and when our beloved gives us something that clearly demonstrates being in tune with our true needs or desires, we feel especially loved. There's also nothing more gratifying to the giver than to hear the exclamation "It's just what I always wanted!"

Giving gifts can also become tainted by complex motivations. At traditional gift-giving occasions, we and our mates may wonder if we're giving because we want to, or because we feel we should. Gifts can also be used as bribes or as diversions from the emotional stinginess of a relationship. The beginning of a liaison can be a particularly awkward time: an expensive gift would clearly be inappropriate, yet divining what someone may appreciate is difficult. The next couple illustrates one playful way of learning about each other through gifts:

Helen and Carl enjoyed window shopping with a creative twist: occasionally each of them would choose a pretend gift for the other. Sometimes they would even go into the store and ask questions about the item or try it on for size. At some point they would talk about why they had chosen this specific present. Sometimes the gift was for laughs, like the time Carl picked out the most garish brooch in the store or when Helen "gave" Carl pink-framed Devo glasses. At other times, as with the pedigreed golden retriever puppy and the Hasselblad, each was really touched by the other's thoughtfulness.

Spontaneous gifts that have nothing to do with birthdays or holidays can be very romantic. For example, while on a walk together in the woods, some couples give each other interesting things they have found, like a piece of birch bark, an attractive rock, or a small bouquet of wildflowers. One man would occasionally leave an unwrapped gift around the house which his partner eventually found. Once, for instance, she discovered a new cactus plant, with a note saying, "A cactus for my flower." The point is to look actively for gift opportunities rather than wait passively for the next birthday or anniversary to roll around.

Some of the best gifts are those that have a very personal touch:

> *"One of my favorite gifts of all the things that my husband has given me is a tattered copy of Pablo Neruda's love poems. He had originally gotten it for a college course in Spanish literature, and the margins were full of his pencilled comments from when he was nineteen years old (we met about ten years later). Neruda is one of my favorite poets, and on my birthday Nick gave me this book. I feel like I'm seeing through Neruda's eyes but also through my own and my husband's adolescence—starry-eyed kids, experiencing love for the first time. Nick kids me sometimes about buying me a replacement for this "second hand" copy, but the one with personal history is much more valuable to me."*

Another husband made a tape recording of many of the "oldies but goodies" that he knew his wife loved. He went to friends' homes to tape the recordings that were no longer available at record stores. Some of the songs reminded them both of times and places they had been together through the years.

Sometimes, when the "perfect gift" is too expensive for your means, it is still possible to give your partner a taste of their fondest wish:

> *Alice was not especially interested in acquiring expensive possessions, which was fortunate since neither she nor Steve were well off. The one exception, however, was her favorite car: a Porsche.*
>
> *One Friday afternoon she went to Steve's place after work and stopped outside his house to admire a shiny red Porsche that she had never seen parked there before. Inside, Steve greeted her with a small package, which contained a teardrop diamond necklace and car keys with the Porsche logo on the keychain.*
>
> *"We have to return the car on Monday," Steve said, "but the necklace you can keep."*
>
> *The rest of the weekend they spent driving around the New England countryside, looking at the fall foliage. On Monday Alice drove to work as usual in her beat-up Chevette, but she always had the necklace to remind her of her magical weekend with Steven and the Porsche.*

Freedom to Play

One of the qualities that people look for in a relationship is the freedom to express normally suppressed behavior. If you're involved with an ax murderer, this could be a problem. But most of us are generally *too* constrained, too worried about what others might think. We never allow ourselves to be silly, childlike, or risk-taking in healthy ways that could invigorate both us and our relationships. The romantic are the daring: not that you have to go skydiving and tongue kiss your partner at twenty thousand feet while you wonder if your parachute is going to open. But you can, and at least once you should, go skinny-dipping together, scream your heads off on a roller coaster, go horseback riding on the beach, or sing songs even though they're out of key. It's not only arousing to try new things, you can give spin to familiar ones by lifting them out of a usual context. An afternoon off to go to the beach in the middle of winter is an entirely different experience from going on a busy weekend in August. As John Updike phrased it, "Romance is, simply, the strange, the untried." One couple I know occasionally gets up to watch the sunrise; at other times they'll bathe together by candlelight. Another creates variety by eating in different styles, for example sitting on the floor Japanese style and experimenting with exotic mixed drinks, wines, and cheeses. You could decide to go wine-tasting, take a field trip to some place you've never been before, such as a rum distillery or construction site, or go to a type of sporting event you've never seen before, whether it be horse racing, a roller derby, or a frog-jumping contest. It seems, unfortunately, that we become sightseers only when we visit exotic surroundings, forgetting that there are interesting sights around us all the time if we could only see where we live with fresh eyes. The purpose of seeking such novelty is to wake ourselves up so we can shake off habit and see *our partners,* too, with fresh eyes.

To be free to play and to allow your partner the same freedom means to let yourself be a child again.

> *"My happiest moments with my husband are when we can be like two kids. We might be out on a fall day raking leaves and start playing in the piles—we like to bury each other under them or lie on our backs on a great bed of leaves and watch the cloud formations. We'll imagine things up there and describe aloud what we see.*

"In the summer, there's water play. It gets hot in the Shenandoah Valley, and washing the car becomes an excuse for turning the hose on each other. We also love a walk in the country in the rain, getting soaking wet, then coming home and peeling off our clothes and toweling each other off."

The stricter part of you may have trouble with this and will mutter, "Grow up," but you don't have to forfeit your mature side by such behavior. It may help to remind yourself that you are not being childish, only *childlike*. William Wordsworth believed in this continuity of a child's joy with maturity:

> My heart leaps up when I behold
>   A rainbow in the sky:
> So was it when my life began;
> So is it now I am a man;
> So be it when I shall grow old.
>   Or let me die!
> The Child is father of the Man;
> And I could wish my days to be
> Bound each to each by natural piety.

The following is an unusual example of how one couple learned about each other through children's play:

Bob and Jane met accidentally, by introducing themselves to one another on a sidewalk while waiting for a streetlight to change. Wishing to make an impression, Bob gave some thought, before their first date, to how to break the ice.

They met after work, and Bob asked Jane if she would accompany him on a shopping spree. As they went to his car he told Jane that they were going to a toy store. He presented her with a crisp new ten-dollar bill and produced one for himself as well. By

*the time they arrived at the toy store he had de-
scribed his intent: he wanted each of them to spend
ten dollars on toys in the space of fifteen minutes.
Each was to buy whatever they wanted, as many or
as few toys as they wanted, within the ten-dollar
limit. Afterward they would go back to his apartment
and begin to know each other by describing why they
had selected those particular toys.*

*The mission accomplished, back at Bob's apart-
ment he poured glasses of wine while they dumped
their bags of toys out on the floor. Bob had bought a
number of small toys: a pink rubber ball, baseball
cards, Sen-Sen, and a Humpty Dumpty watch. Ann
had bought one large toy: a red dump truck. The
remainder of the evening they talked about the toys.*

*Ann said that as a child she had always wanted a
dump truck but that "in those days girls weren't
given such things." Bob said that the ball and cards
reminded him of happy times playing stoop ball and
flipping baseball cards in the schoolyard. The watch
related to his feeling the pressure at his newspaper
job and wanting to rebel against the intractable
deadlines. Contrary to previous reports, Bob said,
Humpty-Dumpty had been pushed.*

Bob's toy idea was a risky step for a first date, since
there was a good chance that someone who didn't know
him would think him a bit strange. But in this instance it
enabled the couple to get to know each other in unorthodox
fashion that made for a more lively first date than either of
them had ever experienced.

For many couples, their play together is an evocation of
memorable times growing up:

*"When I was a child growing up in a small town in
Minnesota," says Margot, "the ponds would freeze
over in the winter and we'd go ice-skating. I came*

from a large family with more kids than money, but with plenty of love, and our recreation had to come from whatever was free and near at hand.

"I still love going skating with my husband and kids. Sometimes my husband and I go alone at night. We have those old-fashioned skating lanterns that you can set down on the ice or carry along. The only sounds are the wind and the scraping of our skates. It just feels so free and timeless."

Private Language

The language of love—both verbal and nonverbal—inevitably borrows much of its expressions from the wider culture. A gift of flowers, an after-date invitation in, a ring, have well-known meanings. A couple draws closer not just by performing a series of timeworn rituals but by developing their own idiom or, if you will, a unique dialect. Terms of endearment gradually replace the lover's given name, although they're typically used only in private. The new name is a rechristening, a statement that your lover stands in a unique relation to you that is known only to the twosome. These pet names are often unusual, reflecting a playful spirit that grasps subtle qualities of the couple in a way that only poetic metaphor can. "Honeydew" and "Melonhead," "Durable Woman" and "Captain Jack," "Bagelman," "Toadface," and "Uptown Toots" evoke rich associations whose specific meaning to a couple forms a private bond. For example, in one couple the nickname "Bunchcrackles" means "I love you a bunch, you crack me up." For a couple to have nicknames means that your feelings for each other are serious but that your mode of relating can remain playful. You may also develop other words that have special connotations:

Joanne and Bob had just met, but they both felt so in sync with each other, as if they had known each other for a long time. On one of their dates they repeatedly experienced the same feelings about what each of them said, and they playfully began saying, "Ditto," as a shorthand for "I feel that way, too." The next day Joanne returned home from work to find a box of roses with a note that had one word written on it: "Ditto."

Private language is used mostly when a couple is alone with each other. The bond of secrecy around such communication confirms their uniqueness, sets them apart from other people, and helps establish a boundary. When private language is used in public, it tends to involve words in common usage whose private meaning escapes those around them. One couple's outward code, for example— "Let's go home and watch TV"—really meant "I want to have sex with you."

Couples can also develop nonverbal communication that has special meaning only to them, such as using sign language to say "I love you" or more elaborate play:

Rick and Bette have pantomime rituals that provide a special way of communicating their affection. For example, they have elaborate ways of winking to each other, as though they belong to a secret fraternity. In another mime routine one of them blows a kiss to the other, who pretends to be a frog catching a fly in midair with his tongue. At other times they make up all kinds of scary and funny faces. In this way they have become exquisitely attuned to subtle nuances of their facial expressions.

This couple provides an interesting counterpoint to the way in which animals adopt a playface to signal "This is play." Humans, too, use facial expression for subtleties of mood, but instead of being stereotyped, as in animals, the healthy play of couples is a richly idiosyncratic form of communication.

Romantic notes are another form of playful communication. One partner left erotic messages on the other's answering machine, another mate sent perfumed love letters to the office, and a third used "invisible ink" (lemon juice) and coded messages that had to be deciphered. The following Valentine's card would not win any literary awards, but it certainly has a personal touch:

> *Ode to a Fickle Lover*
> What twisted joke hath faith doth played
> To have us live the plans thus laid,
> To share life not as friends but foes
> Never content in peaceful repose?
> As lovers united against the night,
> Wake facing the challenge of the fight.
> Hark! The gods I question of,
> Can this be real, can this be love?
> A curse or blessing in disguise?
> I know not where the answer lies,
> But ah, such sweet, sweet misery,
> To be blest with such a man as thee.

Is bad poetry better than mundane prose? Is it better to call your Gladys "Rosebud" and your Herbert "My Snugglebear"? As the French say, *Chacun à son goût* ("Each to his own taste"). Private language is but one way of many described in this chapter of enhancing communication. What matters is not that you adopt any particular way of relating but that you be playful in your approach, shifting as you and your partner's needs require from one mode of relating to another. Romantic play provides alternative ways of contact and in the early stages of a relationship creates psychological bridges between the two of you. Through play you signal and confirm a feeling of connection. It enables you to become more intimate. I am fond of romantic play, if for no other reason than that it makes relationships between adults more profound. Play enables us to live closer to the dream. It wreaks havoc with habit and demands that you create a personal, idiosyncratic form of love, rather than a repetition of social customs. There are surely risks of indulging in fantasy and communicating through metaphor, such as a loss of clarity and a tendency, at times, to mistake illusion for reality. But I think the trade-off of precision for expressiveness is worth making.

As Shakespeare has it, "They do not love that do not show their love." One may ask, How are we romantics to indulge in shows of affection without affectation? I can offer only two wise men's suggestions. Henri Stendhal, who understood love's illusions better than anyone, had this to say:

> The whole art of love reduces itself, it appears to me, to saying exactly what the degree of intoxication of the moment suggests, that is to say, in other words, to listening to the dictates of one's own heart.
> . . . Where there is perfect naturalness, the happiness of two people becomes commingled.[11]

The other advice comes from Hecato, a Stoic philosopher of the second century B.C., who said, "I will show you a love potion without drug or herb or any witch's spell; if you wish to be loved, love."

It is not fancy footwork or footprint dust that we need but our own voice to express caring for another. Stendhal and Hecato are, of course, both right. But if this simple advice were so easy to carry out, more Prince Charmings and enchanted princesses would live happily ever after. My own experience in love is closer to what Hermann Hesse has Steppenwolf lament, "All I wanted to do was to follow the dictates of my own true self. Why was that so very difficult?"

Even fairy tales have their witches, but let us keep searching for our yellow brick road.

CHAPTER THREE

Making a Commitment

Love you. Naturally. Only real woman in the world. Other two point one billion women pale imitations. Marry me, Saturday 3pm, Cumberland Courthouse. Wear blue.

Your Knight-in-Amour

I like to picture the telegram arriving. Did she go? Of course, and Saturday no doubt a cloudless summer day. But then I wonder what happened afterward to the woman in blue and her romantic admirer. If they are anything like the flesh and blood people I know, they found following the promptings of their own hearts an unreliable way to continue to chart their love's course. Their feelings became inconsistent and conflicting. My sense is not that falling in love is always a false start, but rather that we are all quite a bit more complicated than any idealized portrait. In time we must all face the reality of the other person, as distinct from how we need them to be. We likewise, being less than perfect, do not always love or speak the whole truth, even the part of it we know. Ferlinghetti, in his whimsical way, captures this disillusionment:

See

    it was like this when

        we waltz into this place

a couple of Papish cats
        is doing an Aztec two-step
And I says
       Dad let's cut
but then this dame
       comes up behind me see
        and says
        You and me could really exist
Wow I says
     Only the next day
     she has bad teeth
      and really hates
         poetry

Even if our dream lover really possesses the quality that we so admired when we first met, the very virtue later often seems to be a vice. The wonderfully appealing extrovert turns out to be always entertaining others; the solid, imperturbable hero now reveals himself as taciturn and unable to show any weakness. I remember Adelaide, my first infatuation, in second grade, which lasted all of two days. No seven-year-old ever looked so dainty in a party dress. But Adelaide could tolerate no rowdy fun or dirt and was a bore at games during recess.

Another fiendish trick of nature is that the qualities we seek in a mate and wish that we owned, we unconsciously repudiate. The clinging vine who needs a tree's strong limbs for support may envy what the tree can do and she can't. Grafting onto ourselves an alien trait is always a tenuous arrangement: there is a psychological counterpart to the difficulties of organ transplants—each cell of our being is poised to reject what it recognizes as not-self.

In our disappointment that our love is not so fair, we may turn on them for what we now regard as false advertising. Their other unattractive qualities may become magnified in our once-fooled eyes. As Albert Camus has written,

"We always deceive ourselves twice about the people we love—first to their advantage, then to their disadvantage."

The death of idealization can be catastrophic, or it may be a lingering demise. You know something's happened when you begin a love note with "To whom it may concern," and you know the scales have dropped from your eyes when you find out that your pen pal, whom you're madly in love with, has plagiarized his best stuff from Elizabeth Barrett and Robert Browning's letters. It's just as well that idealization dies. Our fall from grace hopefully lands us square on our feet so we can set about the work of a relationship. Your lover may arrive on a great white horse, but committed love turns out to be an infantryman.

Romantics want only tapestries and fog-shrouded vistas. They wax poetic at the sight of the Great Pyramids and the Taj Mahal but are not interested in the blood and sweat lost in their construction. It takes a romantic to *conceive* of the notion of such wonders, but he then needs help to give substance to this vision.

To hold tight to idealization requires too much violence to truth. While we can and should protect our fantasies—natural preserves where our imaginations can run wild—we must not perceive consensus where differences exist, nor always blur the outlines of painful experience. We must not be afraid to step backstage behind the illusion and draw the curtain to see where the Wizard of Oz sits.

Commitment that is founded only on romantic illusion cannot last, as Hollywood stars' frequent marriages attest. Increasingly, since people are marrying at a later age and many live together before marriage, they are making decisions about whether to stay together without the momentum of romance hurtling them to the altar. But what criteria should you use to choose a long-term partner, and how can play help you move toward commitment?

Theories of Mate Selection

In the nineteenth century, consulting a phrenologist was one way to determine a suitable mate. The posterior regions of the brain were considered most crucial to matrimony, since this is where "conjugality," "inhabitiveness," and "amativeness" supposedly resided. Thus, if an admirer caressed your head, you could never be sure if she just liked to run her fingers through your hair or if she was checking out your conjugality. Another way to tell whether someone would make a vigorous lover, without actually trying him out, was to notice the prominence of his jaw. Most marriage manuals of this time, however, emphasized objective scrutiny of a potential partner's personality traits, not just his cranial anatomy. Thus, to pick a model wife:

> You want a wife brave, practical, industrious, with a hand for life's common duties, yet crowned with that beauty which a strong and noble soul give to any face. You do not want a toy wife.[12]

As for choosing a husband, there were many traits to avoid.

> Idleness, intemperate use of intoxicating drinks, smoking, chewing, snuffing tobacco, the taking of opium, licentiousness in every form, gambling, swearing, and keeping late hours at night.[13]

In this century sociologists have gone to considerable lengths to determine whether men and women are attracted to each other because their make-up is similar or complementary. Nineteenth-century marital counselors had already figured out what people should do:

> Wherein, as far as you are what you ought to be, marry one *like* yourself; but wherein and as far as you have any marked *excesses* or defects, marry those *unlike* yourself in the objectionable particulars.
>
> ... The secret of fitness of marriage is opposition of temperament with identity of aim.[14]

Contrary to what romantics may believe, Cupid has less to do with our final selection than does supply and demand: the person we choose falls somewhere between our ideal and what we feel we deserve based on our own "value" in the marital marketplace. Cultural norms also influence our choice of mate far more than either romantics or logical positivists would like to think. Most people marry others who come from the same social class and who have a level of education and religious background similar to their own, although they may choose someone with a contrasting personality. In one study of marital attraction, height emerged as the most significant factor limiting marital choice: only 3 percent of men and women felt free to date if the man was shorter than the woman.

But such cool appraisal of static characteristics, while it narrows the field, does not create a match. Otherwise, computer-dating services would have put marriage counselors out of business. Two people must interact to discover each other, and from the very first, play enters in, initially to signal interest, and soon after to compare values.

> For their first weekend away together, Mark and Sheri went to Nantucket Island, where they stayed in a rather fancy guesthouse. Both of them were eager but also a bit apprehensive. Sheri was recently divorced and unused to starting a relationship, and Mark knew her well enough to realize that he badly wanted to get involved.
>
> At dinner they found themselves overhearing bits

and pieces of conversations about yachts, stocks and bonds, and summers in Europe. The voices had an aristocratic air, and the dress was decidedly preppy. Sheri and Mark were unpretentious products of working-class parents who earned everything they got. While at dinner they rolled their eyes and giggled. Later, back in their room, they caricatured their neighbors with much amusement.

"Oh, dear, I do hope Edna and Charles will sail down here for the race this summer. They're such divine bridge partners."

"I don't know if they'll come. There's just not the right kind of people here, anymore."

This new couple affirmed their common ground by playing "We're not like them." Such searching for mutual compatability may also take place through playful fantasy.

Peter and Teri are both young professionals who, when they first met, had aspirations but not yet the financial wherewithal to buy their own house. Both of them talked about being fed up with living in apartments and dealing with landlords' always raising the rent. On one date, while sitting over wine and cheese in an outdoor café, they began musing together about what kind of house each of them wanted to own. They both became quite animated discussing their fantasies about their "dream houses." As they became more involved with each other, the fantasy became "our dream house," which incorporated features from both of their ideal houses and was really a hybrid of past homes they had loved and their hopes for their future family. They would ponder the merits of greenhouse windows, sleeping lofts, spiral staircases, and stone fireplaces, at times realistically discussing their priorities, at others letting their imaginations run wild.

These two stories point out that through play couples discover each other's values, but that they also find out ways to collaborate and to what degree they share a similar sense of humor. The ability to laugh together and to play off each other's fantasy lives is one sign of an intuitive connection that has deep implications for the couple's potential to achieve a joint enterprise. There is a difference, though, between such reciprocal play and a relationship in which one partner always entertains the other with humor. The latter couple may find that they share a similar sense of humor but the collaborative element is less apparent.

Play is not the only way to assess the quality of your interaction, but the capacity to play may also set the stage for other types of sharing by enabling you to feel accepted and comfortable with each other.

The Meanings of Commitment

"Commitment" is a serious word with weighty connotations, and people do not always have the same meaning in mind when they use it. The question "Are you committed to our relationship?" may be asking for a promise to stay together; it may also refer to an attitude of devotion. Then again, to be committed may signify a feeling of attachment. Traditional vows of matrimony are solemn declarations, as in the *Book of Common Prayer,* which dates to 1662:

> To have and to hold from this day forward, for better for worse, for richer for poorer, in sickness and in health, to love and to cherish, till death us do part.[15]

While more modern wedding vows are not always this grave, we still refer to an incipient attitude of commitment as "getting serious," as if a long-term relationship and playfulness were mutually exclusive. In fact, in ancient

Rome, young brides would bid a ceremonious farewell to their dolls and offer them up to the gods. Similarly, in some parts of Japan it was customary that several days before her wedding, the bride's parents would burn her toys, symbolic that play was over and work had begun. In contrast, in a traditional Russian wedding, the groom gives his bride bread and salt (both representative of life's necessities), but also an almond cake to indicate that he will provide her with some of life's sweet frills. In this country, nineteenth-century marriage manuals also exhorted a husband to love and honor his wife in playful ways:

> Try to make her happy . . . never carry chills and gloom into your home. . . . Take home with you picture books, nicknacks and a cheerful heart so you will add to the happiness of the household.[16]

This prescription is a bit condescending and trivializes the relationship between man and wife. The real problem that couples face is how to cultivate an attitude that still maintains, when the chips are down, "this is important, but we can still have fun."

Couples need time to feel their way into a commitment, so that individual psyches can get used to the idea of being a twosome. Some couples play at being committed as a way of experiencing how they might feel about it:

> *Early in their relationship, Bill and Ellen used to take a lot of weekend trips—skiing, going to the ocean, hiking. They are both very athletic, enjoy outdoor activities, and jokingly describe themselves as looking as if they are "right out of an L. L. Bean catalog." In one of these trips they experimented going by one of their last names. Thereafter, they would both go by Bill's last name on one weekend and by Ellen's on the next. Although they socialized with other people on those weekends, it gave them a*

*sense of a shared secret and was a kind of testing the
waters as to how they felt about being seen as a couple. For Ellen, who had some strong feminist views
about not wanting to have her identity subsumed
under a man's, her discovery that Bill could be flexible about last names was very important in enabling
her to make a commitment. Eventually when they did
marry they both took a hyphenated name.*

At some point in a relationship each must deal with the
uncertainty about making a long-term commitment. Part of
the hesitation may involve wishing to give yourself totally
but also not wanting to be taken for granted. Often one
person may appear to be the pursuer and the other the pursued, but in most cases both partners have some doubts
about, as well as wishes for, commitment. Playfulness can
disclose important underlying concerns and help you gradually define the specific nature of commitment that is right
at any given stage of the relationship.

Weddings

A sure way to turn a carefree relationship into a sumo
wrestling match is to plan a big wedding. Even small weddings can turn into big headaches since parents and in-laws
invariably have a different notion than you of the ideal
wedding. Since you, hopefully, will be doing this only
once, it's also hard to get away from the feeling of wanting
it to be perfect. I'm convinced that it's best to resign yourself to the fact that unless you are really planning this thing
entirely by yourself you're just not going to have enough
control over the event to make it turn out exactly as you
might like. Not that weddings can't be a success, but it's
more often by luck than by design, and the guests usually
enjoy the occasion more than the bride and groom. Planning a wedding provides ample opportunity to practice

maintaining a sense of play, including not taking the occasion so seriously that a relationship no longer is fun.

Jim and Debby wanted their wedding to have a sense of grace but without being too traditional. Thus, they began looking for a professional photographer who would take primarily candid rather than posed shots. The search turned out to be a lot more difficult than they had anticipated: the first three photographers they interviewed each had slick albums and manners to match. Each time the standard line was "I like to tell the story of the wedding." Unfortunately, the story turned out to be the same for everyone, with each picture part of a pre-scripted piece. After looking at a few of their albums, Jim and Debby felt as if their own faces would merely have to be pasted on, like pictures taken at fairs where you stick your heads through stage sets. At first they became depressed, but then they were able to joke about it, exaggerating the photographers' sickly sentimentality. In so doing they became more aware that their pursuit of the perfectly scripted wedding had not left sufficient room for spontaneity.

Shortly before my own wedding, I had a dream that a train station had just been moved next to my house, which in reality is quite secluded. In the dream I was outraged at this invasion of my privacy. When I awoke I knew immediately what the dream was really about: I felt that the upcoming wedding was an invasion of my personal relationship. After all, there would be all these people there whom I barely knew. My sense is that most weddings inherently pose the dilemma of how to reconcile the wish to have an intimate moment in the midst of a public event. A relationship is at heart a very private matter between two people, and even close friends and relatives may know only a fraction of what it is really all about. The presence of an audience inevitably creates a sense of performing and this also limits the extent to which a wedding can feel intimate. One solution is to find ways of creating moments of intimacy sometime during the occasion. At a large wedding, for example, it would be impossible to make meaningful contact with everyone there. It is better to decide in advance on five people with whom you want to make sure to spend some private time.

Another couple I know had a playful way of creating intimate moments: the groom's family had a long tradition of making elaborate toasts; anyone who chose to was given the opportunity to raise a glass and speak. The toasts invariably were humorous, but people also spoke from the heart, particularly when they had been fortified by champagne from the previous toasts. My sense is that this medium for sharing worked so well because there was an awareness that everyone was performing. By creating a play within a play, it became possible to touch the audience in a less self-conscious way because there was less pretense that this was the same as private sharing.

The Problem of Constraint

Having formalized their commitment, two people ever afterward face the question of whether they are together because they choose to be or because they must. As the French maximist La Rochefoucauld put it: "In love there are two sorts of constancy: one arises from our continually finding in the favorite object fresh motives to love; the other from our making it a point of honor to be constant."

Two traditional wedding customs—the honeymoon and the groom's carrying his bride over the threshold of their house—are vestiges of the obsolete wedding by capture. Men used to drag away the woman of their choice, and she had little or nothing to say about it. Although both sexes may still use psychological clubs to bludgeon their mates into submission, the problem of constraint has become much more of an internal issue. Especially in dual career couples in which both partners could easily support themselves, albeit not in the style to which they have become accustomed, both partners have the capacity to walk away from a marriage, and there is much less social disapproval attached to divorce, even when children are involved. Still, there is a very real feeling of constraint attached to marriage that makes many couples feel much less free than when they were just dating. In 1174, at a French "Court of Love," the Comtesse de Champagne answered the question "Can true love exist between married people?" by saying:

> We state and affirm, by the tenor of these presents, that love cannot extend its rights over two married persons. For indeed lovers grant each other all, mutually and freely, without being constrained by any motive or necessity, whereas husband and wife are holden, by their duty, to submit their wills to each other and to refuse each other nothing.

In reaction against the inhibiting effects of a formalized commitment, some couples maintain an open partnership without legal ties or have a succession of short-lived relationships. The lack of any sense of commitment other than to the moment or to one's own growth, however, can rob people of their freedom as well: the situation may feel too tenuous to risk confrontation. The solution, then, is to find some middle ground between too onerous a sense of constraint and too fickle a promise. Again I find playfulness to be a good model for a relationship, since its nature promotes freedom within limits.

> *"We had lived together for over five years, and finally we just decided that it was time to either get married or split up. I was ready to get married, but*

*Kirk, just as he is with other kinds of major life deci-
sions, wasn't sure. It was a very painful time as we
struggled over Kirk's mixed feelings. I felt hurt that
Kirk wasn't sure about me, and he resented my pres-
suring him. He couldn't feel good about choosing me
or giving me up. At last, Kirk eased his way into the
decision to get married, but even after we had set the
date and were planning the wedding I could tell he
was uneasy.*

*"One way I coped with his ambivalence was to
make believe that when the key moment came to exchange vows, I would cross my fingers behind my
back. That way he would end up committed to me,
but I wouldn't really be committed to him. Of course,
this was his worst fear, and by my caricaturing it he
was able to let go of it a bit and realize that the
reality wasn't so bad. I have to admit that I also
enjoyed turning the tables on him after all he had put
me through."*

This story illustrates how healthy play enables both
partners to express their inner needs: the woman took on
her fiancé's role, which allowed her to experience some of
the ambivalence that she herself felt about committing herself to such a capricious lover. She also had a chance to
vent some of her frustrations. But the play also worked
because the man felt more understood than criticized. His
inner life was being played with but not mocked.

The capacity for such an exchange of roles can help free
a couple from an impasse. In a marital system one partner
is often unconsciously "chosen" to express a feeling for
both, as in the above couple's ambivalence about commitment. Polarization increases as the two sides of an emotional issue are felt to be embodied in separate people. But
by playing out each other's feelings you can learn to see
the tug of war as an intrapsychic dilemma in which both of
you have different mixtures of similar feelings.

Some marital therapists recommend that couples who are anxious about getting married should make up a "divorce agreement"—a fantasy of what should occur if the marriage ends. The purpose is not to minimize future legal fees but to help clarify emotional concerns about commitment. As one woman put it, "It was only after we talked about the worst possible outcome and made that less unknown and scary that we could feel freed up to take the plunge."

Like wedding vows, the divorce agreement is a joint resolve, a way of defining the nature of the relationship, in this case by making explicit the underlying wish to have a way out.

Separateness and Togetherness

According to a well-known source, God created the heavens and earth in six days and on the seventh day rested. The latter is not entirely accurate, because while resting, He or She had a chance to think about what had been created and had some second thoughts. Thus, on the seventh day was created Ambivalence. Whether or not this version of creation is accurate, ambivalence has been around as long as original sin and shows no signs of being eliminated by the progress of civilization. Take, for example, "The Bachelor's Soliloquy," written in 1796:

> To wed or not to wed, that is the question:
> Whether 'tis better still to rove at large
> From fair to fair, amid the wilds of passion;
> Or plunge at once into a sea of marriage
> And quench our fires—To marry, take a wife,
> No more—and by a wife to say we quell
> Those restless ardours, all those natural tumults
> That flesh is heir to;—'tis a consolation
> Devoutly to be wished.—Marry a wife,
> A wife, perchance a devil:—ay, there's the rub.

This horny, ambivalent soul clearly felt himself to be a kindred spirit with Hamlet, himself no stranger to feeling pulled simultaneously in two irreconcilable directions. In part, ambivalence is related to our comparing the real with the ideal and being unable to embrace imperfection. But it also has to do with another fundamental aspect of our needs for one another: we desire closeness, but we also need to feel separate. To enter into a relationship always holds a threat of depriving us of one need while it may satisfy the other.

> An engineering student in his twenties had fallen in love with a woman several weeks before she was to go to Europe for three months. While she was away they wrote passionate love letters to each other. The man's thoughts were constantly on his girlfriend—missing her, lusting after her, looking forward to the day when they would be reunited. They made plans to live together.
>
> As the day of his lover's return approached, his excitement began to shade into an edgy sensation in his stomach. It felt to him as if his love had been like a huge wave that had crested and had washed over him, leaving him weak and uncertain. The night his girlfriend's plane arrived he got lost on the way to the airport, and he found her waiting in the terminal. They moved in together, but two months later they had separated. He told her he wasn't ready to settle down.
>
> This man went on to have a series of affairs, with the pattern always the same—infatuation followed by disenchantment as soon as he was faced with making a commitment. In between his affairs he felt desperately lonely. By nature an aloof intellectual, he needed to feel in love with a woman to be able to express emotion. "Without women," he remarked, "I feel as if I've lost my voice."

The truth was that he was never able to love any-one—he was a lover of fantasy.

D. H. Lawrence has a beautiful passage in *Women in Love* where he describes this same yearning for and fear of intimacy, in this case, in the relationship between two men, Birkin and Gerald:

There was a silence between them, and a strange tension of hostility. They always felt a gap, a distance between them, they always wanted to be free each of the other. Yet there was a curious heart-straining towards each other.

In large measure the direction in which we lean psychologically—toward closeness or distance—is a function of our past experience in relationships, going back not only to our earliest rapport with our mother, and father, but also to our most recent loves. Our past shapes the dimensions of our adult loves, and in some cases this can be taken literally:

A very bright and successful public relations man, Crane was forty-five years old and had never been married. He was attracted to women and did not lack opportunities to settle down. But he was obsessed with women's breasts. He was always in search of better or bigger ones, a compulsion that he felt apologetic about, even guilty, but that he could not control.

When he was eight, his mother had frequently called him in to the bathroom to shampoo her hair while she sat with a turkish towel draped loosely over her large breasts. His parents got divorced when he was ten and his mother then took on several lovers.

As an adult, he appeared to be a mature man,

admired by many of his friends as a "Don Juan." In reality, his relationships with women were characterized by his feeling like a needful and naughty little boy.

Rock songs are full of laments above love's dangers. Although some are philosophic ("Momma said they'll be days like this," "Everybody plays the fool sometime"), others, like this Beatles song, caution against getting involved too hastily:

> If I gave my heart to you
> I must be sure from the very start
> That you would love me more than her
> Cause I couldn't stand the pain.

The play of everyday life can be very revealing of inner conflicts about closeness. For example, early in a relationship one partner may be feeling warm and cuddly and use a term of endearment, such as honey or darling, or perhaps a more idiosyncratic nickname. If the other seems to cringe at such words, it may well be because the degree of intimacy associated with this kind of playful talk is not comfortable. (Other instances of how play can reveal difficulties with intimacy will be discussed in Chapter 10.)

Some kinds of romantic play reflect the choice of an opposite solution—the couple fuses into one identity and ignores the need for individual autonomy. Thus, wearing the same clothes or rejoicing at moments of intuitive anticipation of each other's thoughts and feelings, in themselves are not harmful. But if they are part of a general orientation that ignores differences and seeks to promote continual merging of identities, individuality becomes straitjacketed. This wish to fuse into one is just as illusory as the idealization of your partner, for most adult needs cannot be satisfied by such a Siamese-twin way of relating. Real sharing involves two people talking about what is going on inside of each of them in order to discover how they differ, as well as how they may be the same, and it is only then that intimacy takes place. As the oft-quoted Kahlil Gibran advises, "Stand together yet not too near together, For the pillars of the temple stand apart, and the oak tree and the cypress grow not in each other's shadow. . . . Let there be spaces in your togetherness."

While play can represent problems with intimacy, it can also contribute to healthy resolution:

> Andy was twenty-seven years old and Alice twenty-five when they first moved in together. Neither one had ever lived with a lover previously, and because both had been living on their own for some time, they each resisted it.
>
> "I was a lot more insecure in those days," Alice commented several years later. "Moving in with someone was frightening to me then. I was afraid of giving up my own space and of losing my identity." However, at the time they had been going out together for almost four years and were spending practically every night at one or the other's apartment, which was getting very inconvenient.
>
> Neither had an apartment large enough for both of them to move into. One of Alice's requirements was that she and Andy each have their own room as a study or retreat. She used to quote Virginia Woolf's essay "A Room of One's Own" in support of her argument.
>
> Getting a place big enough for each of them to have a room meant moving to a less expensive neighborhood, but Alice was adamant. The process of finding a place was also more time-consuming because such large apartments were hard to find. Andy volunteered to go without a separate room, but Alice wouldn't let them settle for a smaller place.
>
> By the time they eventually moved into a suitable

apartment, the issue of "a room of one's own" had become a touchy one. Airing his feelings in a playful way in the first weeks after they had moved in, Andy bought several printed signs and posted them on the door of Alice's room: Do Not Disturb, No Exit, Enter at Your Own Risk, and Warning: Radioactive Area. Alice took this ribbing good-naturedly and put up a sign on Andy's door in retaliation: Hard-hat Area, which she felt succinctly expressed her feelings about Andy's difficulty in understanding her position.

In retrospect even Andy felt that their separate rooms contributed to the success of their living together. At the same time Andy's playful signs helped to defuse what was, at the time, a loaded issue for the two of them.

It is often the case that partners must feel that their individuality will be respected before they're able to move toward greater intimacy. Paradoxically, we usually can't feel safe to be a "we" until we know that two separate "I's" can exist independently. In the previous example, the play around this issue of private space helped resolve the problem by facilitating Andy's and Alice's communication.

Coming to Terms with Other Relationships

Another way that issues involving closeness and distance are expressed is through regulating relationships that partners have with other people. Commitment requires some pulling away from old ties, in terms of the amount and quality of time spent with friends. It also involves the mourning of relationships from one's past. To choose someone means that you have not chosen others, and it is natural to feel tugged at by loyalties to old intimates, which may extend to parents, to friends, or to old lovers.

Ellen is an actress who had lived in several cities and countries. Before she met Tom, her life was much more chaotic and transient than it has been since she settled down with him.

"I was attracted to Tom in part because he came from a loving, conventional family, which I did not, because he was settled in his profession, and because he offered me a promise of commitment and stability."

Before Tom, Ellen had had numerous lovers. "I had had a more exotic past than Tom and I still work with some of my old lovers. People in show business come and go from city to city and from play to play. You never know whom you're going to bump into." Ellen's colorful past proved awkward to integrate into her new life-style. "I didn't want to pretend that the past didn't exist. I couldn't do that to myself. After all, I still have many good friends from the old days, and if I was dishonest with Tom I'd feel like I was still carrying on an affair. I just wasn't sure how to refer to it. Should I say, 'in my former debauched days . . . ?' That didn't sound right. So I started referring to 'my merry-go-round years.' This was a palatable phrase which captured both the pastiche and immaturity of that era of my life. Best of all, Tom was comfortable with this playful phrase, which allowed me to refer to my past while at the same time distancing myself from it."

Couples sometimes need rituals to help them navigate suitable compromises between the demands of the partner and outside relationships. Otherwise, one set of needs usually gets ignored. This next couple's solution illustrates just another of many possible approaches:

When Jill and Tony began dating regularly, they would spend several nights a week together as well as the weekends. Before they began seeing each other intensively, each one had a busy athletic and social life. While they both enjoyed the deepening commitment to the relationship, they were also hesitant to give up their former separate existences. At the same time, it was difficult to find time for the couple and each of their outside lives.

As a compromise they designated Wednesday nights as "Independence Night" and always kept this open to do things separately. Tony used the night to meet friends for squash games or to go out drinking with a group of the guys he had grown up with. Jill used the time to go shopping or to dinner and a movie with her girl friends. "Independence Night" was a playful way of formalizing a need both partners felt to preserve some of their separate identities, at the same time as they were spending more and more time together.

Old lovers and current sexual attractions to other people are such sensitive issues that many couples find it impossible to talk about them at all. Perhaps if we were fully realized beings we would be able to transcend jealousy and give each other permission to have other lovers. The problem is that few of us come close to shedding the possessiveness born of insecurity. We may also be cursed with a primal sense of exclusivity that dates from Cro-Magnon days, when men were men and women were sexual objects. Nothing short of trading genes with a fruit fly is likely to eliminate this trait. But in relationships in which there is a modicum of trust and in which partners feel sufficiently satisfied with each other that unfaithfulness does not feel like an ever-present threat, it may be possible to use play to dance around the edges of this topic.

While their sexual relationship was very satisfying to both of them, Zack and Teresa still found that they enjoyed looking at other people and imagining them as lovers. They had talked about what these attractions meant and realized that although they found each other very appealing, each of them had imperfections that, of course, these fantasy lovers made up for. There was also something alluring about the unfamiliar, the untried. When they were feeling especially comfortable with each other, such as after a satisfying time making love, they were able to talk about some of their fantasies about other people. Teresa wished for a taller man, and they played out how really big Zack was by comparing his hands and feet with Teresa's, in a sense reassuring her that she really had what she wanted after all. In turn, Teresa pretended to cooperate in Zack's securing any woman he desired, "as long as she's stupid and can't talk."

There is a subtle line between joking as a way of avoiding tensions and play that allows a sensitive topic to be shared, thereby becoming less threatening. Zack and Teresa's play did not lessen their commitment but in fact helped strengthen the bonds between them. I don't recommend that you take lightly each other's concerns about affairs, especially if there is a real threat to the relationship. Similar to the way in which animals and children play only in a secure setting, healthy play is most likely to occur when both partners sense that they can safely be vulnerable.

Money

The ways in which couples handle their finances are another facet of commitment. Early in the relationship understandings are established as to who should pay for what, but as an expectation of permanence settles in, these understandings are negotiated. One potential source of mis-

understanding stems from the different meanings that
money may have for people. For example, to a man, who
traditionally is supposed to be the provider and whose
earning power is regarded by the outside world as a measure of his potency, money represents identity. To a
woman, especially one who has staked a claim to a career,
money may mean that she need not depend on a man for
her financial security. To each of them money is tied up
with self-esteem and power, and to relinquish control and
blur distinctions of ownership may feel like a significant
loss to both of them. Deciding not to pool money, however, creates a sense of separateness that may feel out of
sync with the degree of sharing achieved in other areas of
the relationship. Once again the best resolution is one that
meets both partners' needs for togetherness yet autonomy,
and play can help foster the kind of flexibility that is necessary to achieve these delicate compromises:

> Even after they were married, Sally and Carl
> agreed to maintain separate bank accounts. Sally
> was a broker for a large Wall Street firm and was
> proud of the financial success that she had achieved.
> She had learned from hard experience that most peo-
> ple assumed that the man was the real money earner,
> and she wanted the world to know that when she paid
> for something, such as her first new car, it was her
> hard-earned money. Carl, who judged his worth in
> terms of reviews of his novels and not financial suc-
> cess, would have preferred to pool all their money.
>
> The compromise that they eventually devised was
> called the Swiss Bank Account. While they main-
> tained separate checking accounts and separate in-
> vestment portfolios, they had a third account in both
> their names that each periodically put money into
> whenever one of them had a windfall, such as a tax
> refund. They called it the Swiss Bank Account, be-
> cause whenever money was put into the account, it

no longer was his or hers, and they jokingly referred to it as "laundered" money. It also acquired this name because it was intended to be used primarily as mad money, for extravagant purchases and gifts. Calling it the Swiss Bank Account gave license to their whims, which ordinarily would be kept in tighter rein.

Creative Commitment

Commitment loses its value to enhance love and sexuality when it becomes static. Passive commitment is associated with involuntary confinement, as in commitment to a mental institution. You may naturally look to time-honored conventions to shape your own commitment in a relationship, because it's likely to be territory you've never crossed before; but creative commitment can occur only when you actively collaborate with your partner on your own definition rather than fall into roles and images from the past or borrowed from the media. To be able to play gives you a chance to tap your own sources of creativity and to shake loose from automatic behavior. At a time when women have broken the oppressive spell of stereotyped sex roles, it is too late to reinstall old marital icons. Both men and women have a legitimate right to expect that marriage should enlarge their repertoire of roles rather than diminish their identity.

The romantic is worth preserving, because it helps create intimacy and softens the inevitable conflicts and crises that a life together brings. Being the romantic, though, can also lead to fuzzy thinking; and once the initial state of bliss is honed by reality, there's no use trying to return to it. Romance is a kind of dress rehearsal for true love and as a relationship grows must share the stage with many other emotions. In time idealization should give way to respect for differences, care, concern, and compassion for our partner's pain and failings.

At my own wedding I wanted two passages read. One was Shakespeare's sonnet that includes the line "Love is not love which alters when it alteration finds." The other was from Rilke:

> I tell you that I have a long way to go before I am—where one begins. . . .
>
> You are so young, so before all beginning, and I want to beg you, as much as I can, to be patient toward all that is unsolved in your heart and to try to love the *questions themselves* like locked rooms and like books that are written in a very foreign tongue. Do not now seek the answers, which cannot be given you because you would not be able to live them. And the point is, to live everything. *Live* the questions now. Perhaps you will then gradually, without noticing it, live along some distant day into the answer.
>
> Resolve to be always beginning—to be a beginner!

I could never commit myself to another person if I was committing myself to some vision of the past or if I had a sense that the relationship could not improve. To me, creative commitment means a belief in the possibilities that my partner and I have within us, and that each of us pledges to help emerge. As with any developmental process, we can have only a hazy outline of where we're headed, and chance will have a hand in our growth just as much as our desires. Rilke reminds me that commitment requires a certain amount of surrender as well as determination.

And what of play? Theodor Reik had a beautiful notion that love (I would say play) is an attempt to change a piece of the dream world into reality. We need to give the dream life credence but not be sleepwalkers, and to find ways to reconcile reality to the dream, and not always the other way around. In a beginning relationship fantasy becomes confused with reality—we see our lover as we need them to be rather than as they are. But in a mature, playful relationship, fantasy comes to coexist alongside of reality. *We discover rather than invent our lover.* The difference between fantasy that limits versus fantasy that allows a relationship to grow is analagous to going to a movie or play that distracts us from our cares and entertains us as compared to one that teaches us something about ourselves and gives renewed meaning to our lives.

Keats, that great romantic, saw the concrete and the ideal as one and the same and felt that it is only through the concrete that the ideal can be worked out. Similarly, Zen mystics do not look for spiritual awakening in cloud-shrouded mountains but in the slicing of carrots, in the poignant tendernesses of everyday life. Uplifting the ordinary is not easy, of course, as John Updike is well aware:

> There is no more praise of my heroism in fetching Sunday supper, saving you labor. Cunning, you sense, and sense that I sense your knowledge, that I hoped to hoard your energy toward a more ecstatic spending. We sense everything between us, every ripple, existent and nonexistent; it is tiring. Courting a wife takes tenfold the strength of winning an ignorant girl.

One way to lighten such leaden and predictable intentionality and to keep in touch with the dream without holding tight to idealization is through play. So it is that while you may not reasonably expect that the two of you will be always happy, perhaps, reminiscent of Ferlinghetti, there will still be times when you will turn to each other and with a sense of wonder say, "You and me really *exist.*"

CHAPTER FOUR

Accommodating and Tolerating Differences

One of the occupational hazards of being a couples therapist is that I work more often with couples whose relationships are deteriorating than with couples whose relationships are doing well. There are certainly days when it seems as if every couple's destiny breathes disaffection and disenchantment. But I'm too much of a romantic to embrace a cynical view of love's possibilities—I not only always cry at weddings, I sometimes even start to tear up just driving by one. Yet I know that the couples who show up in my office are no different at heart from those radiant newlyweds, so filled with hope and naïve devotion; they merely represent stages, like snapshots in an album. It's unsettling for me to realize that neither my love relationship nor anyone else's that has become dear to me is immune to such alienation of affection. Why is it so difficult, then, for two mature people to live together intimately, without sacrificing a significant measure of their sanity, or without resort to therapists, lawyers, clergymen, and Ann Landers? Why is it so illusory for us to "live happily ever after"?

The Indian poet Rabindranath Tagore offers one reason in his beautiful statement "Let my love see you even through the barrier of nearness." Physics provides some analogies: at distances we can orbit peacefully, but as we draw closer to Earth we hurtle irresistibly toward collision. A version of Heisenberg's uncertainty principle is also opcrative in intimate relationships: not only does our close observation of an intimate partner change the way he or she behaves, but we are changed as well—intimacy activates mutual "transferences" or distortions based on experiences in past relationships. I don't believe that familiarity always breeds contempt, but it does seem to make it harder to put problems into a loving perspective. With age we require emotional bifocals, for we need to get sufficiently close to someone to really know them, yet be able to step back and see them clearly from a broader perspective.

The Bible blames Adam and Eve, and psychoanalysts believe in a modern-day form of determinism, claiming that our marriages are not made in heaven but in the unconscious; that is, despite our wish to romanticize our attachments, we are endlessly attracted and repelled, like poles of a magnet, by atavistic forces that operate outside of our awareness.

We mustn't settle for any less charm and devotion in our relationship than was present in our earliest infatuation. But divergent views and needs, arguments, ambivalence toward our loved one—such falls from grace are inevitable. Far too many couples who are going through a hard time experience an additional burden of feeling that they are inadequate or that they have a bad relationship. In fact, differences need be feared far less than indifference. My goal is to stimulate your thinking, in as playful a way as possible, about the role of play in dealing with problems in your relationship. For I believe it not only possible but necessary to be both hard-headed and soft-hearted in handling intimate conflict.

Let's first take a closer look at how things can go wrong. This fictitious scene opens as the husband is just returning home from a typical, tiring day at the office. The wife has also just arrived home after a grueling workday. Both of them are looking forward to a quiet, relaxing evening and some tender loving care from their partner.

Husband: Hello, darling.

Wife: Hello, darling. Boy, did I have a bad day!

Husband: (Trying to sound interested but hoping she'll make it brief) Oh? What happened?

Wife: Well, you know Harry . . . (Goes on for several minutes despite the fact that he's too hungry to be really listening.)

Husband: My day was wretched, too. You know Irving . . . (Goes on for several minutes despite the fact that she's too tired to be really listening. Then, hopefully) What's for dinner?

Wife: Do you have any ideas? (This is code for "Don't you think it's your turn to cook?")

Husband: (Ignores wife's gambit) You look great. Where's the newspaper?

Wife: (Charmed, but determined not to be manipulated) Perhaps you could go out and buy a newspaper and pick up some groceries.

Husband: (Sits down and puts feet up on hassock, a code for "I can outwait you.")

Wife: By the way, the garbage needs to be taken out, Fido wants *you* to walk him, *you* didn't pay the gas bill, and it's *your* turn to clean the bathroom.

Husband: (Exploding) You *never* make dinner during the week!

Wife: *You always* expect *me* to do the dirty work!

Husband: My father warned me about marrying a *career* woman. You're just as selfish as your mother.

Wife: I never would have married you if I knew you were such a male chauvinist pig. I suppose you learned it from your father.

Husband: Don't you dare criticize my father. (Said despite the fact that he knows his father is pigheaded.)

Wife: Don't you dare criticize my mother. (This said despite the fact she knows her mother is selfish.)

Husband: (Pout)

Wife: (Pout)

Husband: (Appeals to reason, in order to demonstrate what a fair guy he really is.)

Wife: (Puts on emotional display, effectively canceling out appeal to reason.)

Husband: Let's make a deal. I'll walk the dog if you make dinner.

Wife: How about I'll make dinner or take out the garbage if you buy the groceries now and make dinner tomorrow?

Husband: Okay. (Actually with only weak intention of making frozen dinner tomorrow.)

Wife: Kiss, kiss.

Husband: Kiss, kiss.

In the heat of circumstances, despite being basically sensible people who are reasonably sophisticated at working out problems in the rest of our lives, we've all resorted to similar tactics with those we love. A small disagreement about what kind of stereo to buy somehow drifts into unearthing old hurts and grudges that you thought had been safely buried; a weekend getaway is spoiled by a fight over who was to blame for the wrong turn that took you through an industrial park instead of the shore drive; you start arguing about money, kids, or your mother-in-law and realize you've been down *this* same dead end many times before. Of course, you have alternatives—there's no shortage of folk wisdom about how couples *should* cope with problems.

"To err is human, to forgive divine." True, no couple could last more than one week without forgiveness. But when people forgive they usually mean "I forgive you this time, but don't you dare do it again!" It's a lot more of a strain to forgive when your partner makes a habit of erring. And since few of us are candidates for canonization, we need some other way to deal with our annoyance at our partner's *faux pas* and flaws of character.

An old Danish proverb suggests that "A deaf husband and a blind wife are always a happy couple." Ignoring problems can buy a fragile and temporary kind of bliss. We all need to blink sometimes in the face of the cold stare of reality, and Ecclesiastes would probably agree that just as there is a time to weep and a time to laugh, there is a time to postpone. Short-term accommodations, though, have a way of becoming lifelong adaptations. Some couples arrange such extended holidays from the hard work of a relationship that they end up married not to each other but to an illusion.

Couples can also learn something from children's ancient approach to solving disputes: "One for you and one for me." Negotiation and compromise can resolve many conflicts. But human feelings don't always fit neatly into an equation. It's hard to barter things that admit to no equivalence: she wants more emotional warmth in order to have sex, he wants more sex in order to get to his feelings; he wants children so that he can be a father, she wants a career so that she won't feel trapped by a family. Although marriage is often referred to as a contract, it is really more of a covenant in which two people may share assets and responsibilities, but, more importantly, a vision. It is only when you lose sight of the joint goal that the two of you are working toward or when you lose touch with trust in each other that rights are insisted upon and ledgers kept.

A more recently coined folksaying that has gained much currency is "Let it all hang out." No "truth," no matter how painful, is withheld; no catharsis, no matter how ill-timed, is restrained. Spontaneity is embraced as the greatest virtue; brutal dumping on your partner is justified by the Trojan Horse of open communication. In defense of letting it all hang out, it must be said that too many couples err on the side of side-stepping the truth in misguided attempts to spare their partners (really, themselves) discomfort and other necessary accompaniments of emotional growth. But just as the exhibitionist lets people know who he is in such a way as to drive them away, sincerity can also be a double-edged word.

Finally, conventional wisdom holds that you always be a good listener and empathize with your partner, that you "put yourself in his or her shoes." Who could be against such a loving doctrine? My point is that, like other tools for solving problems that I have mentioned, they are essential but not sufficient. Sometimes you can be too close to a problem to get perspective, so caught up in empathy that your partnership becomes a *folie à deux*. The problem is analogous to the way that your parents and siblings, who supposedly know more about you than anyone else, often don't really know who you are at all. Through time and familiarity, closeness can diminish the capacity to see someone else clearly and to allow them to change.

Such venerated approaches to dealing with problems in your relationship have their virtues. But just as I would not want to do without any one of them, so would I not want to be confined to them. The British psychoanalyst W. R. D. Fairbairn has pointed out that in mature love relationships partners have *multiple* pathways of reaching the other person. Any *one* style of problem solving pursued too single-mindedly eventually becomes a liability. Intimate relationships are dynamic, constantly changing systems, in which partners respond to each other simultaneously on many levels, only some of which are conscious. There are times when you must accommodate one another, changing in order to please your loved one and to make the relationship work more smoothly. In other situations, you or your partner cannot or should not change, and some way must be found of tolerating differences. To walk this tightrope requires an exquisite balancing of problem-solving attitudes and techniques. *Playfulness is your balancing bar*.

Play is not only compatible with open communication, empathy, and a spirit of compromise—it encourages them. In play the starting assumption is that your relationship is basically good-natured and healthy. It does not assign blame or invoke guilt for a conflict, but rather concentrates on the problem and seeks to alter it creatively for the benefit of *both* partners.

I would like to offer a few stepping stones that may help to guide you in trying to integrate playful problem solving into your relationship. These stepping stones are a path, a way of thinking, that is not the straightest line between two points but one that makes getting where you need to go more fun.

Stepping Stones for Playful Problem Solving

Play More, Work at It Less

Relationships require effort, but continual striving can make change impossible—devotion to the work ethic allows insufficient leeway for spontaneity and the serendipitous breakthrough that is favored by relaxed meandering. Developing the capacity to shift into a playful way of thinking about problems is ultimately more valuable than learning playful techniques. Play introduces flexibility where there has been rigidity and gives birth to creativity instead of knee-jerk reactions. Sometimes you need to have fun together first in order to resolve a problem.

> *"I remember Ronnie and I used to have such struggles over things," reports Beverly. "We'd argue over some misunderstanding, obsessing over and interpreting our every phrase. One night we'd been at it for a couple of hours, and I said, 'Look, let's go dancing and talk about this another time.' We changed and went straight to our favorite disco and danced into the early hours of the morning. I forgot completely about our argument.*
>
> *"The next day Ronnie brought up the subject and I thought to myself, Oh, no. Here we go again. But it*

wasn't the same old argument. Having had such a good time together helped us both to lighten up."

Acceptance without Resignation

Change isn't something that's planned for one person by another. It's something that can happen when you feel loved and accepted. Paradoxically, acceptance opens up the possibility for change. But how do you find that place of tranquillity when your partner is displaying his or her most unlovable traits? What do you do when you look at your carping, unkempt mate, who, unfortunately for you, forgot to brush his teeth, and you silently wonder, "Is this the same person I married?" It's as if people become afflicted with a psychiatric condition called Capgras syndrome, in which they feel as if the people closest to them have actually been replaced by imposters. You may feel that you've married an alien from outer space or that they've been hatched from a pod in some grade B science-fiction movie. But *you* have changed just as much as she.

I think you have to start by looking at why a particular issue bothers you so much. In most instances the degree to which our partners' foibles get on our nerves has something to do with our own peculiar emotional vulnerabilities. For example, your moral outrage that your new living partner is a slob may be related to the fact that in your own family *you* wouldn't get dessert if you didn't pick up your own clothes or hold your fork just right. When at odds with your partner, you may feel that he or she is the problem. If only he or she would act or think differently, how much better things would be! Perhaps you've even indulged in the fantasy of sending your mate to a marital reform school, run by Caligula and Dr. Ruth, which would guide him to see things the right (that is, your) way. Occasionally your partner may even agree that she alone is to blame. But as long as you're looking only outward and not inward at yourself, or vice versa, you haven't a prayer if you want to learn what's going on. To use a well-worn phrase, if you're not part of the solution, you're part of the problem. The more you avoid looking at your contribution to an impasse, the more likely it is that it's significant, whether it be 10, 50, or 90 percent of the problem. Acceptance does not mean resignation to things as they are. It does not mean giving up or giving in, but it does mean giving.

Often what stands in the way of acceptance is that we don't want to part with our idealized image of our partner. We need them to be perfect, and any deviation feels like a betrayal, any difference from us as an attack on our own self-worth. Unfortunately, the closer we get to someone, the harder it is for them to cover up or for us to ignore their blemishes.

> Sally and Bob had been going out together for two years when they decided to live together. "I always thought Bob was a very neat, meticulous person, until I lived with him," says Sally. "When we weren't living together, whenever I'd go to Bob's place it was always like something out of House & Garden. But when we shared a place, he'd leave rooms a mess and only clean up after I reminded him several times. I was embarrassed to have people over.
>
> Bob had a different perspective: "When we had separate apartments I'd always clean up just before Sally came over. I wanted to impress her. But basically I'm a casual guy and neatness isn't my thing. I thought Sally was a casual person, too. She never used to give me a hard time about anything."

The romantic sense of being totally merged into one is lovely to re-experience from time to time. But in order to tolerate your partner's faults, whether they be slurping her soup, insulting your friends, or wearing his Levis to your cousin's bar mitzvah, you have to recognize that you have a distinct identity. Most couples have made hostages of each other's self-esteem. Your former soul mate might become your cell mate, because whatever "crimes" you find him guilty of you feel you also have to be ashamed of.

There is no easy way out of this, but the first step is to accept that you, not your partner, are the one who is ultimately responsible for making you feel okay. You might also ask yourself whether you're latching onto a particular issue because of your own fear of intimacy—better to fight, your inner voice might be saying, than to risk vulnerability.

A measure of acceptance is a prerequisite for healthy play. Many of the forms of play described in this chapter won't work if you're still grating your teeth and thirsting for revenge. You don't have to be a saint. Acceptance also gradually deepens through play.

The Medium Can Change the Message

Play expands our repertoire of communications over time. Relationships may start to stagnate and partners' senses become dulled—we hear one another, but we're really not listening because we think that we've heard it all before. Nevertheless, we persist in broadcasting at the same frequency, not realizing that our partner's response may be preordained by the staleness of our message. If this happens, there are many other wavelengths on which two people can tune in to each other.

"We each do things that drive each other bats," says Claudia. "Jim always 'forgets' to wind the electrical cord around the vacuum cleaner after he's finished with it and it seems like once a week I'll be sitting on the toilet and find that there's only one sheet of toilet paper left clinging to the cardboard roller. No matter how many times I cajoled or yelled at Jim to shape up, it didn't do any good. Jim has his complaints, too. For example, I'm always late. Then

there are the bigger issues that we've argued about for years.

"One way we deal with these perennial irritations is by talking in exotic accents. 'Dollink! Vere iz ze toilet paper?' or 'You weel be velly solly, honorable wife.' Sometimes we'll curse at each other with foreign profanity that we know or have made up. Sometimes we'll have a serious discussion using foreign accents when something is very sensitive or when we've tried talking about it many times before and we need a new approach. It's as if we try to shift into a different gear."

Note that this couple has not used play to avoid discussion but as an alternative when more conventional approaches are inadequate. Play, like poetic metaphor, has impact—the same message conveyed through play can render your partner more receptive.

We Need to Be Illogical to Deal with the Illogical

I am not an advocate for the noble savage—the human psyche is driven in part by deeply primitive urges that, without reason in the saddle, can stampede us toward dark places. But in many of the problems that couples encounter there is a thoroughly irrational element, one that no amount of common sense or reason can help.

"Sometimes I bring up a particular problem with my husband repeatedly, like how much progress he's making with his doctoral dissertation. It's not that there's anything new or profound to say. We already have driven it into the ground. And I know there's not much to be gained by talking more about it. But I just can't help myself. At times like this my husband pretends to scream and bang his head against the wall, as if he just went crazy. I'll do something simi-

lar when he tries to give me reasons for why he won't quit smoking."

The next couple illustrates a more titillating form of spontaneity:

> "In the ten years that Redmond and I have been married," says Ellie, "he's gotten totally irrational only a few times. Once it was over the fact that our neighbors erected a fence without consulting us about its design. It was an ugly prefab fence that clashed with our colonial house. Another time it was because the IRS kept on billing us with computer letters over and over, even though we had sent in our payment months before.
>
> "In both instances, Redmond just completely lost it. He was practically foaming at the mouth. I didn't blame him for being upset, but he just couldn't let go of it, and his ranting and raving were beginning to get wearing. So I did a bizarre thing. One night when Redmond was getting himself all worked up, I said in a somewhat frustrated but light-hearted tone, 'You're right. I have to take my panties off to this!' and I reached under my dress and ripped my panties off. This stopped Redmond in his tracks. I suppose I was showing how strangely he was acting by going him one better. Maybe he also realized that he was driving me nuts. Also, on both occasions I did this we had sex together later in the evening, which we hadn't done for days because he had been so moody."

Play enables us to deal with the illogical such that we can learn its language. In this way, we can have a personal relationship with our irrational side rather than railing at it for leading us astray.

From Zero Sum to the New Math

During drawn-out disagreements couples tend to become more and more committed to their points of view and unwilling to consider alternatives because it feels like conceding. A situation that each sees as having only a "zero sum" outcome, in terms of one winning and the other losing, will only create resentment. Play can help change this no-win situation into one in which both can win and are changed in the process. Play provides an atmosphere in which partners can feel safe to explore options rather than asserting rigid positions. The next couple illustrates how playful exaggeration can change a couple from being adversaries to problem solvers.

"My wife says I'm compulsive. We still argue about it, but over the years I've mellowed a bit. For example, whenever we fly I'm a nervous wreck until I'm actually at the departure gate. My palms start getting sweaty the night before our flight. I'm at my worst in foreign countries—I'm sure that the way to every airport is a jungle of police checkpoints, dirt roads, and seven-car accidents. It's amazing to me that anyone makes it to the airport on time.

"Recently we were in Milan, where the airport is a good distance from the city, just the situation where my fertile imagination could run wild. The desk clerk suggested we allow three hours to get there. Since our flight left at two P.M., that meant leaving by at least eleven. My wife was pleased that she could get a little shopping done in the morning.

"I awoke at six and shaved and showered by six thirty. I went into the bedroom where my wife was just waking up. 'I've been thinking about our flight,' I said. 'Maybe we should leave now.' She looked as if she was about to have a fit until she saw that I was *grinning. We left at ten thirty, which gave her a chance to do some shopping and gave me a little reassurance on the way to the airport."*

The goal is to devise creative solutions, not necessarily to win a partner over to your point of view. For even were you to manage agreement on content, there can be lingering resentment if the solution is felt to be imposed. I imagine this explains why some states feel it is more humane to offer convicted murderers a choice of being hanged or shot —they may not like the solution, but presumably they're appreciative that they've been consulted. As the family therapist Jay Haley has pointed out, couples disagree not only about the rules that govern permissible behavior in their relationship; they also struggle over who makes the rules. The American psychiatrist Harry Stack Sullivan defined the mature relationship as being characterized by collaboration.[17] Intimate play invites collaboration. It is not an attempt to manipulate or trick your partner into doing what you want them to do.

Go with the Resistance

In order for change to occur in longstanding patterns, you must have considerable respect for what psychoanalytic theorists call resistance. Without getting technical, resistance means the unconscious psychic forces that limit our awareness and integration of experiences that are potentially painful, embarrassing, and incompatible with how we need to see ourselves. People may consciously oppose change, but it is usually the unconscious forces that resist change which are most problematic. One of the tricky things about resistance is that the harder you try to get rid of it, the stronger it becomes, much as in the Chinese finger puzzle in which the more you try to extricate your fingers by pulling, the tighter they become bound.

June and Henry Benson had lived in their house for more than twenty-five years. It was the only house they had ever owned, and they had raised their children there. Now nearing retirement, they had decided to move to a condominium. June accepted that they had to move to a smaller place. But as the date approached for their move she became paralyzed. She kept on putting off the packing. At first Henry ignored her procrastination, then he became concerned, and finally exasperated. He had begun some of the packing himself, but a lot of the things, like their fine china and June's many "collectables," she wouldn't allow him to touch.

One night they talked about June's feelings about the move and her unhappiness at leaving the home that had so much history in it. At the end of this talk, Henry made a suggestion: "Why don't you pack just one box tomorrow? But don't use a big box or pack it with lots of little things—that would be too much to start with. Take a very little box and fill it with one or two big things." June had to laugh at Henry's proposal, but she agreed to try it. She labeled the box "Henry's First Box."

"It still took me a long time to do the packing," said June, "but I had made a start, and the rest of the job gradually got done."

Many of the playful strategies of problem solving that I will describe are diplomatic ways of dealing with resistance. Play encourages without insisting on change.

Aim at a Change in Awareness, Not a Change in Behavior

When an impasse occurs and both partners feel unable to effect any movement, further insistence that the other person change his behavior is usually counterproductive. Attempts to change the way a partner acts are usually experienced as manipulative and coercive. Behavioral flexibility more often follows a change in one or both partners' way of looking at the problem. As the family therapist Virginia Satir points out, action requires a separate negotiation: it often follows, although it is not an automatic response to, understanding. Rather than ask yourself, How can I change what my partner is doing, ask How can *we* better understand what underlies the behavior? Breakthroughs can involve a new awareness of why either needs to act in a certain way, or of how each might experience the problem. Thus, you must approach your partner's behavior with empathy and with an appreciation for his or her perspective, as well as with a willingness to learn something new about each other.

> One couple developed a phrase, "Warning, conflict area!" to signal that one or both of them was being testy or acting defensively because they were having trouble dealing with a sensitive issue.
> "We say it in a light, not an accusative, way that gets the other's attention without forcing them to deal with it. It's an invitation to be self-reflective. There are often things that you're sort of aware of, but then you forget, or they crop up again and you need a reminder. This is our reminder to each other."

There are exceptions to focusing on a change in awareness; for instance, sometimes people remain stuck even when they understand all they will never need to know (psychoanalysts are quite familiar with this problem), and there are couple systems in which attitudes are terminally intransigent. In such situations effecting a small behavioral change may serve as a catalyst.

Dare to Be Different

Some people insist on a "three yards and a cloud of dust" approach to a problem. Woody Hayes was a success-

ful head football coach at Ohio State University whose offense consisted almost entirely of running straight ahead,
each play gaining about three yards. This worked out well
except when his team fell behind and needed a big play.
When asked why he never passed the ball, he replied,
"When you pass, three things can happen and only one of
them is good." Playfulness often involves a willingness to
add new wrinkles to your game plan, the equivalent to a
flea flicker or the Statue of Liberty play for Woody Hayes.
Stepping out of your accustomed role temporarily does not
mean you have to stop being Woody Hayes, if that's who
you're most comfortable being. Play gives you license to
depart from your norm, to try out the unusual and unexpected.

Playful Strategies

Most couples, once I've introduced them to the notion of
playful problem solving, become excited about the possibility of incorporating more play into their daily lives.
Every couple has impasses that remain impervious to conventional problem-solving approaches, and while I know
that no technique can make a relationship easy, I really feel
that most people can be better equipped through the power
of play to effect change. Unfortunately, play does not lend
itself well to a cookbook approach—there's an inherent
paradox in methodically attempting to be more spontaneous. But starting with a few recipes may help give you
greater daring to adopt a new approach and further stimulate your own creativity. My aim is not to cover every
conceivable type of play but to show by example how play
can be applied to a variety of common problems and sensitive issues. Some of the examples may seem as though
they are drawn from your own life. Others may seem quite
foreign. The important thing is to be creative in your approach to problems in your own relationship.

Play encourages a freeing of hardened positions and

changes the Gestalt in which a problem is perceived—in this case, by putting a frame around a conflict so that it is contained within a loving context. The purpose of play is not so much to avoid a necessary confrontation or to have your point of view win out. *In true play there is always a tension between mastery and submission.* In order to reconcile divergent views and needs so that your loving connection becomes enhanced, neither side must yield alone; rather, both must change.

Laughter can reduce tensions and help establish a more relaxed atmosphere. Similarly, play can help clear the air after a couple's argument. A playful nickname, tickling, acting silly—these can all be flags of truce that invite a renewal of tenderness following a serious confrontation. "I know it's still too soon for real intimacy," our playfulness says, "but even if my entire self is not yet acceptable to you, how about this playful little piece of me that always used to make you laugh?" This very simple form of play illustrates some of the basic dynamics that you will see at work in the vignettes to follow. With this broad picture in mind, let the play begin.

Relabeling: To Touch the Truth Lightly

One of the ways that play can be a creative form of compromise is that it can enable you to communicate about a touchy area in your relationship in a way that your partner can receive. The truth is not glossed over or baldly stated but touched lightly, for example, by using a paradoxical nickname:

Jim, an electrical engineer, tends to tightly control his feelings; whenever he's feeling vulnerable—sad or hurt or criticized—he clams up. On many occasions this leads to fights with Teri, who needs him to be more expressive. While recognizing, in the course of his therapy, that he needed to open up more, it was not easy for Jim to change. But at a time when one of Jim's close friends had died, his customary stoic façade relaxed and he was able to cry. Teri comforted him, and, noticing that he seemed a bit sheepish to have her see him cry, she kidded him, "Don't worry, you're still my invulnerable hero."

Subsequently, at other times when Jim was able to show his vulnerability and to share his fears, she would joke similarly. "But of course, we know you're really an invulnerable hero and that you're not really feeling afraid." Such play was not used as ridicule but as a signal to both of them that this was an instance of Jim's dealing with his problem.

Things that are revealed as sensitive points in a partner during a fight, issues that are difficult to talk about, can later be played with from different directions. The nickname was a play on Jim's characteristic stance, highlighting the absurdity of being so rigid. At the same time that a criticism was implied, it was paradoxically relabeled as a virtue (being a hero) rather than a fault, making it easier for Jim to accept. There is also a second paradox implied by Teri's addressing Jim by this nickname at the times when he was allowing himself to be more vulnerable: Teri was implicitly telling Jim, "When you are *vulnerable*, you are just as much of a hero to me." The next couple further illustrates this use of paradox:

Norma and Andy were both doing well at their jobs in architectural firms until one day, unexpectedly, Andy lost his job. Andy was stunned—he thought that he was completely secure professionally, destined to move quickly to the top. Norma was equally stunned but was then able to anticipate how hard it would be for Andy. During the six months that Andy was out of work he was offered a variety of jobs, but they were all either steps down or not in the

*specialized field of industrial architecture that Andy
was interested in. Although they were not what Andy
wanted, it was hard to decide what to do, since at
least they offered real work.*

*Andy's job loss touched upon deeply felt family
issues. Andy's father was a small-time building con-
tractor who always regretted not having had the
money for a degree that he believed would have
given him the extra status to make it big. Much as
Andy was aware of the unreasonableness of being
expected to fulfill his father's dreams, it did influence
him. Thus, he became moody and preoccupied.*

*Norma's playful approach was to nickname him
"the unemployed genius." At times when Andy was
trying to talk himself into accepting a job that he
really wasn't interested in, Norma would say, "Now
what would an unemployed genius want with such a
job?" At times when Andy was feeling down about
his job prospects, she would hug him and call him by
his nickname. It was all very private—nothing like
this was said in front of anybody else.*

As in the nickname the "invulnerable hero," the "unemployed genius" involves the use of paradox—in this case,
the coupling of the man's sense of failure (remaining unemployed) with his greatest hope—being a genius of an
architect.

Paradoxical nicknames are helpful in relabeling situations in which a partner or couple is feeling pulled in two
different directions. Both of the men in these examples
drawn from my research interviews are trying to reconcile
conflicting forces: for Jim, the problem is how to be more
expressive while still feeling manly; Andy needs to feel
successful, but both being unemployed or accepting a less-
than-ideal job make him feel like a failure. The paradoxical
nicknames touch on both horns of the partner's dilemma
such that he feels understood and accepted while being

gently encouraged to change. Such play provides an alternative to either attacking a partner ("You always hide your feelings," "No job will be good enough for you") or avoiding the whole issue as too explosive to deal with. Play provides a gentle confrontation that surfaces the underlying issues in a helpful way while conveying to your partner that you're on their side.

Touching the truth lightly may serve couples well in dealing not only with such subtle psychological conflicts, but in more mundane matters, such as who does the cooking, washes the dishes, puts out the garbage, and so on. Inevitably, conflicts arise not only over who does what but *how* things should be done. ("Thank you for washing the dishes, but would you mind getting the egg yolk off them next time?") Since things like household responsibilities are a daily issue, you need to be creative in devising ways to cope with your differences so that troublesome tiffs don't continually arise, as in the following example of relabeling:

> For Linda and her gourmet cook boyfriend, Darrell, the problem of how to split up the cooking was complicated by the fact that he was so expert while Linda was just an average cook. When Linda cooked he constantly made critical judgments on the dishes she prepared: a dash more salt here, less vinegar there, a tad warmer, and so on. Darrell's perfectionism frequently ruined the meals for Linda, who argued back that he was just being a perfectionist and a bully. Many meals ended in stand-off silence, which was good for neither their palates nor their relationship.
>
> Linda realized they were getting nowhere, and so she changed her approach. Instead of dwelling on her hurt feelings and retaliating directly at Darrell's criticisms, Linda began calling him by the nickname "El Exigente," after the "exacting one" in the coffee

commercials. This playful response to his perfectionism made her feel less vulnerable and made him a bit foolish in his peevishness, without provoking him into wounded withdrawal. He, in turn, dubbed her "Ms. Microwave," a jibe at her meal-in-a-minute specials. Thus, instead of ending in silence, their stand-offs concerning Linda's culinary skills became spiced with humor.

In this example the nickname worked not because it involved a paradox touching on the partner's subtle conflicts but because it exhibited an appreciation along with the criticism. "El Exigente" compared Darrell to a debonair aristocrat with very high standards, rather than lambasting him for his carping. But it is also the humor in such play that makes it easy to receive. Play leavens the deadly seriousness of our problems, enabling us to take a step back from ourselves and see things more clearly.

Since each couple's dynamics are unique, you will have to experiment yourselves with nicknames that "touch the truth lightly." The real lesson of relabeling is that *half the battle may be to redefine the problem* by casting it in tongue-in-cheek but compassionate terms that help you enjoy your weaknesses. That is, when your partner experiences your criticism as a verbal slap, put on a velvet glove. The key is to try to see the situation with a sense of humor, to caricature and exaggerate it. If you are able to see your partner's problematic behavior as being, at least in part, benevolently motivated, your playful criticism is more apt to be sympathetic. Most nicknames emerge spontaneously by your being open to irrational associations and images. Then a testing-out process follows, in which you need to be sensitive to how your partner receives the nickname. The goal is not to stick them with a name that pleases you but to implicitly or overtly agree to a way of relabeling the problem. Ideally, there will always be a delicate balance between tolerating your partner's being who they are and accommodating—that is, influencing and encouraging them to change.

Another way of touching the truth lightly is through the use of negation—instead of stating a criticism directly, say the opposite, as in the following story:

> Jenny had a habit of talking for Rob, even in his presence: "Well, Rob thinks that Mr. Greenjeans should be elected," she would offer, or "We thought that the Mona Lisa was a bit trop." If Rob tried to ignore what she was doing, he still felt resentment. Telling her directly at the time it occurred embarrassed her in front of their friends, and if he waited till they were alone she had a selective memory for what she had said. Rob figured out a response that seemed to work better: whenever she spoke for him, he responded with something like "Isn't it wonderful how Jenny speaks on my behalf? It's such a bother to have to express myself," or "Thank you for speaking for me, I never realized I had such intelligent opinions." He would then make eye contact with her and wink.

Rob is certainly expressing some sarcasm, but the purpose is to open the door, not to try to score points; if the tone is hostile or bitter, it won't be received kindly. Nonverbal cues are essential to express support and reassurance. The intent should be to make light of the problem, while unmistakably calling attention to it. The indirect approach enables you to do an end run around your partner's defensiveness—it suggests to them rather than insists that something *might* be true, in this case that you don't want to be spoken for. Certainly, it would be important for you and your partner to have talked seriously at some point so that the offending partner knows that the other is bothered by what he or she is doing. Once a problematic behavior has been identified, a delicate touch may be more effective than a continual frontal assault. As G. K. Chesterton put it, "Angels fly because they take themselves lightly."

Changing the Medium

Just as touching the truth lightly can enable you to talk more hospitably and productively about sensitive issues, so may nonverbal strategies be a valuable tool. I'm often impressed with the fact that during so many arguments more talking is counterproductive. Feelings have been hurt, positions have become rigidified, and either we persist in going over the same ground or we avoid the unpleasant business altogether. Many of the couples that come to me for therapy are trapped in a "blame" system. Whenever they begin to talk about anything that they're unhappy about, their perspective is that someone (usually their partner) is at fault, and most discussions soon degenerate into runaway accusations, denials, and counteraccusations. It's as if their relationship were a car and one partner feels as though the other has deliberately damaged it; he retaliates by tearing off a fender. The other ups the ante by pulling off the bumper, and before long there's nothing left safe to drive. It's painful for me, even as an innocent bystander, to watch as two people who care for one another tear the relationship or each other apart. It's destructive, hurtful, and leads nowhere. Nevertheless, it's very difficult to convince a couple to give up the blame system that they know, for a "no fault" approach with which they're unfamiliar. The next couple taught me a technique for interrupting a war of the words, and I have since used it effectively with other couples.

> *Jack and Trudi had lived all their lives in New York City, where they were both lawyers. When they retired they moved to a small town in Florida, where they hoped to escape the pressures of the city.*
> *"When we moved to Florida we suddenly had a lot*

of time on our hands, and we tended to get into senseless spats about things," said Trudi. *"At first they were just silly arguments, and I think they passed a certain amount of time. But then they got more nasty and bitter. I didn't know what was happening. We'd never argued like that before. I was so exasperated.*

"One day, I don't know what came over me. We had been arguing all morning. I came out into the kitchen and I was so upset. I thought, We can't go on like this. Jack was in the living room mumbling away, still stewing. I began rummaging around in the cabinet under the kitchen sink. I don't know what I was thinking of. Maybe I thought I would wash the kitchen floor to take my mind off things. But I'd already washed it, too many times. There I was, so distraught, and then I did the strangest thing. We store new light bulbs in the cabinet under the sink. I took a lightbulb out of those flimsy little shmattes they come in and I carried it into the other room. Jack just looked at me, kind of cross-eyed, as if saying, 'What are you doing?'

"I carried it across the room to where he was sitting and I handed the light bulb to him. Then I sat down on the couch, real neatly, and kind of pulled myself up. 'What the hell is this for?' he said. 'I don't know,' I said, and I was about to cry and maybe he could tell.

" 'It's a bright idea,' I said.

" 'What do you mean, it's a bright idea? What do you want me to do with it?'

" 'I want you, I want us, to stop fighting,' I said. 'That's the bright idea.' He looked at the light bulb and he looked at me like I'd gone crazy. I thought I was going crazy. Then he laughed nervously and said 'All right, we'll try to stop.' And we did. After that

whenever we got into a ridiculous argument one of us would say to the other—he began saying it, too—'I have a bright idea,' which, of course, meant that the bright idea was that we should stop arguing, because it had gotten out of hand.

"Once we'd put a brake on the arguing we were able to talk about why we had been arguing so much. We decided we had a lot of expectations about our new retired life but no plans. We were, in fact, at a loss to fill our time after being used to a busy life in the city. We resolved to explore the countryside and get involved in some local activities, which has worked out very well."

To call a halt to your own destructive arguments, you and your partner should decide in advance on a signal, ideally some kind of absurd word or phrase that has special meaning to the two of you. You must agree that when either of you speaks it, you both have to stop talking until you've had a chance to calm down. The amount of time that you wait is up to you, but either partner can invoke the absurd word whenever you feel that things are getting out of hand. This technique won't solve the underlying issues, but it can help set the stage for a more productive dialogue.

I have also used other techniques to help couples put the brakes on destructive arguments: note writing and foreign language. Writing things down provides a kind of buffer, which de-escalates a war of words. Further, when you have to write something down, you're more likely to become aware of what you're saying from the viewpoint of your partner. One way to use the note-writing technique is to sit across from your partner and to alternate writing notes to each other, the rule being that no talking is allowed. Another way is to write "letters" to each other about the problem whenever either feels moved to communicate; you can then talk with each other about other things and carry on normally in all other ways. Writing notes also lends itself well to injecting a sense of humor, which can help restore good feelings:

> *Joan and Liz came to adapt note writing to their own individual styles. Joan had a taste for Victorian novels. Thus, when she wanted to remind Liz about cleaning up the bathtub after herself she would write "My esteemed Elizabeth, the bathing pool has a ring of unmentionable origin halfway up its side. Kindly see it is attended to at your earliest convenience."*
>
> *Liz, whose father often sent her Godiva chocolates for Christmas and her birthday, would become annoyed when she realized that Joan was pinching the chocolates when Liz was not around. To put an amicable stop to this she placed a calligraphied, religious-sounding note inside the Godiva box, which read, "Thou shalt not steal thy neighbor's goodies . . . at least not too often."*

Another playful way to change the medium of an argument is to conduct the discussion in a foreign language, ideally a tongue with which both have some acquaintance but are far from fluent. The results can be quite comical and can change the whole tenor of the encounter.

Changing the medium not only helps couples deal better with quarrels that have already begun but also averts potential flare-ups. The principle involved is analogous to touching the truth lightly, but in this instance the medium is nonverbal. For example, the couple in which the wife (Jenny) had a habit of speaking for her husband (Rob) developed playful nonverbal language as an alternative to addressing the issue aloud when other people were around. When either of them was doing something that annoyed the other, he or she would bring it gently to their attention by twirling the wedding ring on their finger. Besides being an effective secret signal, this particular gesture probably

developed because it expressed a partly serious impulse—
"If you don't stop doing that, I'm going to have to divorce you."

> Shannon was determined to lose thirty pounds
> after her pregnancy. She announced this to Jerry one
> morning when she couldn't find a single pair of her
> old slacks that would still fit. At the time he just
> grunted, but the next few days, as he saw that she
> was serious about dieting, he thought about how he
> could lend his support without pressuring her.
>
> One day Shannon noticed a picture on the door of
> their refrigerator. It was a picture of a svelte model
> in a bathing suit cut out of the Sunday paper. Jerry
> began this ritual after his wife's first significant
> weight loss—ten pounds—when she felt she was
> really on the road to success. Thereafter, every week
> he would take down the previous week's picture and
> replace it with a new one. His intention was to con-
> vey to her the idea that "this is what you want to look
> like" whenever she went near the refrigerator.
>
> Shannon appreciated the fact that Jerry was think-
> ing about what she was trying to accomplish: "At
> first I thought it was kind of bizarre, because neither
> of us likes advertisements in which women's bodies
> are used to sell goods. But then I realized that his
> inventiveness meant he really cared about my diet. I
> was glad he didn't tell me straight out at the begin-
> ning that he wanted me to lose weight, too, though
> his humorous way of urging me along got the mes-
> sage across in a gently encouraging sort of way."

Body images are a very sensitive area that can be hard
for a couple to share with each other. It's difficult to talk
about something you don't like about yourself when you
haven't accepted that part of yourself in your own heart.
Our culture is so body-conscious—the media perpetuates

the myth of physical perfection—that having less than ideal attributes feels like something to be ashamed of. My big nose and receding hairline were great sources of private anguish for me for many years. When I was finally able to talk about my preoccupation with how terrible I thought I was, I found that women were far more forgiving than I was of myself. My experience as a therapist is that everyone has a secret "ugly me," and that an enormous amount of energy is wasted in worrying about people's, including our partners', evaluations of our "ugly me." Shy people find it especially difficult to talk about these hidden parts of themselves. It's a paradox, because on the one hand they think that other people are constantly homing in on these ugly attributes, while on the other they imagine that if they don't mention them they won't be noticed. Play offers ways to enable reticent partners to open up more with each other.

A good exercise that I have used to help couples share hangups related to their bodies is that of drawing self-portraits. You don't have to be a good artist, just have a willingness to be playful and to let down your guard a little. Each of you takes a large piece of drawing paper, such as newsprint, and some crayons and tries to draw a large picture of yourself in the nude, emphasizing parts of yourself that you like and those that you don't like. You can draw side by side, but initially you're bound to be a bit self-conscious so you may prefer to work on opposite sides of the room. When you're done, both of you talk about what you see in your own and in your partner's drawings. If your partner's creation looks more like Jabba the Hutt than Sleeping Beauty, remember that a lot of care and gentleness is essential in order to make him or her feel comfortable in unveiling some of their secrets. Artistic ability is irrelevant—a child's drawing can be more self-revealing than a talented artist's.

Changing the medium can also help you to accommodate to changes in life circumstances, such as a move to a new city, retirement, or illness. Such readjustments are often complicated by personal inflexibilities that tend to become exaggerated under the new stress, necessitating playful strategies:

One of the most difficult crises Tom and Margaret faced arose after Tom was in an auto accident. After the accident, which nearly cost him his life, Tom was confined to bed for several months. During these months his active sports life and a busy professional life were reduced to a sick room. What was even worse was that given the seriousness of the injuries to his leg, they knew he would probably have to give up much of the sports, such as marathon running, that had been an important part of his life.

Margaret was very supportive, but his convalescence was hard on her as well. In addition to taking care of him, she also had responsibility for their three children and a full-time job. She really needed help, but Tom was a very proud man, bred in a Maine family whose watchword was self-sufficiency. As a way of getting help, in a way that Tom would not find unacceptable, Margaret secretly got in touch with many of Tom's relatives and old friends. She wanted to develop a sense of community and support, so she asked each of them to make one square of a patchwork quilt, each depicting a memorable event or achievement in Tom's life. "I told them I wanted to keep the quilt a secret from Tom until it was finished," she said. "Naturally most of his relatives and friends came over to reminisce with him about whatever it was they were going to illustrate in the square. Tom really enjoyed those talks although he didn't know until the end what they were all leading up to. The project gave me a great focus, too—it was a way of working through the change in our lives that the accident would mean. I don't know who benefited more from it—Tom or me."

On receiving the completed quilt Tom was very touched. All of their friends and relatives that could came over for the presentation and Tom was very moved by the symbolism of the quilt. It was an important morale booster for him during the long months of recovery. For both partners the playful project helped mobilize a support system of caring friends and relatives, which was extremely important at this time in their lives. It helped provide a sense of mastery in a situation in which they would otherwise feel like victims.

Changing the medium can enable you to get through to your partner when serious discussion would be ineffective. As a therapist, I love words—they are my livelihood—but I have also come to learn that songs require music.

"All the World's a Stage": Changing the Context

Sometimes, removing yourselves from the setting in which an argument has been taking place can be beneficial. This is analogous to the effect of changing the shape of the discussion table during collective bargaining or international negotiations. Whether we are perceiving each other as adversaries or allies, it's important to remember that much of what we call personality isn't static. The way a person behaves changes constantly, depending on context.

A California couple developed a ritual for handling potentially touchy discussions or situations in which they had to make a big decision. They lived in a house high on a hill overlooking the ocean. Whenever a potentially divisive issue came up, they would go down the winding trail of wooden stairs to the sea and walk along the beach while having their discussion. "The expanse of the Pacific coast would have a calming effect on us," they said. "Somehow it helped put problems into perspective. It made them seem small, which is a great attitude from which to discuss them. We both felt so much more conciliatory in our bare feet, walking along the beach."

You may not be fortunate enough to have the Pacific Ocean available in your backyard whenever you need to have a serious discussion. You don't have to fly off to Paris for every delicate negotiation. But there's bound to be someplace nearby that can serve the same purpose of setting the two of you at ease and helping to put problems into a more cosmic perspective.

One couple that I interviewed, who lived out in the country, would go out on a hill at night and look up at the stars. Dawn and dusk are propitious times for enlisting nature on the side of conciliation, and I've also found that skipping stones over the water together is a good tranquilizer.

Changing the context can also mean putting off a discussion or interrupting a nonproductive one until after you and your partner have connected nonverbally. Some couples who jog together find that it diminishes tensions and establishes a kind of brother/sisterhood of sweat. If you have a vegetable or flower garden, spending some time weeding or putting in some seedlings can also serve to remind both of you of the positive things you share. It is also well known that "music soothes a savage breast." Playing music together can be a way to reconnect, and I, for one, find it impossible to remain unreasonable after listening to Bach's Violin Concerto in E-major or to Maria Callas singing *La Wally*.

An alternative strategy is to agree to allow yourselves to engage in a particular problematic behavior, but only in a defined, ridiculous context. For example, one couple confined their nasty arguments to the bathroom during a bubble bath. They would wear bathing suits so that sex didn't get associated with unpleasant feelings and also to heighten the absurdity of the context. This couple recognized that they had a tendency to enter into destructive conflicts and used context to limit such behavior.

Through experience you and your partner can build up a repertoire of ways to change the context. Eventually, the hard issues will still have to be faced, but the process is more likely to strengthen rather than divide.

Exaggerating Annoying Behavior

In every relationship, at some point each partner inevitably finds that some aspect of the other's behavior becomes annoying. This is especially liable to happen soon after a couple begins living together. When the relationship is new and they're still basically discovering each other, they tend to moon over the things they like in each other and to overlook "little things" that might be annoying. Then, after a lot of the crucial discoveries have been made, there's a transition period, and they come back to earth to negotiate the everyday details of living. For example, that ghost outfit your partner looked so cute in at Halloween may become a bone of contention when you continue to find holes in your new bed sheets. As in any partnership, there's a certain amount of tension, which tends to focus itself on little things. Often the conflicts were present all along and went unnoticed. It may be the way she hums soft-drink commercials or grinds her teeth or his tendency to leave lights on or to dress like a slob—whatever it is can get blown out of proportion because of other issues in the relationship. Oversensitivity to petty annoyances gives a clue to how irrational our reactions to them are, and why we need something as irrational and as powerful as play to deal with them. When a couple is at odds over something like this, it is often only the surface of a deeper problem, such as tension at work, low self-esteem, or difficulty with intimacy. It can be useful to focus on examining the annoying behavior first, because it may lead to the deeper issue; if left unaddressed, the annoying behavior may become a divisive force in itself. My favorite example was shared with me by an old friend:

Alice was always the neater of the two. In fact, she had to take some ribbing for it over the years. Her first roommate in college said she was obsessive-compulsive and "anal." It was a trait she was aware of and managed to keep under control. Bob had been a bachelor for several years after college and had never bothered too much with cleaning up after himself.

Bob had a habit, which drove Alice mad, of leaving his dirty clothes around the bedroom. Alice tried everything to get him out of the habit but nothing worked. Then one day she got the idea of doing it back, but in a kind of exaggerated way that would be sure to get his attention.

When Bob returned that afternoon from work there were Alice's clothes strewn all about the bedroom, especially her underwear. There was a bra on all four bedposts, and panties hanging from the light fixture. They both had a good laugh at this absurd scene. Thereafter, Bob tried harder to clean up. Occasionally, Alice would remind him by leaving an item of her clothing in an odd place, such as in the refrigerator. This would make them think of her "panty raid," as they referred to it, and it would take the edge off the issue for both of them.

Another seemingly trivial behavior of Bob's that drove Alice into a frenzy was his leaving the cap off the toothpaste. "I hated the little trail of toothpaste that always leaked out onto the sink after Bob left the cap off the tube," she said. "It always hardened like cement, and there would be half a dozen of them to scrub off the sink every time I cleaned it. I felt like a professional charlady scrubbing those damn lumps. I had compromised about a lot of other things, but this was too much."

Once again she resorted to a dramatic gesture to impress upon Bob how much this bothered her. Whenever Bob left behind a trail of toothpaste she got out a pastry bag, filled it with toothpaste and used the largest size nozzle to make a half-inch-wide parallel trail that was five times as long as Bob's original creation. The ugly sight of the long, pudgy toothpaste trails was enough to turn Bob's stomach. "Seeing how gross it could look blown-up," he laughed, "I guess I realized how equally ugly a small amount could look to someone more sensitive to it."

Play can break up automatic reactions, enabling a partner to stop and take notice of his behavior in a way that nagging or tirades can fail to accomplish. In some instances play can have a dramatic impact on a relationship, facilitating rapid change in behavior or perspective. There is a kind of "Aha!" experience in which we see things with new eyes. It is analogous to the experience in psychotherapy or Zen Buddhist training when the balance shifts from rational thought processes to more unconscious, intuitive faculties, such that a limiting set of perceptions and assumptions can be transcended. Such cosmic realignments are rare. It is usually the case that people, who have taken years to become the way they are, are capable of changing only very gradually. At times the request to stop an annoying behavior may not be fair; it may be preferable to let your partner hold onto his or her cherished ritual. A playful approach, on the other hand, may have a gradual effect, and in any case may dissipate some of the annoyance that one of you is experiencing. For example, a person who suffers from low self-esteem may repeatedly belittle themselves. No matter how much reassurance and encouragement they receive, their self-deprecating negativism can be hard for them to give up. Inevitably, this tendency to "kvetch" (complain) begins to grate on their partners, like a phonograph needle stuck on the same groove. One couple's playful response to this behavior was this:

Kvetch: My life's a mess! I'm getting nowhere! Nowhere! Just the same old thing day in and day out.
Partner: Yeah. You're the worst husband I've ever had, too!
Kvetch: Everything's going wrong. What am I going to do?
Partner: You know, considering how bad a day this is going to turn out to be, our first mistake was getting out of bed this morning. Let's not check the mail. I'm sure there's going to be some bad news.

Because the partner's response is so unexpected and so gently mocking of the Kvetch's perspective, it can be more successful than reassurance in pointing out the absurdity of his position. Notice also how the partner takes the position of siding *with the other person,* yet gently attacking the *behavior,* as if to say, "We're in this together." There has to be a real sense of caring behind the sarcasm; otherwise, a partner is likely to feel belittled rather than encouraged to change.

The process of change is analogous to the imperceptible but steady erosion of a rock by falling drops of water. I'm not suggesting you submit your mate to Chinese water torture, but that you view playfulness as a long-term approach to characterologic change.

Even if you're not dealing with a deep-seated pattern, friendly caricature can be useful in short-circuiting self-defeating behavior:

One woman developed a habit of complaining to her husband as soon as he arrived home: the washing machine broke, the children seemed like monsters, she was altogether fed up. While her husband was supportive for a while, he had started to tune out. One time, however, he looked mischievously at her and began to sing: "It's been a hard day's night! And I've been workin' like a dawwg." She burst out laughing, and they had an affectionate hug and talked things over instead of enduring a dreary sounding off.

Playful exaggeration and caricature provide a constructive outlet for your frustrations about a partner's behavior. At the same time, they hold up a mirror to your partner, which, like a fun-house distortion, is not always flattering but, in the proper context, is both amusing and hard to ignore. As Henri Bergson observed, "A character in a tragedy will make no change in his conduct. . . . But a defect that is ridiculous, as soon as it feels itself to be so, endeavors to modify itself, or at least to appear as though it did."[18]

Our willingness at times to mock ourselves, as in the example of the man who exaggerated his own need to leave early to get to the airport, attempts to reassure our partner that such play is not done with malicious intent: just as you should not always make yourself out to be the fool, playful caricature is not a license for shaming your partner. In order for play to be truly caring, you need to recognize some aspect of *yourself* in your partner's foibles. Cicero's empathetic credo best expresses the attitude to bring to your relationship: "Nothing human is alien to me."

Auditioning for a New Part

Shakespeare reminds us that not only is all the world a stage, but "all the men and women [are] merely players.

They have their exits and their entrances; And one man in his time plays many parts."

At times you may have to try on a new role in order to break out of the mold that you're stuck in. At first, you may not feel entirely comfortable with this idea. After all, Shakespeare also exhorted, "This above all: to thine own self be true." But what I am suggesting entails neither deceit nor game playing but a flexibility of spirit. Auditioning for a new part means *temporarily* venturing into your partner's world or experimenting with a style with which you're unaccustomed.

At times when you and your partner are at an impasse, you may think that you're hearing what they're saying and that you understand where they're coming from. But can you have enough genuine humility to admit that maybe you have some things to learn? Exchanging roles is a form of play that encourages empathy; it also fosters a more flexible atmosphere in which each of you can become more receptive to the other's needs. Here are some guidelines:

1. Physically exchange seats (preferably sitting across from each other), and silently try to imagine that you really *are* your partner. For a few minutes put aside the issues you've been discussing. Try to assume their posture and feel into what it's like to be them.
2. Still in silence, bring your new perspective to the situation that you're trying to resolve, and when you feel ready to speak as your partner, signal to them. Your goal should be not to imitate but to speak from your heart.
3. Each of you in turn make brief "I" statements, speaking as if you are your partner. These statements may refer to feelings or perceptions. You may also ask the other person a question. Stay with your new role for a while, and try to avoid switching back to being yourself in order to correct your partner's portrayal of you. Remember that it's only an interpretation.

4. When you're both ready, physically return to your original seats, and share what the experience of being the other person was like, as well as your experience of your partner's portrayal of you. You don't have to accept or reject any part of the portrayal—just regard it as potential new information about both of you.

5. You can switch back and forth between being yourself or taking the role of your partner as many times as you like. Just be sure to be consistent about the place you're sitting, and don't slip in and out of role without the two of you agreeing that it's time to switch.

A variation on verbal role-playing is to adopt the problematic behavior of your partner.

> *One of Karen's favorite ways of pampering herself was to eat cookies in bed. Unfortunately, she tended to scatter the crumbs, so that her partner's sleep was occasionally disturbed by Oreo remnants or an especially pointy chocolate chip. Rather than try to take away her cookies, he decided to eat some bedtime snacks himself. In time, as his popcorn kernels found their way to Karen's side of the bed, she became more attuned to the drawbacks of munching between the sheets. But since her partner had come to appreciate eating in bed, they both decided to make some rules but not eliminate the habit.*

The purpose of playful adoption of your partner's behavior should not be to "pay them back." I don't think Karen would have found it very amusing if her partner had left a horse's head in their bed. Take the positive attitude that you are going to learn what it feels like to do what your partner is doing. In the process, either you or your partner may learn something about the other's perspective, and the system will be changed. You may want to discuss taking turns performing a specific behavior or role-playing different problematic behavior. In this fashion your partner is less likely to feel that your role-playing is an attempt at manipulation.

The most daring kind of playacting requires you to really act "out of character," that is, to do something that you wouldn't ordinarily do. But just as a wise actor will take only the parts for which he can have some basic feel, your acting should feel like an integral part of you that is not usually expressed, rather than something totally alien to your nature. The purpose is to shake up the couple system and, in the process, to have some fun.

> Arthur and Ann are both teachers. She works in a daycare-nursery school, and he teaches at the local high school. Their jobs have always been secure, and while they have never wanted for anything, they also have never had much extra money for luxuries. But Arthur's concern for penny pinching was excessive.
>
> "I was pretty tolerant of it," Ann related. "I'm pretty easygoing. But then he began to pressure me to clip coupons out of the paper and to go to several different supermarkets instead of our usual one, to save money. I got uncharacteristically annoyed. One Saturday I was in the check-out line and suddenly I saw Arthur coming up to me. I couldn't figure out why he would come to meet me there. Well, he had brought some of the coupons that I had forgotten. I was so embarrassed. You'd have thought we were dirt poor. It was that day that I decided I had to do something outrageous. I had always had fantasies of going on a big shopping spree. So now I was going to really do it up—a pretend shopping spree, that is, since I didn't want to and couldn't afford to keep all the things that I was going to 'buy.' It was all going

to be a show to jolt Art a bit. I suppose it was also my declaration that I wasn't going to take it anymore.

"The first thing I decided to do was rent a huge Cadillac and tell him I'd bought it. I thought that was very clever—a minimum of expense for a very dramatic effect, and of course I'd be returning it. Then I found out that you could also rent fur coats, and I decided that that would be the second thing I'd do. Oh, I thought I was being incredibly mischievous and ingenious. I was also very nervous, to no small degree.

"On the appointed day—it was our anniversary— I went down to the car rental place and checked out this huge green Cadillac. I'd never driven anything that big, and I was scared to death, honestly. I felt like such an idiot driving it. I thought, What if someone I know sees me driving this thing. What if I get stopped by a cop. . . .I had sunglasses on as a disguise, I was so self-conscious.

"Then I went to the department store where they rent furs. As I cruised into the parking lot, I began to get into this—me driving in a Cadillac to pick up a fur—it was like I had won the lottery or something. I was so hasty picking out the fur that the saleslady must have thought I was terribly wealthy. I said, 'I'll have that one,' like I was picking out a loaf of fresh bread, and I said, 'No, I don't want to wear it. Put it in a bag.' I meant to say 'Put it in a box.' "

Ann managed to get home and park the Cadillac very conspicuously in the driveway. She hung up the fur coat in the closet.

"Art came home, right on time, like he always does, at five-thirty. It was dusk out and the car must have looked like quite a sight, almost as big as our house, and my own car nowhere in evidence. When he came in he was all out of breath. 'Someone here?' he asked hesitantly. 'No, why do you ask?'

"He looked at me, maybe wondering if he'd hallucinated the car or something. 'Well, that car,' he asked as he took off his coat, 'whose is it?'

" 'Ours,' I said excitedly. He dropped his coat on the floor. 'It couldn't be,' he said, to which I replied, 'Happy Anniversary!'

"Arthur's face looked genuinely incredulous. I knew that I had already made my point so I didn't need to do the coat routine as well. I told him that I had actually rented the car and the coat. I didn't put it on. Instead I held it away from myself like it was something a little disgusting, or pathetic, which it was at that point. Art just looked at me and said, 'Oh, my God!'

"Then he sort of smiled and said he needed a drink, to which I replied, 'Me too.' We sat and talked about a lot of things we'd needed to talk about for a long time. Maybe we could have had that talk without my having gone to such lengths, but I don't think so. You have to fight fire with fire, and Arthur needed something like that to bring him to his senses. It seems I also needed it to be able to express my feelings.

"Art's penny pinching subsided somewhat after that. He still can't help trying to find a bargain, but he also lets us splurge more often, like on special dinners. At least he doesn't bother me to try to save pennies.

"The strange thing—after we'd had our talk that evening, we went for a ride in the big Cadillac. We sailed across the city laughing and joking, looking out at the lights, laughing at how preposterous it was that we should be driving around in a Cadillac. It was a surprise to both of us how much we in fact *enjoyed a bit of luxury. Arthur will probably always be a penny pincher, but he's less obsessed. And neither one of us will ever forget that ride."*

The unexpected can sometimes shake us out of ourselves and make us open to change. It requires courage—the willingness to take a risk, and maybe look like a fool—but there may be no other way to effect a change. Ann's story also points out that trying on a new role is very different from deliberate manipulation of the other person. *The "actor" is changed in the process, just as much as the "audience."* In street terms, you don't have to know your part by heart from the start. You just improvise as you go along and trust that if there's love in your heart, it will work out.

Change

The playful strategies illustrated in this chapter are alternatives to more mundane ways of handling problems. Take what you can use and discard the rest. In this regard I'm reminded of a Sufi tale about a master potter whose message claimed that what is most important remains after the pot is broken. I don't think he was recommending that couples solve problems by throwing dishes. Rather, I try to communicate to my patients an excitement about the *process* of problem solving and an understanding that we strengthen ourselves and our relationships each time we explore new ways of relating. The spirit of play is to be a pioneer.

Play can be used to avoid change, such as when someone pretends to be easygoing and flexible, only to revert quickly to their habitual ways. Humor may deceive or enlighten. There are other limitations to change. For example, trying to restructure your partner's personality is a doomed proposition. When it has taken them several decades to get the way they are, it's not realistic to expect major renovations in a short time. People don't come like Mr. Potatoheads, with the pieces of their personality capable of being pulled off and stuck on at will. Most of us wish at times that our partners *were* so malleable. We have to hold onto a sense of humor about our need to insist on change, and, as with Mr. Potatohead, try to enjoy our partner's eccentricities.

Change is possible, but it usually occurs in the process of two people's ability to play with a problem rather than by a direct tactical assault. I suggest you experiment with play in different problem areas. Sometimes you need to try to achieve change first not in the area with which you're currently most preoccupied but where it will do the most good.

It isn't easy for any couple to solve problems so that the process and the solutions enhance their relationship. Playfulness is not a shortcut to marital bliss but a subtle and powerful resource that helps your relationship grow from your differences. The challenge remains for each of you to define continually and creatively how much to expect from accommodation and how much to tolerate differences between you and your partner. Play allows you to disagree without being disagreeable, and helps ensure that, in the words of the poet Terence, your "lovers' quarrels are the renewal of love," not its extinction. I have sought guidance here at times from classic sources, but it is a contemporary song whose lines may best characterize what accommodating and tolerating differences mean. In Mick Jagger's words:

> You can't always get what you want.
> You can't always get what you want.
> But if you try sometimes, you may find
> You get what you need.

CHAPTER FIVE

Erotic Play

Most people know little about the insides of their car engines and even less about their own bodies. When you are as ignorant as I am about valve-cover gaskets and distributors, you can depend on a mechanic. If you feel sick, you can go to a doctor, and, as with your car, the cure does not depend on whether you understand the cure although it does seem to matter if you believe that it should work. But when it comes to sex, few people are knowledgeable about themselves, let alone about the other sex, and it's embarrassing to admit to the need for an expert, whether for a timing adjustment, fresh spark plugs, or some bodywork. Perhaps we have something to learn from animals, who spout less poetry, but also seem not to worry about simultaneous orgasms. Female monkeys, for example, when their hormones are juiced up, will make special sounds and gestures, turn their backs and bend forward sharply at the hips, thus riveting their mates' attention on the bright coloration and swelling of their sexual parts. Evolution, prior to humans, decided that reproduction was too important to be left to the individual imagination. But at times evolution seems to sit back and see what happens, and it looks as if we're now on one of its coffee breaks. Hormones and the color of sex skin are no longer automatic releasers of sexual passion. We have just enough free will to torture us, yet not enough to master our desires. The result is that our delicate psyches and our physical equipment often are not in sync.

It would be nice if civilization had perfected the task that evolution left undone, but I, for one, am not holding my breath. In a few cultures, the direct approach still holds— the woman displays her genitals in unmistakable invitation. But indirect, symbolic approaches are the rule:

> As a symbol of their intentions Yungar men send a carved stick smeared on one end with yellow clay. For many peoples in the Pacific the so-called love-rod serves the dual purpose of secretly inviting the girl to copulate and identifying the male requesting intercourse. Each young man carries a distinctively carved stick about with him during the day so that he will be recognized as its owner. At night a man slips up outside of the house where the girl of his choice is sleeping and thrusts the stick through the wall, prodding her with it. By feeling the carving on the rod she can tell to whom it belongs and may accept or reject this invitation to copulate.[19]

Unfortunately, Western civilization came to view pleasure and playfulness as threats to spiritual progress and to the work ethic, and love-rods never came into vogue. Instead, in 1727, the English novelist Daniel Defoe in his book *The Use and Abuse of the Marriage Bed* offered this advice about marital sex:

> That it be moderate, so as to be consistent with health.
> That it be so ordered as not to be too extensive of time, that precious opportunity of working out our salvation.
> That when duty is demanded it be always payed (so far as in our powers and election) according to the foregoing measures.
> That it be with a temperate affection, without vio-

lent transporting desires, or too sensual applications.[20]

In the nineteenth century, societal attitudes toward sexual expression were similarly characterized by rationality and restraint:

> Given abundant time and mutual reciprocity, the [sexual] interchange becomes satisfactory and complete without crisis by either party. In the course of an hour the physical tension subsides, the spiritual exaltation increases, and not uncommonly visions of a transcendent life are seen and consciousness of new powers experienced.[21]

Evidently, these writers had forgotten that St. Augustine, before renouncing lust, had said, "Give me chastity and continency, only not yet."

Marital counselors in the fifties and sixties were much more permissive. Marital manuals exhorted husbands to become masters of technique in order not to shortchange their wives' newly discovered sensuality. But a double standard still operated, for husbands were held responsible for their wives' enjoyment. If a man's penis was too long, a sponge rubber ring could be slipped over it to control the depth of penetration. If it was too small, he was advised to put a rubber band around the base to control blood flow, thereby swelling him to sufficient size. What's more, "[The male] who neglects the love-play is guilty not only of coarseness, but of positive brutality. [He is] unpardonably stupid."[22]

A few of the techniques described in these manuals, while intended to enhance pleasure, seem to have been inspired by a wish to retaliate against such brutish males:

> Before intercourse, the wife places at the bedside a bowl of crushed ice or a handful of cracked ice

wrapped in a wet towel. Both partners strip and enjoy sex in any face-to-face posture with the husband on top. As the husband starts his final surge to climax, the wife picks up a handful of crushed ice or the cold towel. Just as the paroxysms of orgasm start, she jams the ice-cold poultice against her husband's crotch and keeps it there throughout the conclusion.[23]

Reading through such well-intentioned attempts to help couples improve the quantity and quality of their paroxysms makes me a bit hesitant to offer my own counsel, since all previous efforts seem to suffer so from the benefit of hindsight. But while we may learn otherwise by the next century, by which time sex may even have become obsolete, it does appear that the basis for a sounder approach toward sexual enrichment now exists, as contained in many current guides. The only element that I would add is play. Sex is the last great preserve of adult play, where even the dourest pillars of our community are permitted to whisper sweet nothings. If I were to urge you to do but one thing in trying to improve your sex life, it would be: don't turn it into work.

How to Make Sex Difficult without Trying

I think we have to begin not with how we'd like to be but with how we are, or rather how we came to be how we are. In our infinite embarrassment we decided that sex education was too subtle and sensitive a topic to be delegated to schools and artists and should instead be left to trial and error, jokes, porno movies, and bathroom graffiti. I remember my own sex education as consisting of playing Doctor, Spin the Bottle, and Twister (the latter was a game that required all sorts of physical contortions whose net result was to rub other bodies without guilt). I also learned some dubious facts about sexual anatomy and desire from jokes, whose meaning I only vaguely grasped but was never brave enough to ask about. This kind of exploratory play arises from anxiety rather than from relaxed sensuality. My recent casual study of bathroom graffiti in the Boston area has convinced me that little has changed since I was, like Alexander Portnoy, of an age that "went all the way" with the family dinner. Alongside the crude drawings, which had been etched on the metal doors with a blunt object to ensure immortality, I found:

There was a man with a yen
Who could do it again and again.
His prick was immense
And we watched with suspense
As he screwed number three hundred ten.

When in doubt, whip it out.

Your sister is like a bowling ball:
She gets picked up, fingered, thrown in the gutter,
And comes back for more.

If you wipe more than once, you're playing with it.

Life is like a penis:
When it's soft you can't beat it,
When it's hard, you get screwed.

Don't look up here,
The joke's in your hand.

There once was a girl so obscene
She was blessed with excessive wet dreams
She saved up a dozen
And sent them to her cousin
Who ate them as if they were creams.

Clearly, preoccupation with genital size and performance, compulsive sexuality, disgust for women's sexuality, guilt, and anatomic ignorance are alive and well in our nation's bathrooms. It would be comforting to think that such graffiti represent merely the psychic waste matter of our culture, to be easily flushed out of our systems. But I think it more likely that, as with dreams and slips of the tongue, bathroom graffiti express the impulses that we usually closely guard. Our sexual behavior is largely learned rather than innate, and sometimes what we learn stands in the way of healthy sexual relationships, all the more if it is allowed overt expression only on bathroom walls or in porno flicks. The first step to new learning is to look gently but honestly at what we already secretly believe.

Expectations

The American dream is not only that of a chicken in every pot and two cars in every garage, but a perfect lover in every bed, complete with stapled belly button. As with material success, carnal happiness is thought of as something to be individually rather than cooperatively achieved. Our inner worries about our adequacy are dealt with by compulsive sexual acts and self-soothing adolescent fantasies of our omnipotence. "I am genitals, I can do anything" is our credo. In our pursuit of mythical orgasms we focus obsessively on outer attractiveness and how we perform, which makes it impossible to be in the present moment, the only place where we can experience fulfillment.

The alternative is for you and your partner to try to develop a less goal-oriented approach to sex and to focus more on your psychological development than on external markers of potency. Approach sex in the same spirit as play—something done not to achieve anything else but for its own sake.

Ignorance

Most people learn to acquire a veneer of "pseudocompetence" about sex—that is, even though we may be woefully ignorant about it, we become good bluffers. It may be adaptive to strut your plumage in order to attract a mate, but in a long-term relationship such false confidence gets in the way of learning about the other sex. We need to recognize, as the American philosopher George Santayana reminds us, that there are fundamental differences between us:

> Friends are generally of the same sex, for when men and women agree, it is only in their conclusions; their reasons are always different. [Their agreement] does not arise from mutual understanding, but is a conspiracy of alien essences and a kissing, as it were, in the dark.

More playfulness, in the sense of relaxed spontaneity, as opposed to playacting can make you open to learning.

Guilt

The sixties was supposed to be the time when sexual guilt was to become obsolete. If the alternative to making love was to make war, who could object? Open sexual relations would soon render monogamy obsolete. But it slowly became apparent that while sin had been abolished, sex was just as complicated as ever. Neanderthal emotions such as jealousy and shame kept on creeping between our bed sheets, and no amount of "doing it" early and often could free us from conscience. Regrettably, as many flower children found out, psychic evolution moves at a much slower pace. You should not feel alone if you still have difficulty allowing yourself sensual pleasure. Our fantasy life is rife with sexual prohibitions that play can help us to contend with.

Responsibility and Responsiveness

One of the things that struck me when watching some porno flicks as part of my research for this book was that they teach some strange lessons about responsibility and responsiveness. Granted that these are made predominantly by men and for men, with no pretense about their being a balanced presentation, they still reveal deep-seated fantasies. While these films had other memorable titles, they all could have been called "Cult of the Penis." All of the action, moaning, and groaning was centered around The Penis and it was clear that all pleasure—both for men and women, was utterly dependent on it being long, fat, and hard. The men were overtly masters of their female slaves, but both sexes were portrayed as depending on the other to arouse their passion.

Unfortunately, we seem to dwell on the most obvious measures of arousal—erection of the penis and number of orgasms—as meters for passion. In reality, each of us can be responsible only for our own sexuality while being responsive to our partner's needs. On the one hand, to abandon yourself fully to sexual pleasure requires a temporary selfishness in the sense of focusing exclusively on your own erotic sensations. You can't always be a spectator and still be a full participant. To the extent that you can let go of judging yourself by how aroused your partner becomes, you will feel more carefree and able to experience your own pleasure. But to also be responsive *to* your partner's needs requires more than skilled technique—you need to know something about their emotional life and the interplay between your own erotic fantasy and theirs. Some balance must be struck to avoid excessive concern with your partner's needs and preoccupation with self.

The Challenge of Intimacy

You can be "up close and personal" or up close and impersonal. Sex with only passing intimacy is quite easy —it is tension reduction and not much more. But sex with intimacy requires that we relate, and whatever problems we may have with people will haunt our sexual relationship. For example, if you need to compete with others, you will never achieve a comfortable rhythm of subtle give-and-take. If you have difficulty telling another person your needs and desires, your partner will endlessly frustrate you, because their touch will as often as not miss the mark. Sex is a perfect mirror for other issues in an intimate relationship.

To be intimate with another person is to hold a seance: your present closeness summons up memories and behaviors from your intimate past, as if, by pressing up against each other's psyches, an unknown door had suddenly given way. This is one of the reasons why we unconsciously need to erect barriers against those we love, for they threaten us with what they might reveal. Your sex will be only as free as your willingness to bring into your relationship all of your inner world and to welcome the same of your partner. Play can facilitate such opening up through uninhibited mental as well as physical foreplay. Through play your intimacy becomes like a river, which, through its many branches, gets around obstacles to make many points of contact with your partner.

But if sex cannot be separated from its intimate context, is it possible to improve it without working on the whole relationship? Your character and unconscious motivations will surely limit how much you can change, but sex is as good a place to work out problems as anywhere else, and improved sex can lead to changes in other aspects of your relationship. You cannot learn how to respond sexually— this is something you're born with—but you can learn to identify things that obstruct as well as things that facilitate good sex.

> During a particularly rocky period, during which time their sex became infrequent, Jennifer and Sam went into couples therapy. Among the sore points that they worked on were Jennifer's habit of putting Sam down in subtle ways, and Sam's inability to make a career commitment. While therapy helped them understand some of the factors contributing to these problems, it was not easy to change, and it became clear that Jennifer would probably always get bitchy from time to time, and Sam might always be a jack-of-all-trades. But they agreed to try to keep their problems out of the bedroom.
>
> Thus, on lazy Sunday mornings or afternoons when they came home early from work, times when they had often made love in the past, they used a playful signal to avert conflict. Instead of taking up an invitation to an argument, the other would ask, "Do you want to make love or war?" and would tickle the other or playfully wrestle. They still had their battles, but the bedroom was off limits for hostilities.

Playfulness allows you leeway to place arbitrary restrictions on reality, in this case to declare a boundary around your sexual relationship to insulate it from your pet peeves. Problems are not resolved nor suppressed so much as put aside. You may not be able to achieve this psychological split, especially at very troubled times, but try to see your lovemaking as a protected playtime.

Tuning In to Your Senses

Anxiety interferes with sexual satisfaction and also can prevent learning, so it is often best not to focus on genitals and intercourse, which is most likely to trigger apprehension. Rather, begin by becoming reacquainted with your full body sensuality, and try to take the approach of a child, who has no preconceived notions or need to perform but who has unlimited curiosity. Some couples find it helpful to start with a relaxation exercise, such as deep-muscle relaxation, meditation, or physical exercise, and then to explore ways of tuning back in to their senses. One way is to start with giving each other massages, initially clothed and then nude, again staying away from sexually specific areas, and with sensual enjoyment and not orgasm as the final goal. Especially if either of you are feeling especially anxious about sex, it is better to agree not to have these exercises lead into sex, so that in the future they will not acquire anxious associations.

> *"We try to find time when we can be private and be free from distractions. We take a shower or a bath first to help us relax and then towel each other dry. Then we massage each other using body lotion or oil while we listen to some mellow background music. The first time the room was so cold that we both got goose bumps and had to stop, so we've learned to make sure the room we use is well heated. We take turns with each of us being a giver and then a receiver. The receiver's only responsibility is to close their eyes and to experience their body. We try to do a minimum of talking, but if something feels uncomfortable or especially good, we let each other know. Being the giver has made both of us more aware of what each other's bodies feel like and how much creativity there can be in touching—slow and fast, light pressure and deep massage. We've also discovered incredibly sensual areas that we never knew existed, such as inner thighs, hands and feet."*

As both giver and receiver try to concentrate totally on the experience, and if your mind wanders bring it back to your sensations. Let yourself feel everything as fully as possible. After both of you have had turns of about twenty minutes each being a giver and a receiver, take some time to talk about the experience, both what you liked as well as things that were difficult.

This "bare bones" approach is perfectly adequate, but if repeated over time may become habit rather than a new experience. So improvise a little. Instead of hand massage, stroke your partner with a flower or a feather or give him or her a sponge bath. You could also try experimenting with body sensations, such as with a fan, a tuning fork, a vibrator, a warm object, a piece of ice (don't jam this against your partner's crotch). Sometimes you can surprise your partner, but be sure not to shock them with an unexpected sensation. Another variation is to sensitize yourselves to other senses: with one of you blindfolded, the other presents a series of smells or tastes or sounds. You could also take your partner on a blindfolded trust walk. In this exercise, you lead your partner outside by the hand and put them in contact with various things, such as the bark of a tree, a flower, the feel of rolling down a grassy hill, and so on. All of these exercises require you to trust that your partner will not deliberately discomfort you. The trust walk makes you especially dependent: you may have some difficulty fully letting go, but that is precisely what you need to get more comfortable with in your sexual life.

Another way to inject an element of play is to spontaneously make use of opportunities for sensual experience. For example, if your partner is taking a bath, ask if you can shampoo their hair, and while you're at it, drip some warm water over their whole body. A rainy or snowy day is usually a signal to stay inside, but you can take a walk and feel the weather against your skin. Mud has many sensuous possibilities as well, if you can dig it. Otherwise, slopping

some body oil on each other and slip-sliding together or
fingerpainting on each other's bodies are "loosening"
equivalents. These are only a few ideas, but if you tune in
to being a child again, there are endless possibilities.

Overcoming Inhibitions

When I was in my early twenties I fell in love with a
beautiful but bashful young woman, who had recently been
burned in another love affair and was hesitant to get sexually involved. No amount of reassurance and cajoling
could loosen her up, even though she had started to like me
in turn quite a bit. Time was getting short, since she was
leaving soon for the West Coast, when I happened to see
Andrew Marvell's seventeenth-century poem. I sent a copy
to her, along with a rose:

To His Coy Mistress

Had we but world enough, and time,
This coyness, lady, were no crime.
We would sit down and think which way
To walk, and pass our long love's day;
Thou by the Indian Ganges' side
Shouldst rubies find; I by the tide
Of Humber would complain. I would
Love you ten years before the Flood;
And you should, if you please, refuse
Till the conversion of the Jews.
My vegetable love should grow
Vaster than empires, and more slow.
An hundred years should go to praise
Thine eyes, and on thy forehead gaze;
Two hundred to adore each breast;
But thirty thousand to the rest;
An age at least to every part,
And the last age should show your heart.
For, lady, you deserve this state,

Nor would I love at lower rate.
    But at my back I always hear
Time's winged chariot hurrying near;
And yonder all before us lie
Deserts of vast eternity.
Thy beauty shall no more be found,
Nor, in thy marble vault shall sound
My echoing song; then worms shall try
That long preserved virginity,
And your quaint honor turn to dust,
And into ashes all my lust.
The grave's a fine and private place,
But none, I think, do there embrace.
    Now therefore, while the youthful hue
Sits on thy skin like morning glew,
And while thy willing soul transpires
At every pore with instant fires,
Now let us sport us while we may;
And now, like am'rous birds of prey,
Rather at once our time devour,
Than languish in his slow-chapt power.
Let us roll all our strength and all
Our sweetness, up into one ball;
And tear our pleasures with rough strife
Through the iron gates of life.
Thus, though we cannot make our sun
Stand still, yet we will make him run.

She and I soon traded coyness for rough strife. Whether her melting had anything to do with the poem I don't know for sure, but I have always felt a debt of gratitude to Andrew Marvell, whose sense of humor about his own plight had just the right touch.

Play can help you ease inhibitions because it can provide a way of escape, of letting down your guard in ways that you ordinarily would hesitate to do. Sometimes people need to have a structured game to give them this kind of permission, just as kids need to spin a bottle in order to kiss. I know of a couple who broke the ice by playing strip poker. The ability to pretend can also help you to be more sexually bold, especially if your partner responds to your risk taking by trying on a more permissive role themselves:

> A newly married couple who both came from strict, puritanical families that prohibited any experimentation with premarital sex felt naïve and awkward about sex when they got married. A particularly difficult moment for both of them was undressing before going to bed at night. One evening the husband spontaneously fashioned a cowboy hat for himself and hung a cigarette from the end of his lips in imitation of the cool "Marlboro Man." His wife, who was at first taken aback, quickly fell in with the tempo of her husband's play and pretended to be a stripper. By imitating sexually provocative characters, this couple was able to gradually modify their physical inhibitions.

To have to continue pretending so that it becomes the *only* mode of relating, especially if your partner is not aware that you're playacting, can interfere with intimacy. But a playful testing of the waters with another identity can help some couples integrate a freer part of themselves into their personalities.

It can also help you to use visual imagery to create a bridge to less inhibited behavior, for example, by picturing yourselves as lusty characters out of a D. H. Lawrence novel. In one couple, a woman helped overcome her compunctions about oral sex by a kind of classic conditioning, by associating it with pleasant instead of anxious experiences.

> "When we first got married both of us had a lot of hang-ups about sex. We had some notion that making

*it legal would make us relax, but it just doesn't work
that way. The first time we had oral sex was an accident, I mean because of an accident.*

*"It was one of those summer nights in Missouri
when even the mosquitoes are sweating and we were
sitting on the floor naked eating ice cream cones that
were melting faster than we could eat them. The top
of Craig's cone fell into his lap and landed right in
his crotch. He just sat there, looking like a helpless
little boy so I leaned over and started to lick off the
ice cream. He started to get turned on and in spite of
the heat we had some great sex. Since then whenever
I go down on Craig I imagine that I'm licking an ice
cream cone."*

Food play was used by another couple to become more
comfortable with cunnilingus. Instead of ice cream they
dripped honey on the woman's vagina and her partner
licked it off.

Playful desensitization may also take place with language. Most people have some reserve about using explicit
sexual terms, and this reticence gets in the way of directly
communicating their needs. Euphemisms can sometimes
help, if they are such that both partners clearly understand
what the terms connote.

*When Carol first started sleeping with Lawton she
became very curious about oral sex. She had had
other sexual partners but he was the first one she felt
comfortable enough to bring it up with. Her mother
had once referred to fellatio with disgust.*

*"I remember the first time I talked about it with
Lawton. He laughed, and in an attempt to set me at
ease said, 'It's just like sucking your thumb.' A couple of days later we were doing foreplay and I was
really horny and wanted to try it, but I still felt inhibited about broaching it, so I asked, 'Do you mind if I*

suck your thumb?' He knew exactly what I meant and whispered, 'No, I'd love it.' I got carried away and it's been an important part of our sex life since."

With the playful expression "Can I suck your thumb" Carol was expressing her gratitude for Lawton's attempt to lessen her anxiety. At the same time she was still staying clear of being blunt about her impulse. Over time she was able to be more direct about oral sex but still occasionally used the old playful expression as a joking reminder about their early days together.

Playful language was similarly used by another couple to facilitate communication:

One couple had a "numbers game" in which each number referred to a sexual behavior or sexually specific body part.

"I think the idea started from the fact that people commonly refer to oral sex as '69.' Carter's penis thus became '007,' after James Bond, and '7–11,' from the convenience store that stays open all night, meant that I was ready to have intercourse; '8' meant that I wanted to have my genitals caressed, since I liked Carter to trace a figure eight around my clitoris."

Calling out numbers enabled Carter and Lucy to express their needs explicitly while minimizing embarrassment. They also played the numbers game sometimes in public, slyly winking to each other and enjoying the private communication. In time they began to use one, then another of the proper names and the numbers game became a nostalgic joke as they matured and became more comfortable with sexual intimacy.

The origins of sexual inhibitions can be traced to our experiences in our families when growing up. While these prohibitions have become a part of us, independent of their original context, a playful rebelliousness can help a couple to treat them as something outside themselves from which they can then achieve some distance:

> *Dan came from an easygoing, fun-loving family, while Jill's family was stiff and proper. Although they were living together, when they visited Jill's family staying together in one room was out of the question. One evening, while sitting beside Jill at a formal dinner in her family's home, Dan, bored out of his mind, put his hand under the table between Jill's legs. She started to laugh and in answer to her family's impatient response pretended it was because of a funny incident that came to mind. Secretly she delighted in putting one over on the rest of the company and brushed Dan's genitals during dessert. The contrast between goings-on above and beneath the table highlighted the prudery of her upbringing to Jill. Thereafter, they occasionally enjoyed this surreptitious sex play, which helped to loosen Jill's inhibitions.*

Overcoming Habit

But between two particular people, any two people on earth, the range of pure sensational experience is limited. The climax of sensual reaction, once realized in any direction, is reached finally, there is no going on. There is only repetition possible, or the going apart of the two protagonists, or the subjugating of the one will to the other, or death.

D. H. Lawrence's grim vision can become a self-fulfilling attitude. Indeed, many couples become stuck with tepid tedium instead of titillating tenderness out of a failure to see that repetition, like alliteration, can create as well as numb. You may fear to improvise for many different reasons—embarrassment, guilt, fear of failure, or just because you are, like most of us, a creature of habit, who finds comfort in the familiar, no matter how limiting it may be. While we are not programmed to mate like animals, with prescribed tail-feather displays and flutters of our wings, our behavior can become just as rigid. In large measure, this is due less to conscious choice than to the endless ways that the stress of life crowd out relaxed sensuality. We attend PTA meetings, plan dinner menus, and fret about the bare spots on our lawn or the back of our head rather than put thought into our sexual escapade. At times, it's just not possible to summon up the energy for passion, but play can help you make sure your sexual side does not become totally submerged:

> "Our baby is now six months old. Play has helped us move from the noneroticism of pregnancy and the postpartum back toward the resumption of an erotic life. With the laundry machine in our bedroom, one or the other kid always about to wake up, and a nursing mother's tricky hormones, play is of the sexual essence. Sometimes play (a joke, a grope, a dirty ballad) is all the sex we have time or inclination for. But it keeps the intimacy quotient high. Reminds us that we haven't fallen out of favor with each other, and will be grand lovers again."

While such dancing around the edges of the problem is sometimes the best approach, sometimes a bold stroke is needed:

> One long-married husband decided to revive the couple's once-active sex life, which had dwindled significantly over the years. He felt this was primarily because his wife was often too tired at night for

sex. He began to complain to her that it was all her clubs that she had joined over the years that kept her out so much and left her tired when she got home in the evenings. When his complaining seemed to have no effect, he borrowed a life-sized mannequin, dressed it up in sexy clothes, and propped it up in their bed beside him. When his wife came home, he explained that the mannequin was his sex surrogate. His wife laughingly got the point and modified her schedule.

I doubt that the wife's busy schedule was the sole obstacle in this couple's sex life. My experience is that both partners usually arrange to arrive at a status quo. To achieve change both partners must be willing to alter their behavior. In fact, in this couple the husband was demonstrating his willingness to make a change by, in effect, saying, "I care enough about our sex life to go to these lengths to get your attention." You can't expect your sex life to change overnight, but going with a creative impulse may help you both break out of a mold.

Although neither one is an alcoholic, both Richard and Debra are fond of alcohol. They enjoy pouring spirits on different parts of their bodies as part of the ritualization of their sex life. For example, Richard especially likes to suck Debra's breasts after coating them with brandy. "I remember the first time we got into putting alcohol on our bodies," Debra said. "We had planned an evening of wine and cheese and sex. Richard was getting impatient for me to give him a glass of wine, and instead of giving it to him I poured it down my open T-shirt and said, 'Why don't you come and get your glass of wine?' He stopped being impatient and ever since we've often used exotic wines and liqueurs to spice our sex life."

Couples tend to fall into a regimented choreography, with each partner's step a signal for the other in a continuous chain. One way to intervene is to change the first move or the stage set. For example, if the first time you think about making love is late at night while your partner is sitting in bed engrossed in *Xylem Structure and the Ascent of Sap*, you're likely to be disappointed. Instead, make a date so there will be time and energy for lovemaking as well as plenty of time beforehand for mental foreplay.

> A couple who tended to be workaholics found that sex got too easily pushed aside by other priorities. They decided to use sexual fantasy to keep their sex life going. Each of them would take time out during the day to elaborate a sexual fantasy to carry out that night. "I'd imagine using oils or massage or screwing in the shower, for example," the wife reported. Occasionally they would call each other at work during the day and playfully scold each other if one of them had not done their "homework" yet. In the evening they would share their sexual fantasies, which would pique their interests and sometimes set a new direction for their sexual activity. Both of them also found it very arousing to imagine that the other person was having erotic fantasies about them while at work.

Although Woody Allen has remarked that "My brain is only my second most favorite organ," the mind is actually the most erotic zone we own. Sometimes it needs time to get reconnected with your body. Having dinner together while sitting in a bubble bath, giving each other creative massages, or dancing together in the nude are other good lead-ins to sex. As for the setting, I suggest you take a hard look at your supposed pleasure dome. You may find that your wonderful but not very erotic parents are staring down from a picture frame. Those cute pictures of the kids may also be heartwarming, but they won't quicken your pulse, either. You don't have to create a harem atmosphere with incense and a red light bulb, but candles, oil lamp, or other soft touches should not be ignored. You may also have forgotten that music can help set a certain mood. Even if you add nothing new, once in a while it's a good idea to just move the furniture around to give things a new look.

And then there's the matter of clothing and physical hygiene. Excuse me for getting personal, but are you wearing smelly sweat socks or hair curlers to bed? Making love to a woman in high-heeled shoes can be a real turn-on for some men, but I have never heard of a hair-curler fetish. In France, in the Middle Ages, a religious woman often wore a *chemise cagoule*. This was a nightshirt that came down to her ankles but had a small aperture so her husband could impregnate her with a minimum of direct skin contact. During New England winters I have known many a couple to economize on fuel by wearing long johns and several sweaters to bed (why not a ski mask, too), thus achieving the effect of mutual chastity belts. Erotic night clothes are no longer things that you have to send away for and that arrive in plain brown wrappers, unless you live in a sexually disadvantaged area. A playful shopping trip with your partner to a clothing store or glancing through a mail order catalog can renew your wardrobe. Sometimes a surprise gift can work but if all your gift negligees wind up sitting in your drawer because those particular styles make you feel like a moose in drag, some collaborative costuming is called for (men can have some sexy clothes, too). Even ordinary clothes can become erotic when you undress each other or make love partly clothed.

D. H. Lawrence may have been right that the range of sensual experience is limited. But 10^6 is a finite number, too, and you need never exhaust the possibilities. The *Social Register* and the *Kama Sutra* agree that position is everything, which makes sense if you extend the notion from *ways* of having intercourse to *where* you have it.

Some couples make a practice of "christening" each room
of their house, including the linen closet, by making love.
This can be playful as long as you don't make it an obligation and omit the basement if your lover can't stand
spiders. Then there's the outdoors. I find the love scene in
the rain in *Lady Chatterley's Lover* to be one of the great
erotic passages of literature. You may find an old Javanese
custom inspiring: couples make love in the rice paddies to
encourage the crops to emulate their fruitfulness. Alternatively, putting yourself in unfamiliar surrounding can be a
potent stimulus to playful fantasy:

> On one vacation Dick and Jane decided to take a
> long train trip instead of the plane. As they were
> getting settled in their sleeper compartment, they
> built a fantasy that they were on the Orient Express
> to Istanbul. At dinner time they pretended to meet as
> strangers in the club car and adopted foreign accents
> to add to the sense of mystery. The rhythmic sounds
> and to-and-fro movement of the train had powerful
> subliminal effects, making the trip the most erotic
> part of their vacation.

There is something about the *first* time you do something—whether it be position, place, or other erotic variation—that not only renews excitement but also creates a
special bond of intimacy with the person with whom
you've explored this new territory.

The challenge is to continually discover each other, like
an artist who looks at familiar things and sees something
new revealed. You need to create what Walt Whitman
called "the act-poems of eyes, hand, hips, and bosoms":

> On their winter vacation in the Bahamas Jack
> brought a copy of the Kama Sutra, and he and
> Sheara read parts of it to each other at night. They
> particularly delighted in trying out the different vari-

eties of kissing: the "balanced kiss," which is placed on the fingertips or the eyelid, the "demonstrative kiss," which is placed on the great toe, and the "reflection kiss," which is blown to the lover's reflection in a mirror or water surface or to the lover's shadow. From another book of erotica they adopted the "oceanic kiss," in which they touched cheeks and deeply inhaled each other's scent.

They then began to improvise their own versions. For example, in the "ice-cube kiss" one of them kissed the other all over their naked body with a small ice cube placed between their lips; in the "fruit kiss" they passed a piece of fruit, such as a grape or strawberry, to the other's mouth. The "kiss of beautiful dreams" was placed on the lover's forehead while he or she was asleep. Sometimes their creations were "tongue in cheek," such as the "kiss that drops from the bird of paradise," which one placed on the top of the lover's head.

Communication

Sex, while primarily nonverbal, requires the most sophisticated skills to receive and send subtleties of intent, mood, and desire. We need to communicate in order to have good sex, but sex is itself a complex form of communication. Which, then, is the chicken and which the egg? The important point is that we need to make use of whatever means we can to find a common language with our partner. Some people might criticize play as being less direct than more "serious" ways of communicating and claim that it therefore leads to fuzzy messages that cloud understanding. But, in a sense, all foreplay is "indirect," and we don't have to grab someone's genitals for them to realize what's on our mind. Playful communication works best when we can shift easily from play to other modes and back again, to ask for clarification when needed and to be able to say "I want" and "I don't want" in no uncertain terms. At times, play provides a bridge to more direct statements, allowing you to say what you want when bald truth would make you feel too exposed. Guilt about asking for what we want and fear of being rejected are powerful disincentives to openness, and we sometimes need to work around them:

> One couple hit on the idea of a "potluck" approach to letting each other know what they desired. They each thought up six things that they wanted their partner to do for them, such as oral sex, a special dinner, setting up a special erotic fantasy, and so on. They then wrote them down on separate pieces of paper and put them in separate paper bags. Each pulled out an item from the partner's bag and agreed to fulfill the wish within the next week, without letting the other know which item had been chosen. In the rare event that one of them felt unable or unwilling to fulfill the request, they had to pay a penalty of picking two of the remaining items. At the same time, each of them also made a list of several things that the partner had done for them recently—either sexually or nonsexually—for which they wanted to thank them. These items were likewise placed in two other bags from which each of them drew one out.

You may decide to create some of your own ground rules to make "potluck" work for you, and it can be used for all kinds of gift giving in the relationship, including the erotic. Ideally it should not only just meet a specific need, but encourage talking about what each of you wants yet may find difficult to ask for or to give. One thing I like about this approach is that it focuses on the positive. Most people feel painfully vulnerable about their sexual identity and need to be reassured at least occasionally that they're doing all right. It's also important that both of you always feel that you can say no, for as soon as a feeling of coercion enters the relationship, it can become more and more difficult to feel free about saying yes. Take the approach that each of you is agreeing to give the other a gift rather than bartering favors. The problem with making strict equivalence contracts about sex ("I'll wash the dishes if you'll have sex") is that it makes sex into a payment rather than something freely offered, and it can reward manipulativeness.

Giving criticism without hurting your partner's feelings is extremely difficult but just as essential as letting them know what you appreciate. You may find that you hold onto dissatisfactions so long that when you finally let them out you have built up too much resentment to have a gentle touch. I think that most of us secretly resent our partners for not intuitively knowing exactly what we need *so they can spare us the embarrassment of saying what we want.* But if you both can drop the expectation that you already own advanced degrees in sexual technique, you can learn from your partner without feeling that you're being kept after school:

> At the time when Gene's son from a previous marriage was nearing puberty, Gene began to talk with his new wife, Rita, about how they should talk with him about sex. In the process they reminisced about their own minimal early education about sex. Gene's mother had one day said, "Your father is going to tell you about some man and woman things." There was an odd tone in her voice, as if she had just swallowed an aspirin that had caught in her throat. Gene and his father went upstairs into a room, where they both stared out the window for a long while.
>
> "So, you know all about sex, right?" Gene said, "Right, Dad." They talked about football for a while and then went downstairs.
>
> Rita's sex education was just about as informative,

*and they were able to admit to each other somewhat
sheepishly that they still had some trouble talking to
each other, let alone Gene's son, about "the birds
and the bees." So they went to a bookstore and
picked up some illustrated manuals and over a period of weeks went through them together. At times
they would use each other's bodies for what they jokingly referred to as their "anatomy lessons."*

*"We were actually both surprised to find that we
had made assumptions about each other's sexual responses that may have been accurate for past lovers
but were wide of the mark for each other. Although
we felt like two overaged teenagers, it felt good to be
sharing with each other in a way that we had never
done before."*

In this couple's case, they were able to rationalize their
need to read about sex as being for the sake of their son. It
allowed them to recapture a healthy sense of inquisitive-
ness. In a sense, when we begin a relationship we are all
starting from scratch, since every person's body is a bit
different from any other; it may help you and your partner
to reminisce about the limitations of your early sex education and pretend to be teenagers learning about sex for the
first time.

Playful communication also means calling up your lover
by telephone and making love over the phone, sending
erotic letters to each other, even if you happen to share the
same mailbox, or sending an erotic tape recording. Some
couples develop private expressions that allow them to
communicate in public without the sexual meaning of the
message being understood by others. For example, one
husband would say "I salute you," meaning that he had an
erection and desired intercourse with his wife. Many people have erotic pet names for each other, such as "Common
Wench," "Stud," "Man among Men," "Amazon Woman,"
and "HHH" (for "Hard Humping Honey"). One couple

confided to me that the woman was named "Hot Lips" because she was a fellatio lover, while he was nicknamed "Mr. Coffee" because "he grinds so fine." Sexual anatomy is often the basis for nicknames, as in "B.B.," short for "Big Boobs." A woman who felt her partner was very good in bed in spite of his concern that his penis wasn't big enough began calling him "Dynamite with a Short Stick." Sure, all of this seems silly when you step back and dissect it, but these names help to mythologize and personalize a couple's sexual relationship, as well as adding a touch of humor to what can otherwise become an excessively grave situation.

Roles

Lack of communication makes it more likely that couples will respond to each other on the basis of preconceived stereotypes. We all have internalized our culture's images of masculinity and femininity—the Marlboro Man, the *Cosmo* Girl, Ozzie and Harriet, Bogart and Bacall, Marilyn Monroe. Despite the gains made by women in staking a claim for equality, old role behavior is slow to change. Men are still typically the initiators in sexual relations, and while an egalitarian relationship may be many couples' ideal, many people lack the self-awareness to practice it. It's one thing to believe in the abstract that men and women are equal; it's another to have the humility to acknowledge when our pigheadedness gets in the way of being fair. Some differences between the sexes may not be due only to cultural caprice but are deeply rooted in biology. Thus, more often than not, men seem able to enjoy sex without emotional intimacy, while women are less willing to do without the relationship.

When you are one person trying to understand another, it really doesn't matter whether your differences have to do with culture or biology. What matters is if you can deeply empathize with your partner's experience and be brave enough to explore sex-role behavior that you may not have been taught when growing up.

> *Jim always felt that "the man should be on top." This infuriated Alice, who was interested in other positions that provided her with more clitoral stimulation. To get him to switch positions she challenged him to roll together in the middle of intercourse. "Jim is an avid sailor, so I compared it to 'coming about,'" she said. "I'd tell him 'You're still in control of the boom, but we need to switch tacks.'" Jim took the challenge to negotiate the maneuver and Alice got the position she wanted.*

Alice's playful analogy with sailing preserved Jim's sense of control and at the same time introduced flexibility into their sexual activity. The next couple's play was liberating at the same time as it was erotic:

> *Kathleen was taking her usual hour to get herself made up before going out for the evening, and Bob was getting impatient. Even though he wasn't looking forward to going to the party, he hated to be late.*
>
> *"If you had to put on your face instead of just slapping on some Aqua Velva, you'd take an hour, too," Kathleen said.*
>
> *"What's the big deal?" Bob asked. "Let me do your makeup and let's get going. He turned her around from her makeup table and started to put some lipstick on her lips, smearing it a bit at the corners.*
>
> *"The lipstick goes on last, turkey, and don't slop it on." Bob decided he didn't like the color anyway and went rummaging through her cosmetics for a lighter shade of red. With some coaching, he applied base, blusher, eye shadow, mascara, and liner. One look in the mirror convinced Kathleen that she would*

have to start all over again, but Bob was looking too proud of himself for her to wipe it all off. "Fair's fair," she said. "Let me do you now."

Using the most garish shades she owned, she applied different color eye shadow on each eye, and deep purple lipstick. Before she was done they had started to make love, and their bodies were tattooed with the rich colors of their lips.

In retrospect, Bob found that the experience gave him more of an appreciation for what it was like to be a woman.

Another couple experimented with different sexual identities by dressing up in each other's formal clothes and having dinner in their apartment. While both of these examples may feel too kinky for you, I don't think that either of these couples were confused about their sexual identities. In fact, their willingness to risk stepping out of their accustomed roles may be due to a strong sense of self. You don't need to go as far as these couples, however. For instance, you could spend a few minutes silently with your partner, each fantasizing what it would be like to be the opposite sex: what it would be like to have a penis, or a vagina and breasts, to have a menstrual cycle, to wear a dress. Afterward, share with each other what your experiences were, and then return to being yourself again and try to share what your own sex feels like. Try not to judge how well you each empathize, but rather use your fantasies as jumping off points to learn more about each other.

The next couple illustrates yet another creative way of playing with sexual stereotypes:

Joanie and Barry occasionally watched porno movies on their home video system as a prelude to making love. Joanie had somewhat mixed feelings about these films since, while at times she found them quite erotic, she also didn't like the way women most often were portrayed as pure sex objects. Barry had to admit that the films were more oriented toward men, and that the plot lines were unimaginative and repetitious. More artistically done films were hard to find. Thus, one evening after they had each had a few drinks, they decided to create their own dialogue for one of the films Barry had bought, dubbing over the original with a microphone. The results were quite comical. On another occasion, they tried the same thing with an old Doris Day movie they had taped off the TV, this time improvising some sexually explicit dialogue.

To be able to play with sex roles can sometimes induce more empathy and flexibility than earnest discussions, which can end in further polarization.

The Return of the Suppressed

I am the sort of person who hates to throw anything away—my drawers are cluttered with sweaters that I haven't worn in years, my file cabinets stuffed with random papers going back to grade school. Once in a great while, usually under duress, I will painfully weed out a few relics to make room for new acquisitions, but I am haunted by the memory of those few occasions when I went looking for something and remembered that, God forbid, I had thrown it out. I am not really a collector in any organized sense—I never have had trouble seeing stamps as something to be stuck on an envelope and sent into the great beyond—but anything to do with my personal history has acquired squatter's rights.

Our unconscious has the same idiosyncrasy. Freud likened it to the way in which new civilizations are built upon old ruins, with past structures still partially preserved. We are unaware of much of our archaic mental contents, but they are not gone so much as forgotten. One of Freud's other great contributions was to notice that children are sexual beings, and that our early sensually tinged, emotional experiences leave indelible imprints on our sexuality. Like other creatures, we have impulses, a kind of blind primeval urge that may be steered to some degree though not turned off at will. What we begin to acquire from an early age are channels through which these impulses surge or pass more leisurely along. A preference for blondes rather than brunettes, for frilly blouses or boyish looks are signposts placed long ago, marking routes our impulses have traveled. As adults we establish fairly constant pathways of meeting our erotic needs with a partner. But the old, less traveled and uncompleted roads, though perhaps hidden from view by psychic overgrowth, lie waiting. Mature eroticism means that you be willing to explore these old pathways with your partner, to be able to have an adventure off the beaten track and mutually chart your course, while still not forgetting your ultimate destination.

Norman O. Brown, in *Life Against Death,* points out that our extended period of childhood dependency inevitably bequeaths lifelong allegiances to nongenital forms of sexuality, such as licking and sucking. To replace such total body eroticism with an exclusive focus on intercourse is to procreate but emotionally incarcerate; by cutting yourself off from the full range of erotic experience, you foreclose many potential points of contact with your partner. At its extreme, suppression of our erotic imagination leads to the limitation of sensual experience that D. H. Lawrence was talking about and that Henry Miller bluntly describes:

> When you look at them with their clothes on you imagine all sorts of things; you give them an individuality like, which they haven't got, of course. There's just a crack there between the legs. . . . It's an illusion! . . . It's so absolutely meaningless. . . . All

that mystery about sex and then you discover that it's nothing—just a blank...there's nothing there... nothing at all. It's disgusting.

To be bored with your sexual relationship, to feel "there's nothing there," usually means that you are cut off psychologically from the deepest sources of your erotic life. Play allows you to experiment with erotic alternatives —for example, to be voyeuristic and exhibitionistic:

> A couple, both of whom enjoyed pornographic and erotic novels and films, discovered that it was even more exciting for them to write their own erotic stories, each taking turns "writing" the story out loud. Sometimes they would tape-record themselves as well as their sounds making love. They also had several mirrors in their bedroom and would act out fantasies while pretending that they were in a movie or that they were other people than themselves.

Other couples may take erotic pictures of themselves with an instant camera or with their video camera or use bold body language or "strip-tease" to express their more exhibitionist side. A hint of bestiality may also get expressed in play:

> Rick and Carol have an elaborate fantasy in which they act like animals. When Rich is "Growl" or "Bear" he makes strange creature-like noises. Carol is called "Tiger Woman," both because of her compassion for stray cats and her way of "pouncing" on Rick. During their foreplay sometimes one of them plays an animal while the other is a loving animal-handler. At other times they both pretend to be animals, rubbing against each other, gently biting and making primeval, animalistic sounds. They find this play is often an erotic prelude or actually carries

over into intercourse, when they use the rear-entry position.

Sexual fantasy immensely enlarges your erotic repertoire. It helps you tap into your personal releases for passion, and when part of a full sexual relationship, is not at all a sign of frustrated or immature sexuality. Numerous books have appeared in recent years popularizing fantasy as a normal feature of our erotic life. They have provided much needed license, particularly for women, to enjoy fuller sexual expression. But under the banner of avoiding judgment and championing individual freedom, these books don't always help people differentiate mature forms of fantasy that lead more surely to intimacy from those that are more infantile or isolating. A very important issue, for example, is whether your sexual fantasies should be kept secret or shared with your partner. We all need to preserve some islands of privacy. You also have to use some judgment as to whether your partner will be able to handle your attraction to your next-door neighbor or your vacuum cleaner fetish.

But we also need to take some risks to let our lover in on what turns us on. Many times you'll find that your partner will agree: "Whew! you have that fantasy, *too*?" Even if she doesn't share your particular erotic proclivities, she may open up in turn about her own. Sharing fantasies opens up possibilities of greater intimacy, of more leeway for experimentation. Often we need an active "witness" to help us integrate a deviant part of our sexuality. Recognizing that reality will always fall somewhere short of the ideal, I think you should try not to settle for less than collaborative fantasy. This involves searching for common ground but also not giving up your points of difference. It will probably be difficult at first for you to share your fantasies with your partner, so try talking about erotic movies or literature that turn you on. You can also thumb through some magazine pictures together and comment on what images and associations appeal to you. The more you can tune into each other's specific releases of passion through detailed fantasy, the more your love-making will become filled with fresh adventure. Eventually your partner's favorite fantasies will change, and you will have to renew your acquaintance with each other's inner lives and be prepared to modify old fantasies.

You may find it hard to tolerate your partner's fantasy life because you may wonder why the real you isn't good enough to satisfy him or her. It's as if you have a silent competitor against whom you can never measure up. This line of thinking is founded on the faulty premise that you are responsible for turning your partner on. It also fails to recognize that everyone has a secret fantasy life that is larger than one's lover, and your partner's enjoyment of fantasy need not mean you are inadequate. Your partner's bringing a personal fantasy into your relationship for the first time can mean that you are all the more special. While the content of the fantasy may not have to do with you, the act of sharing surely does.

Another important dimension of fantasy is the extent to which it is acted out. The important issue is to find the right meeting point between the illusion—the dream, or fantasy—and the real world. You may prefer not to enact a particular fantasy with your partner or to play out only a part of it. For example, your partner's fantasy of displaying herself nude at the Academy Awards may be translated into your own private viewing, spiced up perhaps by suitable props. Fantasy that becomes too real ceases to be play. There need to be limits, with one of them being that the play remains contained within the privacy of the couple. You can fantasize all you want about being different people or phylogenetic organisms, but once you actually admit someone else past the boundary of the couple, the spell is broken. Intimacy depends on such limits. They are also necessary because in gratifying suppressed impulses we always risk arousing our guilt. To indulge in fantasy can grant us a piece of our dream world, while still allowing guilt to slumber undisturbed.

In fact, many people's favorite fantasies have to do with doing something forbidden, sinful, or taboo. Freud described the basis of taboo as a safeguard against incestual wishes, and, indeed, most cultures have uniformly forbidden sexual contact between close relations. For example, in Melanesia in the nineteenth century:

> If brother and sister meet by chance in the open, she must run away or turn aside and conceal herself. If the boy recognizes certain footprints in the sand as his sister's he is not to follow her. He will not even mention her name and will guard against using any current word if it forms part of her name.[24]

The nature of taboo reveals itself in the fact that cultures don't erect such elaborate barriers to impulses that no one is interested in indulging. Such powerful injunctions indicate powerful wishes. Because the wish remains a rambunctious captive, constant vigilance is necessary to keep it under control—the sad prevalence of incest suggests how tenuous these controls can be. There's nothing healthy about incest, no matter how playful someone pretends to be. But many of us *over*socialized types overdo our self-restraint to the extent that anything remotely titillating is taxed with guilt. We need some harmless outlets from the fiery injunctions of cultural taboo. Play allows for a healthy loosening of such rigid taboos so that elements of past family relationships—erotic and nonerotic—can be woven into your current sexual relationship:

> *As kids, Ann and her brother Jim, who was two years older than she, would tumble about on the floor, Jim would adopt a deep voice and say, "I am*

the steamroller," and Ann would shriek as he rolled on top of her. Only when she said, "I can't breathe," would he roll off. Many years later, as an adult, she happened to share this story with her lover. That evening while she was reading in bed, he plopped down beside her and in a deep voice said, "I am the steamroller." To Ann's delight, he rolled on top of her.

Ann's original play with her brother was not incestuous, but it was erotic, in the sense that they were giving each other physical pleasure. Healthy sibling relationship can permit such freedom since both partners respect limits. Similarly, in healthy adult love relationships, partners can recreate some of these early intimate moments. Through play you can give each other permission to rebel a bit against your inhibitions.

After two years of living together the woman felt she wanted something more. Coy at first, she became braver about livening up her sex life. She decided "what the hell" and went and bought some sexy underwear. Included in her purchases were one red and one black garter. She wore one on each leg and presented herself to her boyfriend. Pretending to be a prostitute, she also used the coarsest language she'd heard and found it marvelously stimulating. To her delight, her boyfriend responded in the same playful spirit.

Some people have fantasies about the innocent one who is seduced by the more worldly and older partner, or in turn being the corruptor of naïve youth. Some are excited at the thought of multiple partners, of homosexual contact, or having sex with tabooed authorities, such as teachers, religious leaders, judges, or doctors. Whatever other meanings these fantasies have, they are often attempts to work through early prohibitions. Playful fantasy is a way of thumbing your nose at the forces of suppression and declaring your independence.

The very act of forming an intimate sexual relationship with another person is breaking a taboo. The person we are most strongly drawn to always possesses some of the qualities that remind us of a parent. To make love to them is thus, in fantasy, to have what we have been so long denied. This is a very tricky bind for a permissive partner. They can either become our ally in overcoming old taboos or be rejected because of our guilt about having forbidden desires gratified. I recommend that you try to use play to loosen up your inhibitions, but there is always a chance that you will have to weather a backlash by your conscience. Consider your play as a probe into unexplored psychic territory. If you find the natives friendly, so much the better. But if you meet resistance, see if you and your partner can understand where the trouble lies.

On Using and Abusing

In a time when looking out for number one has been touted as a moral obligation and selfishness is glorified as self-actualization, using another person to further your own pleasure shouldn't raise too many eyebrows. But surely a romantic, such as I, must be appalled that love could be reduced to using a partner to play out your sex fantasies. Love has certainly descended from her pedestal, yet we still can do her honor. I am not troubled when our use of another is reciprocal, acknowledged, and when it is not the predominant way that we relate.

Some people's favorite fantasy has to do with dominating or being dominated by their partner: you are a member of the sheik's harem, a slave to his every pleasure, or you are an officer of the law free to do as you will with your sex prisoner. Body tattoos and jewelry are some of the tangible ways that "ownership" of the other person is manifested. Some couples act out this fantasy through light "bondage":

> *After several years of living together, a couple found that their sex life lacked the zest they had known early on. Part of the problem was that neither of them took much initiative. Then one of them got the idea of experimenting with tying each other's hands and feet to the bedposts with some thread. This forced the partner who was not tied up to be more aggressive and helped break up the pattern that they had settled into.*
>
> *"Since we knew that the person who was tied up could easily escape at any time, it wasn't scary at all. As we got used to the idea, we started using velvet cords and got into more elaborate fantasies, such as my being Queen and Jake being my handsome courtier."*

Bondage fantasies gratify the wish of the bound person to be sexually stimulated without having to take responsibility for desiring it: "He made me do it." It thus is a strategy for holding your sexual guilt captive. In turn, the one in control can play out fantasies of omnipotence and mastery over his or her own helplessness: "*I'm* not powerless like that one. I can do anything I want." We all need to find ways in life to re-experience our childhood sense of omnipotence, and this is one way to do it. What marks "bondage" as play is the flexibility of the fantasy and the preservation of "pretend." When nothing else but actual chains or permanent skin markings will do, you need to look at whether you are acting out a compulsion and not playing.

Bondage fantasies are often associated with sadomasochism. It's a peculiar fact about eroticism that pain can be pleasurable. Among animals, aggression is often associated with mating. For example, in the three-spined stickleback, the male will initially bite the female repeatedly and the female flees, but as courtship progresses, his attacks diminish. Human sexual passion can be hard to distinguish from violence; it is not by accident that the word "fuck" has a brutal sound and is used as often to curse as to express desire. The *Kama Sutra* compares sexual intercourse to a quarrel, "on account of the contrarieties of love and its tendency to dispute." Some couples find that arguments or wrestling lead into passionate sex, which may speak to the fact that anything that stirs up emotional arousal can be sexy if interpreted as desire. It may also be that some people need to create emotional distance first in order to open themselves to sexual intimacy.

>   One couple used provocative teasing as a way of keeping a spark in their lovemaking. When she undressed, Roberta would leave her underpants on and would make Alan struggle to get them off before "giving in" to intercourse. They would roll around in foreplay, but every time Alan went to remove her panties, Roberta would put up a struggle. This light fighting would force Alan into a more aggressive, demanding role. She would allow him to fully remove her panties only when both of them were sexually very stimulated and she was ready to be penetrated. "It was a guarantee that I got as much foreplay as I wanted before I let him come in," she said. For his part, Alan saw the play as a challenge to stimulate Roberta sufficiently to "open up." Sometimes if he felt that Roberta had made him work too hard, or he was feeling tired, he would roll over and act disinterested. Then their roles would be reversed and it would become her responsibility to maintain his erection and to effect coitus.

Some couples indulge in more aggressive sex play. The next couple's style raises some difficult issues:

"*My partner usually calls me 'Old lady,' but once we get to bed he calls me 'Bitch.' When we first got together he seemed to be really shy and quiet which I later found out he wasn't. I was used to that type of male, so I had him call me things like bitch and slut to see if it would 'bring the tiger out,' so to speak. It finally caught on and he uses these names all the time. Being an ex-hooker I am used to such terms and it helps to keep me from feeling uncomfortable about our sex. Sometimes he pretends I'm a very young girl (about twelve) and that I am so bad I need a spanking. Then if I say I'm sorry and won't be bad anymore he gives me a treat by making love to me or eating my box. Most times we play s&m games. I love to be spanked, slapped, or tied when we fuck, the rougher the better. Sometimes I play the heavy and he has to do anything I say. I still beat him with the belt but when I'm through I reward my slave with some expert head and then a nice long fuck. . . . Rape is a favorite game with us. My husband pretends to break into the house and finds me on the bed in a very revealing nightgown, then tells me he is going to rape me. When I resist he pulls my clothes off and holds me down. About then I stop fighting 'cause I'm as hot as he is, so it really isn't rape anymore. This type of play makes sex something to look forward to and not just something to hurry up and get over with. Also with my husband I can trust him to take the play only as far and as long as I want to, where in the past the situation was all too real. When I left home at fifteen I wound up on the streets and was raped quite a few times.*"

Ideally, our love would be pure of wishes to degrade or injure, but we have to reckon with how we are and not just with how we wished we could be. This couple dramatically illustrates how couples can attempt to work through early traumatic experiences through play. Just as children can play out painful experiences, so can adults achieve some mastery over disturbing events in which they were previously helpless. We don't know what this particular husband's issues were, but what keeps this play is the sense of limits, the knowledge that it is all but a fantasy in which *both* derive pleasure.

It's important to realize that you can be kinky without fearing that you're a depraved, salivating creep. If you're in doubt, you can use four criteria to distinguish between healthy play and perversions. In perversions the primary motivation is often the expression of hostility. Play can include getting rough with your partner, if that heightens your passion. It functions as a kind of brake or modulator, allowing an outlet for the inevitable ambivalence that any person feels in an intimate relationship. We all have old angers, too, that stem from unfinished business in past relationships and which may be expressed in a sexual fantasy. With play the hostility is contained within a more loving context, and eroticism coexists with respect, while with perversion there is a consistent or unrestrained attempt to humiliate, degrade, or injure. The difference is the same as that between the Marquis de Sade, for whom pain is the essence of pleasure, and Vatsyayana (*Kama Sutra*), who sees striking, biting, and scratching as ingredients of passion. The latter would certainly have agreed with the poet Robert Graves that "Nothing, agreed, is alien to love when pure desire has overflowed its baulks." For example, many people enjoy acting out a rape fantasy, as long as strict limits are observed. One couple recognized the difficulty in communicating about limits—for example, saying "stop" might be interpreted as part of the act. They hit upon a playful solution: in advance they agreed on an absurd word—"abracadabra"—to signal when one had had enough.

A second hallmark of perversion is their autoerotism— your partner is not recognized as another person with distinct needs but rather is treated as an object to be exploited. As the Harvard psychologist George Goethals elegantly puts it, "A perversion is something that two people do but that only one of them enjoys." In contrast, intimate play invites collaborative fantasy, so that both partners' needs can be satisfied.

Perversions mistake the means for the end. In fetishism, for example, an inanimate object may totally replace another person. Whatever detours you may take during intimate play, your goal is always to end up in closer emotional contact with your partner.

Finally, there is a ritualistic rigidity to perversions, a repetitive, compulsive urgency that must use the same means and attain the same goal, analogous to the stereotyped mating of animals. Instead, play leads to multiple pathways of making erotic contact with your partner rather than limiting your repertoire. The very essence of play is its creative unpredictability. You're not stuck in one mode, genital or otherwise. A lifetime of making love in the missionary position can be as much a perversion as a fondness for women's shoes.

Mystery and Monogamy

We are creatures that hunger for both tenderness and sensuality. Neither our genes nor our parents have prepared us for how to go about having both in one relationship. It is not just a taste for symmetry that makes us want to meet all our needs with one person, but rather that, with all the potential for intimacy to make sex difficult, it also makes for the most body-and-soul satisfying sex.

Romanticism is often associated with frustrated desire. We seem to need barriers, if not unattainability, in order to kindle passion. Sometimes only in the safety of distance can we acknowledge how important someone is to us. This poses a problem for our poor wife or husband, who may be sweetly loving and anxious to please but who is utterly and always afflicted with the curse of being available. In part our needs for a barrier come out of Oedipal guilt—intimacy is associated with prohibited eroticism with parents and siblings, and so, if our partner is fully available, we must make them psychologically unavailable. We erect barriers also because we are afraid of intimacy—afraid of being hurt, rejected, controlled; whatever bad things may have happened in previous relationships we expect to occur again, only worse.

I don't know what makes the fateful difference between tenderness becoming a catalyst for, instead of diminishing, sensuality. I'm convinced that we have to reckon with our need for keeping a certain distance and find healthy ways of preserving mystery and secrecy in spite of familiarity. Our genitals and our psyches are inextricably linked by the seductive thread of taboo. We are constantly in a tug of war with our conscience—this tension can keep our impulses too tightly reined in, but it also provides much psychic release when we suddenly give in. Our fascination with the forbidden and the out of reach is not just a matter of our unresolved incestual wishes. *Every* secret carries within it the wish to conceal but also the captive wish to reveal. The tension between self-restraint and raw impulse is the taut instrument of our greatest pleasure, which needs constantly to be fine-tuned.

Play helps mediate subtle degrees of intimacy and mystery. It's like a thermostat for regulating how emotionally hot things get. As such it provides a variety of potential solutions that may be right for you at each stage of your relationship.

Most of us are at heart incredibly resourceful, and I feel confident that our inventiveness will always provide monogamy with interesting possibilities. As a so-called expert, I have the privilege of being asked a lot of odd questions about sex, some of which I never even thought of being afraid to ask. The other day I was asked whether it was possible to laugh and have an orgasm at the same time. My first reaction was that the question was an ancient Zen koan—such as "What color is the wind?"—meant to confound the reasoning powers of horny monks vainly seeking enlightenment through the intellect. I then consulted the *Kama Sutra* to see if it described some strange contortion of limbs that could accomplish such simultaneous release. Finally I concluded that, except perhaps in Tibet or remote regions of Albania, where sexual practices are poorly documented, it can be said not to occur.

There is a truth concealed here about play and sexuality: humans, unlike three-spined sticklebacks and fruit flies, have the potential for two distinct kinds of sexual intimacy —one that requires you to take your time, to dance around your lover, and to be open to the sort of loose mental connection that makes humor possible; and one that takes the shortest line between two organs and presses for ripsnorting, instinctual release. I would not want to do without either of them. A good friend of mine told me that the joy he felt in getting his partner to laugh at his wordplay was associated with a feeling of potency very similar to the satisfaction of facilitating her orgasm. My wish for you, then, is many orgasms but just as much laughter, even if they never happen at the same time.

CHAPTER SIX

Coping
with Parents
and the Past

We like to think that in starting a new relationship we can create a new version of ourselves. Last year we were certainly turkeys, maybe even yesterday, but today everything is different. We think we can be born-again lovers. But it's not as simple as laying down some rubber and leaving our past in the dust. Our good intentions and earnest declarations give way to familiar feelings. We soon find that we are governed more by nature's slow pace of change than by our will. Like the planets, we move great distances but manage always to return to the place we started—we can deflect but not choose our character. Like all living things, we are also capable of growth, but we have more in common with oak trees than larvae that can go into a cocoon for a few months and emerge suddenly, able to fly: inevitably, we bring to each new intimate relationship the ways of relating that we have learned before. In fact, intimacy has a way of reactivating our oldest ways of responding, a form of second childhood that does not imply senility and need not preclude maturity.

Coming to terms with our past is very much bound up with putting our parents into perspective. Most people have only one model of a marriage (their parents') to help guide them, and this one is learned at an impressionable age when lessons consist more of absorbing feelings than verbal understanding; that is, this model influences us so strongly in part because it is unconscious. Unfortunately, our past is a jealous mistress that looks on new ways of relating with suspicion. Arguments over little things can escalate into religious wars, because our own past ways of doing things that we have learned from our family feel sacrosanct.

> "Bob insists on keeping our refrigerator well stocked. He's not overweight but he loves to snack," says Jane. "It used to bug me the way he'd gulp down large quantities of orange juice—he wouldn't take a small juice glass but a big tumbler, and sometimes he'd just drink it straight out of the container. When I was a kid, I was the oldest of four girls and there wasn't much money. Whenever I had an ice cream cone it wasn't just for me, I had to share it with one of my sisters. Naturally, I never would have taken a half a quart of orange juice at one time just for myself. So even though Bob and I could afford it, it bothered me when he'd do that. It irked him that I gave him a hard time about it, because to him orange juice was like mother's milk—it was always his favorite drink as a kid.
>
> "For similar reasons we'd get into arguments about choosing presents for our in-laws. I'd argue for real practical and economical things, like heavy winter socks and sweaters, while Bob, who was used to giving and receiving expensive gifts, would think I was being cheap."

Sometimes an argument over who last walked the dog is only an argument over who last walked the dog. But not always. There are often deeper levels to your conflicts that, if they go unrecognized, will make accommodation and tolerance impossible. As the historian Will Durant has observed, "Most of us spend too much time on the last twenty-four hours and too little on the last six thousand years." I'm not suggesting that you and your partner go on an archeological dig or look for the roots of your marital troubles in Egyptian burial customs or Sumerian fertility myths. The most difficult conflicts that you experience usually have to do with both partners trying to get each other to conform to archaic and mutually incompatible notions of how husbands and wives are supposed to behave.

Some of the worst fights Mark and Suzi had were in the car. Invariably Mark would drive and he would expect Suzi to be the "navigator." Then, whenever they made a wrong turn or got lost, he would yell at Suzi for not doing her job.

"I was never good at map reading," relates Suzi, "and Mark's yelling at me made it worse. My father was the one in our family who had the best sense of direction, and he never asked for help when driving. When I confronted Mark on how mean he was being, he refused to see what he was doing; eventually he admitted that he was acting just like his father, who would constantly put his mother down when she made a mistake."

The more wedded you are to your original family, the more difficult it will be to adapt to the different ways of being that your partner cherishes. The family systems theorist Boszormenyi-Nagy calls such allegiances to the past "invisible loyalties."[25] Growing up requires that you shift your devotion from past loves to your partner.

Another reason that the past affects our present loves is because old pain leaves fault lines in the successive layers of our experience. We deny, displace, sublimate, and repress painful childhood experiences that were too overwhelming to bear. These memories and feelings remain active in our unconscious and can errupt into our awareness when situations occur that are similar to the past.

Adam was an avid cyclist and cross-country skier before he met Judy, and early in their relationship he introduced her to these two sports. When they started to make weekend jaunts together, the one thing that marred them was the drive. "Judy became another person in the car when we set out on a long drive," said Adam. "She would get passive and nagging, which was not her style."

Judy agreed. "I wouldn't want to help tying down the skis or bicycles to the car rack or loading up the luggage. I would just sit and watch and criticize. Then in the car I'd complain about the radio music or traffic, the weather or the condition of the road."

"The regularity and the repetitiveness of Judy's behavior began to bother me," said Adam. "I began to wonder what it was about the car and trips that changed Judy. Then one day Judy was describing how as kids they often went camping and how she hated it, because her mother would always bitch on the car rides and her parents would get into big fights."

"My mother bitched a lot of the time," said Judy, "but it was worse in the car, in that confined space, where you couldn't get away from it. When I was with Adam on these trips I knew I was tense, but I didn't make the connection with my parents or realize how impossible I was being. Then one time when we were going skiing and I began complaining about other drivers, Adam said, 'Do you feel like we're going camping? I think it's too cold.' He said it gently, but suddenly I could feel what was happening."

Adam's playful comment to Judy at the very moment when she was reenacting a situation from the past helped her make the connection. You may find that it is more productive to explore this kind of territory with your partner at more neutral moments. Eventually you and your partner will find your own preferred ways of helping each other come to terms with the return of ghosts from your past.

Painful memories and experiences do have their redeeming features. The British psychoanalyst D. W. Winnicott suggested that we all have a kind of deep freeze in which unresolved situations are kept in abeyance. A thaw may occur when our unconscious senses that the new environment—in particular, the people with whom we are intimate—will help us come to terms with old hurts and frustrations. One of my favorite fantasies is being able to travel back in time to anxious moments in my youth and to have a comforting chat with myself as I was then. For example, I'd like to reach across time to that child packing his duffle bag to go to sleepaway camp for the first time, already feeling homesick. I'd also like to have a heart to heart talk with myself before my first date. My wish is not so much to change my history as to provide for that child what he needed. Your painful past is waiting for a similar restitution.

While the past can create conflict, you can use play with your partner to help find its proper place in your relationship, so that it brings richness and intensity. As with all mixed blessings, what matters ultimately is not whether troubling feelings return, but what kind of reception you give them. If you can accept and acknowledge each other's visitations from the past when they occur, your relationship can be enhanced. I'm not suggesting that you try to psychoanalyze each other. Even for trained therapists, there are big pitfalls in trying to interpret your partner's behavior. It is often difficult to use play with sufficient delicacy in situations that have so much emotional power. But if you can adopt an attitude of both of you exploring the unconscious, rather than trying to "find out" each other, you can help each other grow.

Getting Acquainted with Your Unconscious

You can't rid yourself of your experiences with parents or with any other part of your past, but you can become more free by learning about how you reenact your past in the present. This requires that you get better acquainted with that mysterious inner realm that Freud called the unconscious.

If you dissect the brain, you won't be able to locate the unconscious. You can't summon it up for a heart to heart talk when it misbehaves, or do mental isometrics to make it stronger. Freud's approach was to sneak up on it, like a detective who looks for fingerprints and fiber remnants. The unconscious reveals its presence in slips of the tongue, forgetting, and dreams. Fortunately, like a guilty and bumbling burglar, the unconscious always returns to the scene of the crime, and so if you miss it on one occasion, it's bound to reappear in similar circumstances again. This is the reason we have recurrent dreams or find that we always seem to mispronounce the name of an obnoxious colleague. You need not lie on a couch for ten years or watch vigilantly early every morning to recapture your dreams, like a lobsterman retrieving his lines. The unconscious reveals itself in your relationships, in the way that you continue to perceive, feel, and act as if you were much younger, and as if you were dealing with significant people from your past instead of with your partner. The unconscious (or, as some analytic thinkers would call it, "transference") causes you to distort, to impose your inner version of reality, fashioned out of your earliest hopes and fears, on the present. You *transfer* the past into the present. Transference operates in all your relationships, but it is usually harder to see it in transient encounters than in longer term partnerships. You and your partner have a rich opportunity to learn about your inner lives if both of you can have the humility to admit that, despite being mature people in many other contexts, you can be driven by impulses of which you are totally unaware. The next couple illustrates one way in which your play can teach you about the influence of the past:

> Early in their marriage, Jean and John had gotten into several arguments about John's sarcastic "digs," which he was accustomed to use in banter with male friends, but which made Jean feel that she wasn't being taken seriously. She had reason to be sensitive to such behavior, since her father had never been able to say anything affirming to her, instead relating through sarcasm.
>
> John's sarcasm also had early antecedents. He had lost both parents before he was thirteen and had been left with a rigid and controlling stepmother, with whom he could never overtly disagree. Instead, he would vent his frustrations by thinking of sarcastic putdowns that he would never dare utter. Through serious talks, Jean and John identified the individual histories underlying their conflict, and John's playful sarcasm evolved from a divisive influence to one helping bind them closer together.

It's often difficult to recognize that you're seeing the present through the outmoded lenses of your past, because in most situations *both* partners are innocently distorting in different but overlapping ways. It's as if you were a surveying team trying to lay out straight dimensions while both of you are moving. If you can each take responsibility for your own contribution to a problem, each of you will learn something.

Often couples find ways to subvert this learning process. They remain ignorant of the irrational foundations of their behavior. Dealing only with the surface of their bickering is to see only the tip of the iceberg, below which the frozen situations of childhood moor them fast to the past. Their ignorance is a form of silent conspiracy: a couple may appear to be actively struggling with important issues but actually has an implicit understanding that the most painful truths are never explored. Their overt conflicts function as a red flag toward which they will always charge, missing what lies behind it. Another couple may adopt good guy-bad guy roles, in which one of them is seen as the source of all ills. For example, I am unshakable, tolerant, and have all the answers, while you are clinging, moody, and scatterbrained. Such couples perceive any conflict through the distorted perspective of their mutually contrived roles, with one of them seen as the sick partner in need of help—psychiatric, spiritual, or medical. Or they may assign the bad role to someone outside the couple: they're having such a hard time not because either of them is neurotic, but because of Mom, little Johnny, or the IRS.

It's important to realize how powerful yet invisible this conspiracy can be. We are each poised to perceive our partner in a stereotyped way and ignore any evidence that contradicts our expectations. Not only does each partner unintentionally distort the present relationship, but they're often able to induce each other to behave *as if the distortions were real*. Thus, while John may initially have reminded Jean of the way her father treated her because of a few sarcastic comments, in time John may become more and more like her overbearing, oppressive parent. It's as if each partner were a silent director, giving subtle stage directions to each other.

> Early in their relationship, Steve and Barbara had what Steve thought was a minor argument over who would mow the lawn. Steve said that he'd worked hard all week and he wanted to relax over the weekend. Barbara said that she'd worked equally hard taking care of the kids, the lawn had to be cut, and it was Steve's responsibility. Steve was annoyed but

grudgingly said he'd do it and then sat down to read the newspaper for a while.

Later in the day, when Steve was halfway through the job, he came into the kitchen to get a cold drink. Barbara was furious. She said he "had no right to cut off the conversation like that" and that he shut her out by reading the newspaper. She said he was being "icy, cold, and distant." The disparity between how little he intended by his actions and how strongly she felt about them upset him. As he had done in the past when Barbara criticized him, he withdrew and became sullen. Their weekend was ruined.

Several months later a similar episode occurred. After a minor argument, Steve went off to do some paper work for his job, and several hours later when he came downstairs Barbara was furious that he had "cruelly and abruptly cut her off." He again defended himself, and when he saw he was making no progress lapsed into silence. But later he thought about it and began to see a pattern. Barbara had often said her parents had usually ended their arguments with her father refusing to discuss the issue any further, leaving her mother feeling trivialized and wounded. Barbara had always sympathized with her mother and during her adolescence had secretly called her father the ice prick.

Steve sat down with Barbara and said, "I really don't know why you've reacted so strongly to our arguments." He paused and then added, "Perhaps you think I'm another ice prick." Barbara saw the connection and burst into a combination of laughter and tears. She talked about how miserable she had felt as a child when her father had treated her and her mother so coldly, and how vulnerable she felt to Steve's silence or coldness.

After this Barbara jokingly called Steve an ice

prick when she felt he was about to terminate an
argument before adequately resolving it together.

One of the keys to this kind of play is that you have to gently offer an evocative image to your partner. To be accusatory or just to say "You're treating me as if I were your father" won't work. It's the gentleness with which you point out a concrete and evocative image from the past that helps bring them face to face with themselves. This vignette also points out how a problem is usually entwined in both partners' behavior. That is, Steve is not a completely innocent victim of Barbara's reenacting her past—he does withdraw and act coldly at times (a pattern that probably has meaning in his own past)—although Barbara's overreaction pushes him further away.

Often the same characteristic in your partner that you find so objectionable is actually also within you, although it is hidden. By seeking to "manage" your partner's behavior, you are actually working out your own internal conflict. Obviously, trying to assign blame to one of you for a particular problem has no meaning. Although in many of the vignettes in this chapter I will focus primarily on one partner, keep in mind that this is always only half the story. In any impasse each of you has a role, however unconscious it may be. Patterns from the past draw their power not just from old spirits that have never been laid to rest; they are also maintained because they serve some current masters.

It may appear from my description that in trying to come to terms with reality we are no better off than someone stranded in a fun house, wandering from one distorted image to another. But there are some reliable clues, which psychoanalyst Ralph Greenson has spelled out in *The Technique and Practice of Psychoanalysis,*[26] to tip you off to the fact that your present behavior is at the mercy of emotions from the past. For example, if the positions either of you are taking are especially *rigid,* they are likely to be motivated by complex and not entirely conscious feelings. *Extremes of feeling* might also be clues—either intense emotion (especially if it seems out of proportion to the situation) or a lack of feeling (especially if some kind of reaction seems called for). Another tipoff is the *inappropriateness* of a reaction to a present situation. For example, I've learned that often when something has caused me pain, I react with anger, when sadness is what would be the most appropriate response. In fact, I have come to think that many men who are acting as if they were angry are really sad, and that when many women cry they are actually angry. In part, such inappropriate feelings have to do with culturally prescribed sex-role behavior, but inappropriateness is also a calling card of the past. The past is sometimes as *capricious* as a gremlin: your feelings may be erratic and change unexpectedly into their opposite. You may also uncover a *repetitive* pattern in your behavior that seems to have a life of its own, largely independent of current circumstances. Finally, if you find yourself acting in ways that you had *outgrown* (what I've referred to before as regression), you should look carefully for parallels between the present and your past. However, not all regression is a malignant intrusion. When it is contained within limits, is voluntary, and furthers adaptation, it can constitute healthy play.

Clearly, past "apparitions" take on many guises. They may appear as a visual memory from the past, a verbal message from a parent that you repeat to yourself, or as a familiar emotional state. You may experience them as a painful intrusion, or find yourself acting in ways that are alien to your usual way of handling problems. In such situations, your motivation to look below the surface can come from within. You may also experience the hold of the past as a comfortable, but too smug, certainty that you're right about something. In this case, I hope you will be able to listen to your partner's questioning your rigidity. The key question to ask yourself is not whether you are right or wrong in your attitude, but *why are you so sure*?

The most important ally you and your partner have in becoming acquainted with your mutual distortions is your commitment to each other. When things get tough, you can either get going and move on to a new relationship, which you imagine will be free of irrational and uncomfortable situations, or you can try to learn about yourself. You can look at the reappearance of the past in a long-term relationship as a kind of perennial plant that takes a long time to grow. You will inevitably see it sprout up again in another relationship, but it will usually take some time. Thus, rather than seeing it as a bad thing, look at it as a sign of the depth of your relationship and an investment that will have to be written off as a total loss if you don't learn from it. People who can't commit themselves to anybody are sadly like Marley's ghost, in Dickens's *A Christmas Carol*, who was condemned to wander forever after death wearing the chains he himself had forged. But, unlike Marley, they drag the weight of their past in this life rather than in the next.

Partners as Parents

I was talking during a recent holiday season with a young couple, and both of them lamented the fact that they were going to have to visit their families. "Thank God they don't live with us!" said the husband. I thought about how much both spouses were still enacting their pasts in the marriage, and I said, "Are you sure?" They laughed and the wife recalled that her husband had recently sent his mother a Mother's Day card, but it had come back to them because he had sent it to the couple's *own* address.

One of the more disturbing discoveries that we make as we get older is that some of the qualities that we found so difficult to deal with in our parents have become a part of us. In growing up we need to psychologically take in large chunks of our parents, just as much as we need Wonder

Bread and peanut butter to feed our bodies. We can't be expected to be discriminating about what we consume, and so we wind up with the equivalent of junk food as well as wholesome ingredients. One of the ways of coping with a recurrent, painful interaction with a parent is to adopt their behavior, a strategy known as identifying with the aggressor, or "If you can't beat them, join them." Since all of these identification processes function largely outside our awareness, and since no one likes to admit that they've become so much like their parents, we tend to have a lot of blind spots. Our partners, however, inevitably bump into them and can help us gradually come to terms with ourselves through play.

Greta had complained to Charley many times about her mother, Ann. In particular, she hated the way her mother would act like a martyr. Ann had had an unhappy life, including putting up with a husband who seemed interested only in bowling and baseball, and she used her unhappiness to play upon Greta's guilt. She never could say straight out what she wanted, instead maneuvering other people through passive-aggressive displays.

Early in his relationship with Greta, Charley noticed that she sometimes did similar things with him, but she couldn't see it. One time, when Greta, after sighing heavily, said that she didn't mind doing the laundry again, even though it wasn't her turn, Charley gently asked, "Oh, really, Ann?" Greta stopped short and then started to go into a caricature of her mother, which made them both laugh.

As Greta became more aware of her tendency to try to "guilt" Charley into doing things she wanted, she was able to catch herself. However, it also became clear that part of what maintained her indirect appeals was that Charley would get annoyed if she accused him of not doing his share. In some ways,

Charley acted like Greta's father. Thus, at times when Greta found herself resenting having to do the dishes for the third time in a row, she would do her "mother imitation": "I really don't mind doing them again. These hands were made for washing dishes and doing the laundry." Charley would usually fall into the same playful spirit and get the message.

Sometimes what we transfer from the past into our current love relationship are not characteristics of a parent but a style we developed to deal with a problematic parent, as illustrated earlier with Steve and Barbara. It is as if we keep in place the tidal walls originally thrown up to contain storms long past. Any sign from our partner that we interpret as familiar clouds on the horizon sends us scurrying for cover.

Play helps you deal with such sensitive issues for several reasons. It provides a break from serious discussion without ignoring the problem, and it also sets a tone in which both people can feel more relaxed. Your partner's playful message is saying "You're doing it again," but it also implies "I understand where you're coming from, and I can still accept you." Play also works because it introduces new perspectives in the same manner that a cartoon caricature highlights certain features that we were only dimly aware were present. When I interviewed Greta and Charley, they described the way play fit into their problem solving like this:

"Usually after we have a fight, we talk about it in a straightforward way. But the problem still feels a little scary or tender. It's at that point that play comes in. Instead of having another serious discussion, we'll play around it. We need to have first agreed about something, though, and defined the problem, in order for the joking to work.

"Things that are revealed as sensitive, vulnerable

points in the other person during a fight, which are difficult to face, can later be played with from different directions, such as teasing or exaggerating. It is the recurring play around that issue that makes it easier to receive. We never joke about a problem while one of us is really angry, but through play we see if it still hurts and bring it back slowly without its being a crisis. It helps us gradually integrate a solution into our relationship."

My experience is that playful approaches are usually more helpful after a problem has already been identified through serious discussion. You are more likely to avoid the trap of "playing therapists" with each other if there's some kind of mutual understanding of the nature of the problem and the ways play can be of help. Further, as Greta and Charley suggest, change takes place very gradually. If you're tapping your foot, or stamping it, in expectation of your partner changing rapidly, you won't get anywhere.

Another couple, who had had some experience with psychodrama, used the techniques they learned to handle partners acting like parents:

Melissa and Michal had battled for a number of years over Melissa's whining and Michal's tendency to lapse into silence whenever he was upset about something. They had argued with little progress about these traits, each acquired from their own parents, until they started addressing the problem through play.

When Michal became silent or Melissa started whining, the partner would put one hand on the other's shoulder and attempt to put into words the feelings that underlay this behavior—in Michal's case, feeling vulnerable, afraid, or angry; in Melissa's, feeling needy or resentful. For example, Mi-

chal would suggest that Melissa really meant "Your forgetting to go to the post office must mean you really don't love me." They would adopt thick Yiddish accents that were reminiscent of their grandparents, which made them laugh and which made it easier for them to acknowledge their falling into an old family habit.

It is essential, as in both of the couples illustrated here, for you to really have compassion for where your partner is coming from. Melissa and Michal taught me something else about why play can help couples deal with such sensitive issues. In their words,

"Satirizing our families is an undoing. Taking the things in our families that have been and still are painful and making fun of them with each other is a safe thing. It purges. The joking reminds us that we are together, and we have something better than we had in our original families."

Comically exaggerated playacting serves as a ritual celebration of your being *different* from parental models. It allows you to acknowledge your being caught up in unconscious forces from the past while also placing some distance between you and them. Your playful alliance with your partner can produce change in the same way that a child in play therapy gains a feeling of mastery by actively playing out a trauma that he had earlier passively experienced. It may also have dynamics in common with the comforting effect on children of fairy tales, in which wolves and witches (fantasy representations of "bad" psychological forces) are ultimately subdued.

Whenever I see my own or someone else's relationship limited by the unconscious hold of the past, I find it comforting to remind myself that these constraints, once fully understood, can become an asset. For instance, the victim of a controlling parent can gain a special sensitivity to how manipulation—instead of allowing autonomy—can stunt natural growth; whoever has experienced a loss, for example, can more deeply sense another's need for constancy.

> *Randy describes coming from a "stiff-upper-lip WASP family, in which certain things simply weren't discussed and emotions were swept under the carpet." Elissa describes her family as a "New York Jewish family in which everything was discussed, and I sometimes felt as if I didn't have enough privacy. When we started dating, I taught Randy that he didn't have to bottle everything up all the time, that he didn't have to go run five miles every time he felt upset about something. I used to playfully tell him, 'You don't have to be Jewish to kvetch about things.'"*
>
> *In turn Randy helped Elissa feel comfortable about just going off by herself from time to time, to read or take a walk or listen to music. He would affectionately call it her Robert Frost time, an allusion to a poem in which the poet talked about good fences making good neighbors. This helped Elissa to overcome her feeling guilty if she was at all secretive or didn't share everything with Randy.*

Elissa's and Randy's family backgrounds helped each of them appreciate more keenly the need for a proper balance between intimacy and distance, so that they both had alternatives to sharing everything or sharing nothing. Many people consciously or unconsciously choose partners whom they see as having a quality that they lack, in the hope that they will thereby be able to incorporate into themselves a missing piece. In contrast, people sometimes choose partners who have come from families with similar problems, such as having critical, unsupportive parents. Inevitably, they repeat these problems with their partner, but they at least have the feeling that their partner *understands*. You don't always have to have had the same painful experience to be able to empathize with your partner, but it can help.

Sometimes it will be difficult for you to identify with your partner's unresolved issues from the past. Much of your ability to help each other grow beyond each of your pasts, whether by "serious" or playful means, depends on your seeing in your partner some reflections of yourself.

Partners as Children

While growing up has its advantages—I like being able to stay up to watch the "Late Late Show" if I want—we also lose some things: for one, the comforting feeling that a bigger, older, and wiser person is there to take care of us. Responsibilities can be gratifying, but it's nice not to have to be responsible *all* the time. For me it was a lot easier to skip school than it is to skip work. We can't go back fully to being kids without forfeiting some adult goodies, but you and your partner can provide excursions back to childhood for each other.

> *"Sometimes when both of us are feeling really tired and we don't feel we can face things, we become a little childlike. For instance, it might be a cold Monday morning and the alarm will have gone off, and neither of us wants to be the first one to get up. The floor's cold, the dog needs a walk, the dishes are sitting in the sink from the evening before. Instead of getting into a struggle over who'll be the responsible one, one of us will pull the covers over our heads and wail, "We need a parent! Where's our parent?" Eventually, of course, we get going, but it's kind of soothing to sit for a moment and recognize*

that we don't want to be adults; we want to be taken care of.

"The same kind of thing happens at other times when one or both of us are feeling all pooped out. Such as when we both get back from work at seven-thirty and find that there's no food for dinner. Sometimes, one of us will volunteer to be the parent that time, if they can summon up the energy. It's kind of understood that at another time, they won't have to be the responsible one."

Particularly at times of great stress or during an illness, you're likely to feel an urge to be more of a child and let someone else make the decisions, make dinner, or just tuck you into bed. These needs are often more difficult for men to acknowledge.

"My parents both worked," says Andrew, "and I always had the feeling that my being sick was a great imposition to them. Unless I was at death's door or had spots all over my body, it was off to school and not much sympathy.

"As an adult, I have rarely missed work. But after I almost caught pnemonia because I didn't stay in bed with the flu, Sally put her foot down. I had always treated her with kid gloves whenever she had the slightest cold. Now she insisted that I have the same treatment—she made me soup and brought me a special treat every day, got flowers, the works. Although I protested a lot, I rather enjoyed it, especially when I realized that she enjoyed taking care of me."

Here's another, similar example:

Bob and Alice just moved into a new house. Although neither is particularly handy, there has been a lot of fixing up to do. Alice well remembers the first time Bob accidentally caught his hand in the pathway of a hammer:

"I heard Bob howl and I immediately went downstairs. He was standing sucking on his left index finger, which he had just whacked with a hammer. I gave him a big hug, which quickly gave rise to his whining, baby talk, and demanding to be taken care of. I was quite taken aback but I pampered him nonetheless. It didn't last more than the ten or fifteen minutes it took for the pain to subside."

For his part, Bob says, "I find it very comforting to be able to be childish from time to time with Alice. I don't do it with anyone else and I think it's a measure of our mutual trust."

It is important that each of you allow the other the leeway for such temporary flights from adulthood. Just as we need to restore our psyches through dreams, so do we need to drift back playfully into childhood. It is restorative. When your partner remains the adult while you are the child, you can experience a wonderful sense of giving up control.

Baby talk is one way that couples may signal to each other that they have a need to be cared for.

Art and Carol ritualized their parenting. When one of them had a particularly difficult decision to make or needed some extra support, they would say, in a somewhat childlike voice, "I need some attention." This was a signal to the other partner that, in effect, meant, "You've got to be strong for me on this issue." Frequently, the other one would respond by saying, "There, there, now," and would put their arms around the other, motion for them to sit down next to them, or some other reassuring, parental gesture. This ritual signaled a basic understanding of which one of them needed to assume the more dependent, nurture-needing role.

The caretaking and trust involved in such experiences may help lay the groundwork for other restorative and letting-go experiences, such as in sexual relations. The next couple had a slightly different ritual for giving the wife a good parent:

> *One couple used the expression "come for a visit" to refer to the wife's sitting on her husband's lap and getting some affection. There was a slight "little girl—big daddy" connotation to the words. Thus, when the wife was upset, her husband would often ask, "Would you like to come for a visit?" There was a special feeling associated with the phrase and the caretaking, probably because neither of them had had a father who had comforted them like this when they needed it as children.*

Such parenting rituals may evolve out of a particularly memorable experience together, as in the next couple:

> *"One time, before we were married, we went swimming in a secluded mining pit that had filled with water. I had rather long hair then and had put it up in pigtails. We had gotten out of the water and we were lying on a blanket nude, talking and waving at a small plane that flew overhead a couple of times. I said something about feeling like a little kid with my pigtails. Chet laughed and said that I did look pretty young and it made for a great fantasy. I played along, acting like an innocent little girl. It was one of those magical days together.*
>
> *"A few months later a thunderstorm frightened me. Something just came over me and I ran to Chet's lap and he comforted me as if I were a little girl.*

Every so often now we play at me being a little girl. I suppose it makes me feel protected and cared for."

The first time that a couple slips into childlike behavior, each partner is looking for the other's response, whether it be accepting or judgmental. If you aren't comfortable with letting your *own* childlike self be expressed, it's likely that you will be taken aback by your partner's baby talk or unabashed needful appeal. See if you can take an honest look at why you may feel threatened or why you may believe childlike behavior is incompatible with being an adult. My sense is that to be *able* to be adult is an asset, but to *have* to is a liability.

Play can provide an opportunity for men as well as women to express their more nurture-needing sides:

David is a sales representative for a medical-book company and has to go on a lot of business trips across the country, often being away from Danielle for several days at a time. The separations are hard for both of them. One way they've developed to ease them is a ritual in which Danielle will pack David's suitcase.

"At first," said Danielle, "it seemed a matter of convenience—David was in a hurry and gave me some instructions over the phone as to what he wanted me to throw in a suitcase so he could dash right over to the airport to catch a plane. Then it became a favor I would do for him. When I didn't offer, he began to play helpless, pointing out how he didn't really know how to fold his shirts so they wouldn't wrinkle or pack things efficiently so he wouldn't have to take the big suitcase. I knew that wasn't really the issue and he wasn't just taking advantage of my good nature. He needed me to take care of him in this way. Once I realized that, I got

into it. I always try to add a personal touch, like a small thing I've baked or a card. Sometimes I secretly tuck in Herman, the stuffed frog we keep in our bedroom. It's one of our 'in' jokes, and it's also a way that he takes part of our relationship with him."

Repairing the Past

One of the truths we can't escape is that few things in life are all or nothing, all good or all bad. No parent can be perfect; all we can hope for is that they were good enough so we can eventually fend for ourselves or, as in the song, get by with a little help from our friends. To realize intellectually the limitations of what your parents can do for you is easy; to really feel it takes much more. It means giving up some long-cherished hopes and fantasies and mourning what wasn't there or can no longer be there for you. It also means not completely turning your back, so that you can acknowledge what, realistically, a parent still may be able to give you. For example, one woman related to me how she had always hoped that if she became a lawyer, like her mother, the affection her mother had always withheld from her would finally be showered on her. "She was really pleased," she said, "and I was happy to be able to please both her and me at the same time. It settled things between us. But I also realized that she would never really understand what becoming a lawyer meant to *me*. We're just very different people at heart, and nothing will ever make us good friends."

You may think you have given up your fantasy of having the perfect parent only to find that you have transferred your expectations to your partner. It's natural to transfer unrequited needs to your lover. Play can help you to acknowledge this process and gain a measure of restitution for what you're missing, without perpetuating a false sense that you can have it all.

"Carl and I both make a good income, but I'm not interested in having a lot of expensive things. We recently bought a very nice house, and we take good vacations. Coming from fairly modest backgrounds, we both look for bargains and don't spend money lavishly. But gifts from Carl are very important to me. I think it partly comes from the fact that my father wasn't really there for me when I was growing up—emotionally, he was always distant, and then my parents got divorced when I was ten.

"There's a lovely thing that Carl does when he knows I'm feeling really down. In a very sweet, soothing voice he'll say, 'I'll buy you anything you want.' Immediately, I'll perk up. 'Anything?' I'll ask. 'Anything you want,' he'll say.

"It makes me feel good all over, like all's right with the world and between us. You see, I know he really means it. And he knows that I won't really ask him to buy me a fur coat or a car or anything at all. I just need to know he would buy me anything if I asked him."

Just as a tangible gift is, most importantly, a symbol of caretaking, so is play. The thought may not be all that counts, but when play is based on real concern, the thought may be enough.

"My parents were very strict when I was growing up. I knew they loved me, but they didn't show it as much as I would have liked. In some ways their being strict was their way of showing concern, although I didn't appreciate it that way at the time. I thought they were just being rigid. They've mellowed somewhat, and so have I.

"There's a way that Sheila and I pretend that I think relates to my parents. Usually it will be after an argument, when I've been critical of her. Sheila will *start to act much younger, as if she were a naughty girl, asking for forgiveness. In turn, I will feel like her parent and act like a stern but forgiving papa. She'll sit on my lap, and I'll stroke her hair while we hold hands."*

It may be, as John Barth has said, that "Marriage is our last best chance to grow up." If so, it is not because you and your partner have learned to put aside childish things, but because you can help each other acknowledge and put into perspective the sadnesses and satisfactions of each of your pasts. In so doing, you free each other of the obligation to make up for the past. John Updike's description of one couple suggests how giving up blaming your partner for not making everything better paradoxically allows you the freedom to be children together:

He marvelled at how light Joan had become. . . . He no longer blamed her: that was the reason for the lightness. All those years, he had blamed her for everything—for the traffic jam in Central Square, for the blasts of noise on the mail boat, for the difference in the levels of their beds. No longer: he had set her adrift from omnipotence. He had set her free, free from fault. She was to him as Gretel to Hansel, a kindred creature moving beside him down a path while birds behind them ate the bread crumbs.

Dealing with Parents

So far I've been addressing the ways in which parents continue a ghostlike existence in your intimate relationships. Exorcism is a complicated business, in part because parents often stick around in your lives as real people, whether next door or at the other end of a telephone. Most of us don't really want to be rid of them—there are loving parts of them and us that are worth preserving, and debts that can be repaid only by the same kind of care and tenderness they gave to us. The trick is how to weed out the troublesome elements—so that they don't stunt our healthy growth. Further, like surgeons, we need a delicate hand to excise the offending parts without traumatizing the relationship.

You and your partner can help each other become more aware of how you relate to your parents. Some of this learning can best take place when your parents aren't around but when some contact with them is about to take place or has recently occurred. At such times, we tend to be in touch with our feelings about them but have sufficient distance so that we can get some perspective. The playful techniques next described are not intended as substitutes for serious discussion with your partner or your parents. Rather, they may facilitate becoming aware and also trying out different ways of relating to your parents. Think of yourself as an actor who can learn his lines only by acting: before you actually go on stage with your parents, you have to have some rehearsals.

Become More Aware

One way to learn about your relationships with your parents is through photographs. You and your partner can gather old and recent family pictures and look them over together. You may be surprised either to learn how much the pictures portray, or by what your partner is able to see that you may have ignored. Does it seem that the same people always stand closer to certain family members? How intimate do people really appear? How do the people in the pictures seem to be feeling? You may also see changes over a period of time. What might account for this? For example, when one couple looked at some old pictures of the wife's family, they were both struck by a picture of her mother, surrounded by four children, all below the age of six. It was immediately clear how difficult a time her mother must have had in the early years of her marriage.

The next couple illustrates a playful way of using photographs:

Jack and Julie enjoyed traveling together, whether for a fall weekend to see the foliage or an exotic trek to Morocco. One of their rituals was to take a lot of photographs; they would spend many happy moments afterward with their pictures, remembering their past trips and planning the next one. Both of their respective parents lived in neighboring states, and they would visit each of them three or four times a year. However, they rarely took pictures on these trips, usually leaving their cameras at home. One time, as they were anticipating what promised to be a dreary Thanksgiving get-together, they decided it might be more fun if they took along their cameras. Suddenly it felt a little bit more like a vacation than an obligation. During the trip to Jack's family's house they joked about how they were going to take their usual quota of "sightseeing" pictures. When their photographs came back in the mail, they were both surprised at how they were seeing Jack's family from new perspectives. Since then they have continued to take a lot of pictures when they visit their families and frequently refer to it as "going sightseeing."

You may find that the taking of pictures while visiting family enables you to gain some useful distance. On the other hand, if your position in the family is already too distant, it may be best to let your partner be the photographer.

Another technique that can help you learn about your family is fantasy. You and your partner should first lie down in a comfortable position and then silently imagine a series of scenes involving your own parents; first, imagine your parents together before you were born, then a scene when you were a baby, a few years later, and so on. Rather than just trying to remember specific incidents, let your imagination create scenes that might have been. You can also try fantasizing about your partner's family. After allowing perhaps a half hour for silent fantasy, you can then share your fantasies with your partner.

Drawings can be a creative way to explore each other's family relationships. For example, each of you can take a large piece of newsprint and, using either charcoal, crayons, Magic Markers, or watercolor, sketch a picture of each of your families doing something together. You can also draw pictures of the house you grew up in. After you're finished drawing, try to put into words what each of your pictures seems to represent, and see what you can learn from what your partner sees in your pictures.

A variation on family drawings is family sculpture, in which clay is used instead of pens and paper. You can also use your partner instead of clay—that is, your partner pretends to be a malleable piece of clay that assumes whatever silent posture you place him in. He or she can be placed in a series of such poses, each representing a member of your family. This is a technique used by family therapists that works best when you have several different people, each of whom can hold the positions that you have assigned to them. However, you may find that it is still valuable to try alone with your partner.

Letter writing may be a more comfortable medium for some couples. The idea is for each of you to write pretend letters to your own parents or another member of your family in which you say only the things you really feel. After you've each written a letter, instead of sending them to your parents, you share them with your partner. Some people find this a helpful vehicle to clarify their feelings about their parents and to let their partners know more about themselves. Eventually, either of you might decide to share some or all of the contents of your letter with the relative to whom it is addressed. But you could also choose not to do so. The first step is to become more aware of your feelings.

In addition to using playful techniques to look inward at your, and your partner's, perceptions of your families, you can also learn a great deal by becoming your family's historian. Let your parents and other relatives know that you're interested in learning more about the family history and would like to interview them. You can compile an oral history by visiting each relative in turn and tape-recording each person's recollections. Another approach is to write letters and ask them to send you their recollections on paper. It's important to make clear that you're interested in learning about the family for your own sake and because you think that they have a valuable perspective to offer. You're not conducting a criminal investigation to find out the "real truth," for you recognize that truth is made up of varying perceptions of different people. In addition to identifying some family patterns of which you were unaware, becoming the family historian may help facilitate your talking with your family about issues that might otherwise never be addressed.

In the System but Not of It

I have always been fascinated by time machines, the kind that H. G. Wells wrote about, which by your setting a few dials, could whisk you millennia back or forward. Recently, I came to the realization that I had been looking in vain toward science for such a device, when all I had to do was go home. Actually, it's a time machine that goes only in reverse, but what it lacks in versatility it makes up for in authenticity. I may go home thinking I'm an adult, feeling like an adult, and possessed by adult worries, but before long I find that I'm acting and feeling like I'm twenty, fifteen, ten, or even younger. If you were to visit my home, it wouldn't work that way for you, but unless you're more of a fully realized human being than most people, you have a time machine at your own home, too. Visiting your parents puts you at the mercy of powerful psychological forces that are curiously difficult to control.

Wayne is a recent business-school graduate who has a steady girl friend and a prestigious job with a Boston accounting firm. But when he visits his parents in Chicago, he enters a realm of time and space, and of sight and sound that we call . . . home.

The visit begins with Wayne's father wondering whether Wayne has lost some weight—he asks if he's been "eating right." Soon after this come concerned inquiries about his clothes. "For such a big shot, you don't dress right," says his mother. Wayne explains that he doesn't have time to do a lot of shopping, and his mother offers to take him to buy clothes. Next comes Wayne's apartment. "You haven't got shades yet!" his mother cries, and she insists on buying him some on the spot. "And furniture?" she asks.

As Wayne explains, "During my first couple of days home, I'm constantly trying to fend my mother off, constantly trying to convince her that I really don't need her help. Sometimes I get angry, but she has a knack for making me feel guilty for refusing her. It reminds me of that old Anacin commercial where the daughter with the headache snaps, 'Mother, I'd rather do it myself!' and then a few minutes after popping some pills acts as if she didn't know what came over her. Eventually, I give in. By the time I get on the plane back to Boston I'm asking myself how I manage to get dressed on my own."

In part the pull of the past is due to parents not wanting their children to grow up. As long as you're dependent on them, they may still feel young, and capable, as well as justified in influencing you. To be able to let go of children requires that they have separated psychologically from their own parents, which they may never have been able to do. Whether you become corporation president, a psychoanalyst, or a Supreme Court justice, your parents may still wonder why you didn't bring home your laundry. Zen monks undergo years of severe training, so that when they return to the outside world they are able to resist all temptations of the mind and flesh. But even they never return as priests to their home town. They're tough, but not *that* tough.

All fault can't be laid on our parents, however. Invariably, the healthy part of them wants us to grow up. The problem is that sometimes we're not so sure *we* want to leave home. Maybe being an adult isn't so appealing after all, and even though being a child may not have been great, we'd like to have another go at what we missed. It's not that these longings get stirred up just with our own parents—people often marry with the fantasy that their in-laws will be the perfect parents they have sought. Whether with your own parents or with your in-laws, you need to try to do the same thing as in binds with your partner: to recognize your own part in the dance.

> For many years Wayne, the business-school graduate with the parents in Chicago, thought that he was the innocent victim of a meddling mother. But when he went over his visits retrospectively, in a slow-motion mental replay, he noticed some things that he was doing to perpetuate his role as a helpless little boy.
>
> "For one thing," Wayne explains, "when I visited home I didn't bother to put my best foot forward. I treated it as a time to let my guard down and relax, when I should have been treating it as a job interview. I knew my parents were looking me over with a fine-tooth comb to see if I was grown up, and I gave

them plenty of opportunity to question my 'application.'

"I thought I was trying to refuse their help, but at times I actually invited it. If I felt depressed about something at work or with my girl friend, I would confide in them. Even though I didn't really want their advice, I guess I knew they felt good if I told them about my worries. It's been very difficult for me to keep my own counsel about some things because it's meant breaking away from them in ways that are hard for me, as well as for my parents."

When you go home, the challenge is to enter the family system but not become part of it. You need to keep enough psychological distance so that you are able to observe instead of always react. Your automatic reactions usually derive from the past and once set in motion become a chain reaction linked to the automatic responses of your parents. You don't have to be as imperturbable as Gandhi, but it's only when you can meditate a bit on what's going on around you that changes become possible. It may help to consider yourself as an understudy for your own part, having to study your role very carefully, because you really don't know it that well. The couple that used photography as a way of "sightseeing" when at home is an example of another playful attitude that can help you be in the system but not of it. Practicing some of the awareness exercises before visiting home may also help you bring a more playful set to situations that ordinarily might make you too tense to respond flexibly. Even if you are able to see only some of the patterns in which you and your family are caught, and begin to make only some connections about the way that you get stuck with your partner, you will have learned a great deal.

You can then approach making changes in your family as putting on a play within a play. There are certainly risks in trying to induce change in your relationships with parents, no matter how playful you are. As Tom Mosson warns, *"Hamlet* is the tragedy of tackling a family problem too soon after college." Psychotherapists are of two minds about the importance of developing a new kind of relationship with your parents, some feeling that it is the only way meaningful change can occur, and others emphasizing that it is the change within *you* that really matters. My sense is that if you can become more of an adult with your parents, so much the better. It's not the only way to grow, but it's worth a try.

Reparenting Your Parents

Many of the playful strategies for problem solving illustrated in Chapter 4, such as relabeling, changing the medium, changing the context, exaggerating annoying behavior, and auditioning for a new part, can also be applied to your relationships with your parents. As with your partner, play is liable to lead to change and to preserving a good feeling within a relationship only if your attempt to induce change comes from a willingness to also change yourself. You need to approach your parents' foibles with compassionate understanding of why they are the way they are; or, at the least, you should be willing to learn. Your parent has a childish side, too, that you need to understand and nurture. You may find it helpful, when your parent is being most difficult, to create a picture of them in your mind as a child—a fantasy caricature—and then to picture yourself as that child and how *you* would want to be cared for. In the stories that follow, couples devise a variety of playful approaches to dealing with parents who belittle, frustrate, and attempt to control them. In general, the goal is not to respond in kind, but to establish an adult relationship between equals.

> *Tom's father has a way of always giving his children advice about the "right" way to do things. For*

example, he'll tell Tom three times in one conversation, "Don't forget to lock up when you go out." When Tom's wife, Cary, once opened a bottle of soda and a little spilled on the table, he commented, "I always open up bottles over the sink." Tom would often get furious when his father made these comments because he felt belittled. Most of the time they were quite subtle. To confront his father usually brought self-righteous assertions that he was only trying to be helpful. Cary pointed out to Tom that his father was probably threatened by his successful son and dealt with his insecurities by asserting dominance in these small, but annoying, ways. Intellectually, Tom could see Cary's point, but he still couldn't feel that his father could be threatened by him in any way.

One summer Tom and Cary had been staying alone for a week at his parents' cottage in Maine when his parents showed up. Tom's father asked if he had gone swimming yet. Tom told him he hadn't, because the water was ice cold. "I would've been in!" his father shot back. Cary then said to him, with a knowing look at Tom, "But you're a real man. Tom is just a little boy." Tom's father seemed perplexed for a moment and then said, "Well, I'm glad to hear that."

Cary's remark and Tom's father's curious response enabled Tom to feel for the first time that his father really did need to see himself as more of a man than his son. Instead of feeling threatened, he could now experience his father's subtle putdowns as coming from a position of weakness. It's hard to say exactly why Cary's comment worked, but it had something to do with the fact that absurd exaggeration can sometimes catch another person off guard. My hunch is that Tom's father realized in some vague way what he was doing. He could acknowledge the truth of Cary's comment because he felt reassured.

One of the morals learned here is that if you can take care of your parents' underlying needs, they may give up the obnoxious behavior that is driven by that need. Parents' understanding of your tactics may not always be necessary. Such play provides a way of dealing with issues in indirect ways that can relieve your frustration without provoking retaliation or angry denial. Further, while it may not fully enlighten a parent, it may sufficiently confuse and disarm him so that the problematic behavior is interrupted.

This story also points out how helpful partners can be to each other. Cary was able to make the playful remark because she was close enough to Tom and his father to understand their relationship fully, but she had enough distance to be able to play. The next couple similarly illustrates how partners can help each other with their respective families:

> "You can never be a heroine in your own family," says Karin. "At least, not in my family. Even though I've earned a Ph.D. and make a great salary, my parents still think of me as their helpless daughter. They ask my brothers about their careers, but they never ask me. Instead, my dad will ask me whether I need any money, and if my husband, Jack, and I are borrowing my parents' car, he'll hand the keys to Jack. Jack feels that his own parents don't recognize his accomplishments, either. His father is a doctor who tends to monopolize dinner conversations with medical talk that Jack, who's an architect, knows nothing about.
>
> "A helpful way we've come to deal with our families is for whoever is the 'visiting' spouse to be a spokesperson for the other person. Thus, if we're at my parents' house, Jack might say, 'It's amazing how

*much positive response Karin has had to her journal
article this month,' or 'You wouldn't believe how
much money your daughter is making.' He'll say it
with disbelief, so as to reach them on their level and
also say things that will make them want to know
more. I'll do the same when we're at his house. We
call it doing PR for each other."*

Part of what's involved in changing your relationship
with your parents is recognizing that they're not bad people, they're just hung up. The next vignette illustrates how
one woman put this awareness to good use:

*Beth's mother didn't mean to withhold from her
daughter, but her own self-denial was so ingrained
that her charitable spirit stopped at home. She was
active in all manner of public service organizations,
but it made her very uncomfortable to be generous
with herself. In large measure this asceticism
stemmed from having had parents who were emotionally unavailable. She had come to make a virtue
out of the necessity of self-denial. Yet, like all wishes
that are long frustrated, her longing to indulge and
to be indulged lay coiled like springs under the tension of guilt. How can you feel okay about asking for
more if your parents make you feel bad about your
needs?*

*Beth was caught in a similar dilemma with her
mother. Whenever she would let slip that she had
bought something special for herself or wanted something "frivolous," she could usually count on her
mother responding with uncomfortable silence instead of the sympathetic joy she wanted. "Do you
really need that?" was her mother's characteristic
phrase. It made her avoid telling her mother about
some happy things in her life, because her mother's*

reserve made her feel guilty. Yet she couldn't give up wanting her mother to change.

"The problem was that my mother and I are so much alike and I wanted her to be different from me. Much of what I was looking to her for I realized in therapy I couldn't get. To some extent my therapist provided what my mother lacked, and my friends helped, too. But I also found a way to get a piece of what I wanted from her. It turned out that if I played up all the reasons why I shouldn't indulge myself—it's too expensive, I don't deserve it, I should wait—she would often encourage me to go ahead. It was like a seesaw. The more heavily I came down on the side of self-denial, the more she would insist on giving. It became a kind of joke between us, because as I exaggerated the reasons why I should deny myself, my mother began to see herself a little more clearly."

Giving

Creative gifts are another way to facilitate change, as in the next example:

Living through the great Depression has left some people with an eternal sense of the fragility of economic security and the necessity of conserving pennies no matter how advantaged they may later have become. Joseph's father, for instance, would worry about every electric light left burning and would buy only chainstore brand merchandise. Joseph understood, therefore, when his father would fret about the length of his long-distance phone calls home, but it irritated him when, three minutes into speaking with his mother, his father would invariably come on the line and say, "Everything fine? Good, I'll get all the news from your mother."

When Joseph was in college, he felt he could argue only weakly. After all, his father was paying the bills. But even after he had become a successful stockbroker, he could hear the anxiety in his father's voice if they talked for very long on the phone. Finally, he hit upon the idea of giving his father a gift of some AT&T stock for his birthday. He presented it as a good investment, but made a big show over the fact that now that his father was a shareholder in the company, he would have to protect his interests by using their services.

"Since then," Joseph relates, "his fretting about wasting money on telephone bills has diminished. In part, my strategy worked because he was faced with a contradiction. How could he be against helping out his own company? But I think it was more symbolic than anything else. After all, it was only five shares of stock. It made my father feel good to own AT&T, and it was a gentle reminder to him that his son is a stockbroker, whom, God forbid, maybe he should listen to for once."

It's not that play can make your parents change, but that by your adopting a more playful attitude, new options can sometimes emerge. The best antidote to rigid patterns of behavior is anything that induces flexibility. To borrow a metaphor from an old children's game, it is the paper that covers the rock.

As with your partner, the most productive place to start to bring about change is in yourself, not in your parents. Many people prefer to complain about their parents and consciously or unconsciously blame them for the unhappiness in their own intimate relationships. They actually don't want their parents to change, for then they would have to look more closely at themselves. As I pass through my thirties, I have increasingly come to think that you don't change your relationships with your parents by trying to change them or by trying to get them to accept you, but by trying to *give* to them. Most simply, it makes me happy to make my parents happy. Sometimes the price is too high. but sometimes it really doesn't take much at all. I'm not talking about giving out of guilt, but I do think part of the satisfaction comes from the sense that you are giving something back to people who have given you a lot. It helps turn your relationship from one of child-parent to a more symmetrical arrangement, and, as parents get older, the roles at times become reversed. I'm not suggesting that there should be a complete exchange of roles: your parents cannot become your children without losing their dignity. While failing health and being out of step with the changing culture can make them need you, they deserve respect for their set ways that, while not making sense for you, are meaningful within their own historical contexts. Your parents may well resist being given to; if so, a bit of playfulness may help:

Audrey has found taking care of her aging parent a difficult task.

"My mother is very passive-aggressive. She puts a nice face on being very manipulative. I always resented this, and I suppose I saw less of her as an adult because of this. Then, when my mother went into a nursing home, the issue really came to a head. When I'd go to see her she'd go on and on about 'Oh, you're so good. You're so busy with your job. I know it's difficult for you to find the time to see me.'

"I'd long ago given up on trying to explain to her what passive-aggressive behavior was or to get her to cut down on it. The nursing home routine really became too much, and I was afraid I would stop going, which I didn't want to do. Then I started to remember some of the good times as a child—one of my birthdays when she arranged a special picnic, an Easter egg hunt, her reading to me before I went to

sleep. I resolved to make things more fun for myself, and, hopefully, for her, by giving to her in some of the same ways. One time I brought a picnic basket of goodies I had made with some of her old recipes. Another time I read to her until she nodded off to sleep, and then I wept.

"Then one day when she was being impossible I said, 'I'm just following your good example.' I said it in a very sweet, daughterly way. I don't know why, but it calmed her down and I find I'm visiting her more now."

Siblings

You have another valuable resource to help you put your past in perspective—your brothers and sisters.

The three Allen children never got along as well as they would have liked. In retrospect they feel that their parents unwittingly played them off against one another. This probably occurred as a result of their attempt to avoid facing their own marital troubles.

When they were in college, the two oldest children, Kathy and Alice, got together one spring break on Kathy's campus. Initially, their visit was strained, much as their relationship at home was. Gradually, they began to talk about things, starting with some of the most humorous moments. One of their grandmothers had been a crotchety old woman who thought children were wayward adults. Whenever any of the Allen kids acted up in the least bit, she would get red in the face and say, "This is the limit!" At times she would curse in German, and Kathy and Alice laughed till their sides hurt as they imitated her.

As they discovered some common ground, they were able to talk about some of the problems in the

family. To encapsulate their negative feelings toward
their parents and to gain some distance they coined
the nickname "The Wardens" for them. This cap-
tured the feeling of their having escaped from being
trapped in negative relationships at home. Thereaf-
ter, when they corresponded or saw each other, they
would refer to "The Wardens," which would make
them laugh and also remind them of the bonds they
felt with each other.

Changing the context—in this instance, two sisters
spending some time together away from home and from
their parents—can help set the stage for a different kind of
relationship. The past can be recapitulated in new ways,
and you may find that you can be more playful than the
more stressful environment of your parents' home usually
allows. I know of two brothers who always dreaded going
to their parents' home on Thanksgiving. One year they
agreed to invite their parents to the older brother's house in
a nearby city, where they prepared the entire Thanksgiving
dinner. The experience was much less freighted with past
tensions, and they've gotten their parents to rotate holding
the dinner at their three places.

My experience with my sister has been like viewing old
films together. I'm often pleased to get confirmation of
how I remember things, but I'm also surprised at how our
vantage points on the same events can be so different, as if
we were filming with different cameras. Your partner can
perform a similar role when you get together with your
family, helping confirm and extend your perceptions of
how you relate.

Humor: The Comforting Parent

My emphasis on the problematic parts of people's relationship with their parents neglects the fact that most of us
are lucky to have had parents who at least were "good

enough." I remember as a child how my mother's cheek felt so wonderfully cool when she kissed me good-night after coming home late in the winter, and in the morning I can recall the muffled, soothing sounds of my family outside my room as I was just waking up—I called them "morning voices." Good parental relationships facilitate having good love relationships as an adult. All of us also have unfinished business with our parents: you might consider your parents' legacy as one in which you're forever stuck as a victim of their deficiencies; another approach is to act as if you can forget, if not forgive, and start with a fresh slate. A more hopeful and realistic position is that all children have to struggle with learning how to grow in ways that their parents were not able to do. You can't do this through will power alone. Loyalties to the past can be modified only by new experiences in intimate relationships. Loving play is a vehicle for such new experiences.

Sigmund Freud, in 1927, wrote that the main intention of humor is to say, "'Look! here is the world, which seems so dangerous! It is nothing but a game for children—just worth making a jest about!'"[27] Such words of comfort, in Freud's view, come from our superego—the part of our psyche that originally derives from our parents. There are other theories of humor, but I find it pleasing to think of humor as a parent that consoles us and protects us from suffering. It is as if our parents, no matter how they may have failed us or left burdens of guilt or fears about closeness, have still managed to give us the essential thing we need to work it all out.

CHAPTER SEVEN

Play and Work

Tom contemplated the boy a bit, and said, "What do you call work?"

"Why, ain't that work?"

Tom resumed his whitewashing, and answered carelessly, "Well, maybe it is, and maybe it ain't. All I know is, it suits Tom Sawyer."

"Oh, come now, you don't mean to let on that you *like* it?"

The brush continued to move.

"Like it? Well, I don't see why I oughtn't to like it. Does a boy get a chance to whitewash a fence every day?"

That put the thing in a new light. Ben stopped nibbling his apple. Tom swept his brush daintily back and forth—stepped back to note the effect—added a touch here and there—criticized the effect again—Ben watching every move and getting more and more interested, more and more absorbed. Presently he said, "Say, Tom, let *me* whitewash a little."

What I find most instructive in Mark Twain's story is not how to unload unpleasant tasks on other people, but that the difference between work and play depends on who's holding the paintbrush. It doesn't really much matter if you're doing the dishes, planning a vacation, or building a new deck—your lot can feel like play or drudgery. Clearly, then, the issue is one of attitude. Part of the problem is that our categories of work and play are as sharply divided psy-

chologically as Fundamentalist notions of right and wrong.
But the arbitrary nature of this dichotomy is easy to ex-
pose. Why is it that working together with someone can
make a dull chore into play? If your partner enjoys taking
out the garbage, does that "count" the same on your balance sheet as your doing the laundry—a task you reso-
lutely abominate? In short, how do you know if you're
working or playing? I don't propose to solve a problem that
has vexed philosophers since the Stone Age. Part of my job
as a therapist is to ask people questions for which they
don't know the answers. That's not just to keep my work
playful, although it's part of the motivation, but it makes
discovery possible. My recommendation, then, is that you
and your partner keep this question of what is work and
what play open, and see what you might learn.

Aristotle suggests that "nature requires us not just to
work well, but to idle well." My impression is that it's
more in the idleness area that couples have trouble. After
the initial surge of playfulness has past, sweeping away
schedules and responsibilities, the honeymoon is over and
we're back on the assembly line on Monday morning. Unfortunately, the assembly line mentality extends to our lives
at home so that we always seem to have time for one more
project but not enough to waste. Later we'll have time to
enjoy ourselves, we think, after the new addition is finished, after we buy the dishwasher, after the kids get older.
Only later never comes.

Work into Play

Ancient alchemists sought to turn base metals into gold,
hoping thereby to allow more time for play and less for
work. Part of the solution I'm advocating is to turn base
work into play. This transformation requires that you cultivate an attitude that values the quality of your relationship
over accomplishment of tasks. I know this is difficult when
it already feels as if there aren't enough hours in the day to

do what has to be done. But do you really want to continue holding your breath until the next vacation? One of the problems with continuing to postpone gratification for so long is that we forget *how* to have fun—our weekends and vacations become further opportunities for checking things off our lists rather than to "idle well." I know a lot of people who are always launching into great endeavors, only to find that what they most enjoy is doing nothing at all.

Let's see how a playful spirit can be brought into your activities that might ordinarily be unrequited drudgery.

> "Doing the laundry has to be absolutely the worst job around the house. It sure helps not to have to go to the laundromat, but it still is a drag."
>
> When Sherry and Dan used to have to go to the laundromat, they got into the habit of doing their laundry on Thursday nights, which they have stuck to, even though they now have a washer and dryer in their home.
>
> "A ritual which we made up to ease the tedium of laundry night, when we were still going to the laundromat, was to observe other people in the laundromat very closely. There were quite a few strange birds there, and we got into making up stories about them. Sometimes, we would base the fantasy on the kind of clothes they had. One of our favorites was a woman whom we called the Purple People Eater, after the song of the same name. She was an obese woman who had a lot of purple clothing. One time we found a purple slip mixed up in our clothes and went into mock hysteria about the Purple People Eater having left her calling card. It kind of epitomized our distaste at having this peculiarly intimate contact with so many anonymous people.
>
> "Now that we have our own washer, when it's time to fold the laundry we sit together and pretend the laundry is not ours but someone else's. We still make

up stories about the kind of people who would have
such things. We've added sipping wine or having tea
and desserts to this ritual, but otherwise it remains
essentially the same. It's a night we have together
just doing relatively boring work and turning it into
somewhat of a fantasy. Some weeks you almost are
sorry to see the last shirt get folded, because it's like
the last page of a book and you don't want to let go
of this rich story you've woven."

It certainly helps if you have a well-developed capacity
to fantasize, but the most important requirement to turning
work into play is staying in the present moment. If you're
fighting the experience, wanting it to be over, you can't
make it playful. But if you can focus your attention fully
on whatever it is you have to do, playful opportunities may
emerge. The next couple illustrates how another tiresome
task became more fun:

After several months of house hunting, the initial
excitement had worn off. The houses that were in
Ron and Marie's price range were either unimagina-
tive Capes that were too small or Victorians that had
been brutalized by the crazed renovations of previous
owners, who had been in the aluminum-siding busi-
ness or who loved Astroturf. Both of them being
working people, their weekend time was precious.
Thus, they hit upon a playful way of letting each
other know as quickly as possible after entering a
house that they weren't interested in getting the
grand tour of the basement and third floor: one of
them would bump into the other.

"Both of us are very polite people," explained
Ron, "and we don't like to alienate people. Frankly,
most real-estate brokers are creepy characters, but
we have to work with them. By 'bumping,' we can
secretely communicate the extent of our disinterest—

the more emphatic the bump, we know the quicker the bumper wants to get out of this place. One time we were looking at a place that was advertised as a 'charming Cotswold with interest.' It turned out to be completely pink inside and decorated in a style that was so jarring to your sensibilities that neither of us could have lived there for five minutes, let alone buy it. We inadvertently bumped each other at the same time, and Marie almost got knocked over. After we left we enjoyed a few laughs thinking of how the real-estate agent must have thought we were the most clumsy house buyers she'd ever seen. We also enjoy the conspiratorial feeling of being able to 'talk' critically about a house without brokers knowing what's going on."

In both of these examples, the play emerged out of the activity and helped change the couple's experience into a less labored and more intimate one. Even solitary chores can be made less burdensome through playful touches. Serving breakfast in bed to your partner is a traditional example. Making the bed may seem less tedious if, at the end, you leave a flower on the pillow, imagining your partner's response when he or she sees it there later on.

There will always be tedium and trivia in a couple's life together, but some of it, at least, can be made to serve the relationship rather than the relationship always being called upon to do the serving.

Sex Role Issues

One of the obstacles to domesticity always being bliss is the stereotyped sex roles that we have learned growing up. Even if intellectually we may repudiate the most male chauvinistic attitudes, we may still function on the basis of what has been most tried if not true. Equality of the sexes does not exist—in most couples even wives who work

have most of the responsibility for housework. Though old
sex roles are still strong, most couples are trying to change,
and the gap between what feels familiar and what seems
fair causes frequent discontent. One of the ways that play
can help is in recognizing and debunking some of the role
models that we are stuck with. The problem is not that
there are good and bad role models, but that when lived out
rigidly they all have their limitations.

Careers

*Beth was a schoolteacher for three years before
her first child was born. "I loved the work. I was a
special education teacher and worked with very
small classes of learning-disabled children. You
could really see the results of your work." When her
first child was born, Beth took a six-month leave of
absence, the maximum the school system allowed.
"When I went back to work the following fall I was
very torn. I had to put Jonathan into day care, which
I wasn't comfortable with, but at that time I wasn't
ready to give up the job. It wasn't until I'd been back
at the job a few months that I began to really start to
think about giving it up. I still liked the work, but I
realized I liked being with my own child even more.*

*"Then came the most difficult part," says Beth.
Apart from her husband, she found little support for
her wish to stay home and rear her children. Her
mother, for example, who had felt trapped by child
rearing, couldn't understand how she could give up
everything she thought she had never had. "You
should see people's faces at a cocktail party when
they ask, 'And what do you do?' and you tell them
that you stay home with your two kids. They look at
you like 'Where have you been, honey?'*

The one person Beth got a lot of support from was

*her husband, Robert. "Robert is a chemical engi-
neer. He makes a good salary but not a spectacular
one. He knew the sacrifices we would have to make if
I didn't work. The thing Robert most helped me with
was my own insecurity about being 'just a housewife.' When I first met Robert I told him all about my
mother whom I used to refer to as 'a domestic basket
case.' Robert sensed that this was what I was most
afraid of. One time we were on vacation on the Vine-
yard and he gave me a gift of a T-shirt with a picture
of a basket and the word 'basket case.' It was done
with such affectionate humor that I just melted and
was able to talk to him about all my fears about my
decision.*

*"I've never really regretted giving up my career,
and I now have two lovely children whom I adore
looking after. Every once in a while when the pressures of caring for children around the clock get to
me, either I'll put on that T-shirt or Robert will ask
me if I'm feeling like a basket case. It seems to
lighten my spirits and helps me vent whatever I'm
feeling."*

More chic role models can be just as limiting and may
also be dealt with through play:

*The boyfriend of a network executive felt increas-
ingly deprived of his girl friend's companionship
during a hectic six-month period in which her work
took complete precedence over her social life. She
herself was frustrated by demands from all sides. By
joking about her being the Cosmo Girl (capable of
fulfilling all her roles without working up an unfe-
minine sweat), both of them had a good laugh and
gained some perspective on the tensions between
them. They would think of other humorous images*

that highlighted the impossible expectations that either she or he placed on her. Thus, for example, doing the laundry was not enough—it had to be, after the French, "la lavage avec la cleavage."

Many women who take on a more competitive, powerful position in the working world are fearful of losing their femininity or, at least, of being perceived as such by men. While their way of coping with this concern may not always be as overt as in the following story, the use of a nickname that playfully captures the two sides of a dilemma may often help a partner to integrate them.

"The contrast between my work self and my home self was nowhere more evident than in my clothing," says Janet. "I work in computers, a field which has been relatively good for women because it is youthful, with a lot of growth and upward mobility. I think I was thrown into an executive role before I really knew what was happening. All of a sudden, within three years of entering the business world I was manager of a department with a dozen people.

"To cope I think I developed a very tough stance to make sure people took me seriously. I was like a drill sergeant in those early days and, especially in my clothes, I took on a managerial appearance, with slacks, ties, suits, and starched white shirts. By contrast, at home my dress became, if anything, more feminine, complete with frills, lace, and flouncy dresses."

Janet's husband, Gary, was the first to point out the contrast. He noticed that she was getting more feminine, even submissive, at home and felt that this might be to compensate for what was going on at work. He nicknamed Janet "the executive bride," to express the two sides of her—managerial and domestic—which he felt were becoming increasingly

*polarized. Janet was grateful for the playful insight.
"Over the next six months or so I gradually brought
these two sides closer together as I became more
comfortable as a woman with authority. Sometimes
Gary still uses the nickname when he feels I'm acting
'uppity' at home. I think he probably does have some
trouble with my being real assertive, but at least we
can talk about it, and his playful nickname has
helped."*

Sometimes career women have to contend with very delicate male egos in their partners. The next couple illustrates
a use of play that represents a compromise. I'm not entirely
comfortable with it, but it illustrates one solution that a
couple might adopt as a temporary expedient.

*Clark is a real-estate agent who comes from a
blue-collar-family background, in which the man is
supposed to be the primary, if not the sole, bread-
winner. During a slack time in his business, when
they were having trouble making ends meet, he re-
luctantly agreed to Jeannette's going to work at an
advertising firm. Initially hired as a secretary, she
rose rapidly to become a branch manager earning a
considerable salary.*

*"Clark is a very traditional man, and although he
said he was proud of me, I knew it sometimes bothered him that I was so successful. It wasn't something we could talk about directly, but I pretended
that my work was really rather insignificant. He had
a career, but I only had a job, and he, cruel man,
was making me go to work rather than it being something I wanted. It was important that he felt like the
one in charge.*

*"He's much more used to the idea of having a
successful working wife, and I don't have to pretend
as much as before."*

Housework

Ideally, partners should be flexible in the tasks for which they are willing to take responsibility, and the overall burden should be fairly divided. But while this may be the standard to try to approximate, in practice some accommodation must be made to individual preferences and limitations for change. Whatever the criterion of fairness that you agree on, there will always be points of contention. It is difficult to make housework fun; if you're feeling at odds with your partner about anything else in the relationship, it is easier not to take out the garbage or not make dinner than to talk about what's bothering you. Even when you have serious talks about who's supposed to do what and you're feeling good about each other, your deeply ingrained notions of what is man's work and woman's work may create problems. It's not easy to make a smooth transition from what you were exposed to in your parents' marriage while growing up, to current notions of gender identity—our feelings lag behind our intellectual positions. Even if both of you are completely flexible, the culture often conspires against us, and a gentle understanding of your partner's situation, coupled with a sense of humor, are essential.

Al and Elizabeth have reversed the traditional male-female roles: Al stays home and minds their three children, while Elizabeth works as a radiologist. It's a relationship both of them are happy with, but which finds few social supports.

"Most people assume I'm a weakling, a sissy, or passive for wanting to stay home," says Al. "In fact, I just love taking care of kids, especially my own."

"I think a lot of people assume I'm a castrating female, an aggressive bitch, to have conned a man into such a role reversal," says Elizabeth.

Both say that their social life has been limited by

their arrangement: "Our few friends are very liberal, flexible people, who make no big deal of our respective roles and just think that it's our business. We've learned to be suspicious of people who think that it's 'neat' but then don't know how to relate to us."

One of the biggest problems for Al has been finding companionship during the day: "I don't fit in at sewing circles," he says. He and Elizabeth have a mutual joke, "There are no sports circles," to express his dilemma.

"The joke, which gets repeated a lot, provides comic relief for the most frustrating thing for Al," says Elizabeth. "I don't know which of us said it first, but we seized on it. Al has a great interest in baseball scores and tennis matches—it really is too bad there aren't more men in his position for him to get together with."

I think it's important to maintain the perspective that both of you are up against powerful psychological and cultural forces when you try to achieve an equitable partnership. From this perspective, you are not so much adversaries as comrades in adversity. This is not to say that we're all incapable of acting blatantly or sneakily in our self-interest, but it is helpful to keep in mind that at least a piece of the problem is "bigger than both of us."

Ellen always felt her mother was enslaved by housework and preparing meals in particular. " 'A woman's work is never done' was her favorite expression," says Ellen. "It captured her chronic sense of never getting out from under the work. My father never set foot in the kitchen.

"I vowed that in my own relationships with men I would not get into such a pattern. John and I have been living together now for five years. We both

work, which gave him less of a leg to stand on, but I think men still expect women to do the greater share of the housework. Early in the relationship he would complain from time to time because the laundry wasn't done or the garbage hadn't been put out. We would argue about it, and he would do some more work for a while. Sometimes I just didn't feel up for an argument, and it was easier just to do it myself. This upset me, but I was determined to try to make a go of it with John, whom I really cared a lot about. I figured if I couldn't make it living with him I wasn't going to be able to live with anyone.

"So I came up with this slogan, 'The slaves are acting up,' as a response to his complaints. I said it with chagrin, like I had little control over it, like 'what can you do about them?' Sometimes we'll launch into a little parody of being slaves on a chain gang, or we'll be the two overseers commiserating about our lazy slaves.

"That slogan put distance between me and the work and allowed me to have more humor and less anger about John's complaints. It captured an important theme for me—that is, housework symbolically is enslavement and I wasn't going to be trapped by it. Finally, it said to John 'We're in this together.' That is, it's the 'slaves' who'd acted up and what were we, not just me, going to do about it. It was one of my best slogans. I wish I could think of more of them!"

Many women have the experience that their partners may be willing to do some house chores, but that they're doing so as a kind of favor; they're participating but not taking responsibility. I've noticed myself acting this way and recognize it as a more subtle version of male chauvinism. Such an individual will do what he is called upon to do but displays no initiative. One couple addressed this pattern as follows:

Making meals was always a loathsome chore, as far as Bob was concerned. Carol felt less strongly, but resented being left with the task because of Bob's relative disinterest. In most areas she did not consider him to be selfish, but she felt that his disinterest was a rationalization for avoiding work.

Bob and Carol discussed the situation and arrived at a creative approach to meal preparation, which Bob went along with, initially half-heartedly: the person who planned a given meal and made sure all the necessary ingredients were on hand was the chef, i.e., the boss for that meal. In return for having taken responsibility for the meal, this person got to delegate the work of preparing it and cleaning up afterward. Naturally, the other person—the worker —was given the least exotic jobs, like beating eggs, peeling onions, and, most important, cleaning up afterward.

Bob reports that initially he went along with this scheme to placate Carol: "I thought it was a fair deal, but that after a while the whole thing would blow over. But Carol persisted, and gradually I realized that I was going to be the dishwasher forever if I didn't get my act together." Bob's initial forays into being the chef were fairly unambitious meals—hamburgers or barbecued chicken—but he quickly graduated to more gourmet meals. "I would have to say that I now enjoy cooking and don't do it just to avoid the menial work. At this point Carol still does more of it, but I cook at least two nights a week. Once I got over the hang-up that cooking was boring or woman's work, I began to enjoy it for the creative enterprise that it can be. I'm not sure that would

have ever happened, though, without Carol's idea of
making me the worker if I refused to be the chef.

Even if you end up doing the work, you won't mind so
much if you feel your partner is appreciative. Part of what
makes "women's work" so oppressive to women is that it's
expected of them. Similarly, if men are only told by their
partners that unless they do their share they're male chauvinist pigs, they will feel like slaves and rebel whenever
they have the chance. I don't believe in keeping a rigid
accounting, but the next couple developed a playful way of
bestowing recognition:

> "I am a martyr. No one, as I see it, ever gives me
> enough credit for anything. Especially housework.
> Especially my husband. So imagine my surprise when
> one day as I sniffed and pouted around the kitchen
> ('Who—me upset? Why would I be upset?'), he turned
> to me and said expansively, 'You get twenty points for
> cleaning the oven.' A small miracle took place. I light-
> ened. I brightened. I smiled. 'Well,' I responded, 'you
> get fifteen for fixing the hole in the screen.' (I am not as
> nice as he is, and anyway, it doesn't pay to tip your
> hand too soon.)
>
> "Many years have passed since then, and we are
> still awarding each other points. Sometimes it is a
> sincere message of appreciation, as when I gave him
> 50 points for cleaning the charcoal grill of the gunky,
> grungy 115-day build up of grease at the end of the
> summer. Other times it is ironic—an end run around
> confrontation—as when he gave me two points for
> watering the tomatoes once during a seven-day heat
> wave.
>
> "Silly? Childish? I suppose. But it is also incredi-
> bly helpful, having saved us from more arguments,
> hurtful comments and subsequent depressions than*

anything I can think of, and as much a part of our life together as the way we furnish our house or entertain." [28]

One of the obstacles to an equitable division of chores is that women are apt to have had more experience with "women's work" and men are more skilled in traditionally male activities. To be equitable doesn't mean that you both have to do the same things, but rigid segregation of tasks can lead to resentment, as well as an inability to empathize with your partner's lot. One couple developed a playful way of introducing some flexibility into their roles:

"After a couple of years of living together," said Serena, "Mark and I had fallen into fairly typical roles. I did the bulk of the housework, and Mark did odd jobs around the house and mowed the lawn. That worked all right until I got a full-time job. Mark's a considerate guy, but he's used to having a woman cook and clean and iron for him. It never ceases to amaze me how grown-up men can be so helpless about these things.

"The idea I hit upon was for us to switch roles, but only for a day. One weekend day he was designated as the 'house husband' and had to do the ironing, shopping, sewing, and so on. In return, I took whatever 'man's work' had to be done. Part of the deal was that, if either of us needed help, we could ask for it. For instance, I gave him lessons in sewing on a button and making thin pancakes, and he helped me lift the trash barrels into our pickup.

"It's led to a little more flexibility in our roles, and although I still do much of the housework, I think Mark appreciates me more. Every so often, when he starts acting helpless, I threaten to declare another 'house husband' day and Mark hops to it."

We need to accommodate our partner's more traditional gender expectations, such as for a woman to iron shirts or a man to split wood, because these small acts often have symbolic meanings. If your wife bakes you an apple pie or sews on your button, you feel cared about in ways that resonate deeply in your childhood. You have to find the right balance so that you are not enslaved to either of your pasts, but also don't neglect their importance. One couple used play to try to find this balance:

> Jim considers himself to be an enlightened man who is in favor of equal rights for women, and he married a physician whom he knew would not have the time or inclination to do all the housework. However, at times he finds himself longing to be cared for by a housewife: "It came out in little things, like wishing Carla would fold my shirts and match and roll up my socks. I mentioned this to her, and she joked about both of us needing a housewife." Sometime after, they both decided to send their laundry out. When it came back, everything was taken care of just as Jim had wanted. He turned to Carla and said, in a gently mocking way, "I really appreciate your doing this for me." She joined the play, saying, "I do it because I know how important it is to you, and because I love you."

As in many of the illustrations of playful problem solving, so much depends on the way in which things are said. If Jim were feeling bitter about Carla's choice not to act like a housewife, or if he was trying to make her feel guilty, his comment would have been a manipulation rather than a playful acknowledgment of the irony in their situation. Carla's rejoinder works only to the extent that she truly feels sympathetic to Jim's need, at the same time that she feels comfortable about not giving up her time in order to satisfy him. Through play Jim gets part of what he's seeking; his gratification comes through being understood and accepted.

There are no sex-linked genes that make women inherently suited to housework or make men allergic to it, but while biology need not be destiny, gender identity is established early in our lives and thereafter is not infinitely malleable. Everyone has their limits, which should be respected, and fairness is best defined not by some objective standard of equality but through sympathetic understanding of each other's vulnerabilities and capacity for change.

The Play Space

One of the most basic ways intimate play serves a relationship is by safeguarding your personal world from outside interference. A couple needs to have a special sphere set apart from the usual norms and constraints, in which special intimacies can take place. As you move from courtship to an established relationship, it is natural to move from a sense of the whole world as a place for you to play, to a feeling of a more circumscribed sphere. Play space is more of a psychological than a physical construct, although it also requires private time and space. It is best described by the metaphor of a "home," as described in Hermann Hesse's *Demian,* when Frau Eva speaks of Sinclair's mystical affinity for her: "One never reaches home. . . . But where paths that have affinity for each other intersect, the whole world feels like home for a time."

The Spanish word *querencia* embodies the rich emotional tone of the home created through intimate play:

> *"Querencia"* . . . means affection for the place one calls home and the sense of well-being that that place gives one. . . . It means the sense of being nourished by a place in which you belong. It means needing that place and having it. . . . Strictly speaking, it de-

scribes the satisfaction of a groundhog surveying his
domain in the evening from his customary post outside his burrow. It describes the tender serenity of the
people on the porch once again noticing the groundhog in the familiar field beyond the porch. Immedi-
acy is the essence of *querencia*.[29]

A home is a special place that has boundaries and that
nurtures many meaningful ways of relating, including play.
The unique intimacy of play has a special role in defining
the boundaries of your play space. For example, a nickname, tickling, or a joke may serve as a transition between
the impersonal world of work and the "home" of the couple. As one partner put it:

> *"I have to be serious all day at work. Playing is a
> way to get to a relaxed level when you come home.
> It's a great way to unwind from the hassles of the day
> to shift to thinking about each other. It establishes a
> relaxed atmosphere in which you can act in any way
> you want, and it leads into making love or having a
> serious discussion."*

Some couples develop recurring rituals as a way of
marking the end of their work week:

> *Paul and Andrea both have demanding jobs and
> often bring home work on week nights. "By Friday
> afternoon I'm always exhausted and looking forward
> to the weekend," says Andrea. "We're generally both
> too tired to make dinner, so for a long time now
> we've had a tradition of going out to dinner every
> Friday night to put the workweek behind us and to
> start the weekend. We usually rotate restaurants but
> have a few favorites that we'll sometimes go to sev-
> eral weeks in a row."*

Paul says that the Friday night dinners help him unwind: "I enjoy being waited on, and so does Andrea. It's nice for us just to have the time to sit and talk in peace. We especially like candlelit, romantic restaurants for our Friday night meals. It helps us forget our jobs and realize it's the two of us for the weekend."

Another couple described this end-of-the-day ritual:

"You know the old fifties movies in which the man comes home and the woman brings him his slippers. Well, my husband and I use a more modern version to signal the transition from the workday to our more private home. Whoever gets home first prepares a light tray with cheese and crackers and two small glasses of wine. That person also gets out both of our slippers. When the other gets home, we go through this ritual where we kiss and hug and then we take off each other's shoes and put on the slippers. We sit on the couch, sip the wine, eat the cheese and crackers, and tell each other about our respective days. Sometimes, if we're in the mood, we get carried away and take off more than just each other's shoes."

When both of you are deeply absorbed in your careers, there's a risk that no one will be an advocate for intimacy. Couples can drift into an amiable but impersonal state of being together in which their play space becomes completely solitary:

Donald is a sociology professor, who works on professional papers and prepares many lectures at home in the evenings and on weekends. Charlene is a registered nurse, who takes her own work quite seriously and appreciates the importance that Donald's work has for him, but over the years she has con-

fronted him on the way work has limited their time together. Characteristically, Donald will head to his office in the den after dinner and not be seen or heard from until bedtime. If Charlene walks in while he's working, Donald will often not even look up, or he'll barely listen to her.

"I would feel quite shut out and hurt until I realized that it wasn't my problem but Don's. Although he knows a lot about human behavior and writes sociology texts, practicing intimacy is another matter. He's really a lot more comfortable going into his clubhouse and playing by himself. That phrase, 'in your clubhouse,' has helped both of us deal with the situation. I'll go into his office and ask, 'Are you in your clubhouse now?' or if I'm really in need of some attention will say, 'You've been in your clubhouse all evening. Come on out and play with me.' It's a light way of recognizing the problem."

For this couple the problem is not due to uncontrollable circumstances. Rather, work became a handy way of avoiding intimacy. "Don't bother me, I'm doing something important" may be a convenient excuse. Play can be a gentle way of knocking on doors closed by your partner's character.

Vocation and Avocation

As zealously as you should guard the boundaries of your play space from encroachment by work, parents, and Fuller brush salesmen, there is no reason to consider the work place as inviolable. As has often been observed in military strategy and football, the best defense is a good offense.

Sue and Bart liked to write secret notes to each other. For example, Sue would frequently enclose "I

love you" notes inside his lunch pail that she fixed
for him each morning. On one occasion she forgot to
put a fork in with the piece of pie and the next morning found a note from Bart: "No forkie, no nookie."
At lunchtime that day he found a piece of pie with a
huge serving fork.

Even brief playful forays into each other's workday can
maintain personal contact so that when you get back
together at the end of a day you're not meeting a stranger.
As one couple described their brief playful phone conversations:

"We achieve a lot of contact in a short time inter-
val, when we don't have time to get close by having a
serious conversation. It provides a spark of something good and new, and a certain release from
problems. There's fun and looseness and a reaffir-
mation of our basic feelings for each other. These
moments of spontaneity are reminders or signs of the
happiness we have and can create for each other."

Sometimes play can be used to acknowledge the inevitable limitations on Eros in the work place. Recently, I was
finishing up a night on call in a hospital emergency room
and overheard part of a conversation between a medical
resident, who had also just spent the night at work, and his
wife:

"Hello there, Dovey. This is your wake up
call. . . . Yeah, it's about six-thirty. It's quiet now, but
it's been a busy, busy night. . . . Have I been thinking
of you? Are you kidding? No one has ever been
thought of as much as I've been thinking of you."

I smiled to myself, wondering how often this doctor
could really have had a chance to think of his wife while

sewing up lacerations, reading electrocardiograms, and forcing nasogastric tubes into people's nostrils. My hunch is that both he and his wife knew the reality but could still be playful about it.

At the end of the day when partners talk about what happened at work, some couples use a lot of play, exaggerating events for comic effect, poking fun at some of the ridiculous character flaws in their colleagues, and so on. This is another way to bring a playful spirit into your work life. Yet another approach is to gently caricature each other's superserious work identity:

> John is carefully blow-drying his hair at the bathroom mirror. He's unusually anxious to get his hair into shape, since he's going to the first office function since joining his law firm the preceding month. His wife comes in, laughing to herself at the sight of her normally placid husband all hepped up. She stands beside him and nonchalantly primps her own hair, imitating him as much as she can without appearing to look at him. She primps away, then she begins humming the music from Saturday Night Fever. Suddenly, he catches sight of her in the mirror.
>
> "What the!" he blurts out.
>
> "Don't touch a thing. It's perfect," she says, laughing and hugging him. He laughs, too, and is much more relaxed setting off for the office function.

Many of the ways that play helps solve problems and improve the quality of your love relationship can also be helpful in your work environment.

> "I work in a high-pressure management position," says Sandy, "and there are a couple of people in my office who really get on my nerves. One of them—I'll call her Jane—is an overweight, pushy pill some-

times, and unfortunately I not only have to work with her often, but she's above me. It really used to burn me up when she'd get real demanding and inconsiderate. What a pig, I'd think to myself. In fact, I'd look at her and imagine her chubby face growing a snout and little pig ears. It struck me as so comical that it made me feel better.

"I had another problem with a guy at work, whom I actually like most of the time. Jerry likes to have his way—he's one of our salesmen, and when all his orders don't come in on time, he pouts. So I started to picture him in my mind as a huge baby sitting in a crib tantruming. It made me feel less defensive."

Sandy's strategy for dealing with annoying aspects of her colleagues is another instance of fantasy caricature. By exaggerating the problematic behavior into grotesque form, you extract a quiet piece of revenge while also gaining some distance from the situation. Sometimes you may also learn something about yourself when you create these caricatures: the people who most get under your skin psychologically already have counterparts deep within you. Just as in coping with problems with your spouse or with your parents, the degree of your emotional response corresponds to the meaning that person has in your own psychic life. Thus, fantasy caricature is a first step: once you have cast a problem in absurd or mythical terms, you need to own whatever parts may belong to you.

The people I enjoy working with and respect the most are those who take their work seriously without taking themselves overly seriously.

Craig Morse and Joanne Zartmann are teachers at a suburban elementary school. Over the years, they've knocked heads many times, for although they respect each other, Craig takes a very rational, pragmatic approach to problems while Joanne is

*more intuitive. One of the ways they have evolved to
soften their inevitable disagreements is to address
each other by their playful nicknames, whose origins
they no longer remember.*

*"Z-Girl, that's totally off the wall and inconsis-
tent," Craig will say, and Joanne will respond toler-
antly, "Captain, I just knew you were going to think
that way."*

In one mental-health clinic, the staff has made a tradition
of celebrating important events—such as a colleague's
leaving or having a fortieth birthday or a new director taking over—by making up a song. They'll take a familiar
folk song and make up humorous lyrics. At their annual
Christmas party they also do some creative play. One year,
for example, before the party a few of the staff used the
video equipment to make a tape in which they acted out a
skit modeled after "Bob and Ray." Many of these same
therapists, who spend their "work" days playing with kids,
have found a daily way of combining vocation and avocation.

Even neurosurgeons do it, although not necessarily better. During incredibly delicate operations on people's
brains, in which a one-millimeter slip could mean the loss
of the patient's ability to speak, they often play music in
the operating room and tell lewd jokes. Admittedly, some
careers have more potential for play than others, but state
of mind is a more important factor than your particular line
of work. In medicine, macabre humor is an important outlet for tension and a way of coping with realities that over-
tax our tolerance for grimness. The life of a medical intern
is an ordeal made up of sleep deprivation, fear of being
unable to handle a medical emergency, daily public recita-
tions to critical superiors, and flogging patients back to
life, many of whom are so debilitated and demented that a
gentle death would be the kindest treatment. In such absurd

circumstances, any opportunity to enjoy a bit of humor is welcome, including joking about patients:

> One group of medical house staff renamed the ward on which they rounded every morning "Happy Palace," a name they adapted from a local Chinese restaurant and which highlighted the bleak nature of the geriatric setting in which they had to work. On occasion, when they would discuss their patients' medical situation outside of their hearing, one intern would sum up the situation with a pithy phrase, in the style of a Chinese fortune cookie, such as "The physician heals, nature makes well," or "You will soon be going on a long journey."
>
> Two sisters were often observed visiting their mother. They both had strange, birdlike mannerisms and looked thin enough to be anorexic. Hence, the nurses renamed them "Anna" and "Rexie."
>
> Another intern working in the cardiac care unit was distraught at having just resuscitated a patient, who was now still alive but clinging to life with about five neurons and two myocardial fibers. When questioned by his fellow interns about whether this patient had "made it" through the night, he didn't know how to answer. After passing by the bed next door of an elderly patient who looked hunched over, with gnarled hands, he renamed the two patients "Quasimodo," after the Hunchback of Notre Dame, and "Quasi-made-it."

It may be distressing to know that young doctors make light of serious situations in this way. But people can't continue to function under such pressures without emotional outlets, and often there is more opportunity and sanction for laughing than for crying or getting angry. I know of one harried internist who got so fed up with his on-call beeper going off that he finally ripped his electronic tormentor off his belt and threw it against the wall. It stuck there embedded in the plaster, still beeping.

My own rule of thumb is that it's all right to laugh at a patient outside of his presence as long as at some other point you can feel what it's like to be him. In play there is often a feeling of triumph over adversity. It can serve to bring you and your colleagues closer together. In the "Happy Palace" situation, play helped the intern group create a sense of community and *esprit de corps*.

Further, in all but the most mundane tasks, play can enhance your creativity:

> Lawrence is an architect who found inspiration in playing with his children's toys.
>
> "Sometimes an architect can get very bored and stuck if he just sits at the drafting table or works with conventional models. Recently I was working on a major commission to design an apartment complex on the outskirts of an urban center. I wanted to do something original, but I was definitely stalled. I wanted to go back to basics in simple design elements, but I just hadn't figured out how to.
>
> "Then one night I was playing with my son's colored building blocks on the living room floor. He had gone to bed, and my wife and I were just sitting in the living room with a fire going. As I played with the blocks I began to work on some simple design ideas. Imagining each block as a two-story unit of apartments, I began to arrange them in concentric rings around an inner courtyard. Then I broke up the rings with a series of walkways, lanes, and small gardens that interlocked and led to the courtyard. In less than two hours of playing with my son's blocks I accomplished more than I had in weeks of agonizing work. My client loved the plan, and the blueprints just got a design award."

It's difficult to spend all of your time at work in highly structured activities and relationships, in which you do very little that is spontaneous or expressive, and then expect that you can readily be playful when you go home. It also seems a waste to be alienated so much of the time from your spontaneous, playful side. Robert Frost, in his poem "Two Tramps in Mud Time," describes an ideal that is worth striving for—to make our vocation and our avocation one and the same:

> But yield who will to their separation,
> My object in living is to unite
> My avocation and my vocation
> As my two eyes make one in sight.
> Only where love and need are one,
> And the work is play for mortal stakes,
> Is the deed ever really done
> For Heaven and the future's sakes.

A couple of examples come to mind. I was recently looking through antique stores for an oak table and walked into one dimly lit shop, where a middle-aged woman, with green eye make-up and dressed completely in black, greeted me. The shop had few items, but practically all of them were unusual, and the owner had a little story to tell about each of them. One was a huge, grotesque metal demon about which she related a myth and then said, "Isn't it the ugliest thing you've ever seen?" There was a very old model of a Chinese sailing ship that she told me had been partially restored by a psychiatrist (I think she also had clairvoyant powers). The proprietor loved all of these things. She had found in this shop a perfect play space for her eccentricity. While she could not afford to own all of these antiques, she could play with them and with her customers.

I'm also reminded of a saleswoman at a large department store whom I observed selling fine china and glassware to an engaged couple. She laid out a succession of services, taking obvious pleasure in matching different combinations of plates, glasses, and silverware. At one point, when the couple was having trouble deciding between two types of glasses, she suggested filling them up with water so they'd see what they would look like. "I'll have to make sure my boss doesn't see me," she said, and cast a furtive glance around her. I suddenly saw a little girl pretending to have a tea party. This adult woman had found a job that would allow her to continue to play.

Very few of us can take off and join the circus or the Harlem Globetrotters or spend our days floating down the Mississippi River on a raft like Mark Twain's Huckleberry Finn. But you can bring your vocation as close as possible to being your avocation, and you should make sure that there are moments of quietude and *querencia* before or after work when it seems that you and your partner are alone on a raft, watching the world go by:

> Next we slid into the river and had a swim, so as to freshen up and cool off; then we set down on the sandy bottom where the water was about knee deep, and watched the daylight come. Not a sound any-wheres—perfectly still—like the whole world was asleep, only sometimes the bullfrogs a-cluttering, maybe. . . .
>
> Sometimes we'd have that whole river all to our-selves for the longest time. Yonder was the banks and the islands, across the water; and maybe a spark —which was a candle in a cabin window; and some-times on the water you could see a spark or two—on a raft or a scow, you know; and maybe you could hear a fiddle or a song coming over from one of them crafts. It's lovely to live on a raft.

CHAPTER EIGHT

The Mature Relationship: A Culture of Two

Many couples lament that playfulness gradually goes out of their relationships. Although my powers of reason may be clouded by my romantic nature, I prefer to think that this loss of playfulness is neither inevitable nor desirable, and that in the most vital individuals and relationships, playfulness will continue to flourish. As one couple in their eighties related about their sex life, "Doc, it's not that it's any less good or better, it's just different." In play, as in sex, I think the key to keeping the spark alive is to find ways to make your history together create culture rather than habit.

While we are all children of our culture and are bound as well as nurtured by its enduring forms, we are also creators of culture. If this sounds like a *National Geographic* special, so be it, because I liken this creation to a voyage of discovery, such as those made by the explorers of the Nile. The voyage I have in mind is that made by two people who love each other and whose discoveries spring from seeing things through the eyes of the other. The symbols and meanings a couple devises to chart their experience is not just a reflection of the wider culture, but a new society. For just as an individual's unique clusters of meaning associated with language might be called a culture of one, the private language, rituals, and shared sense of humor of a couple constitutes a culture of two. This is not a laborious, self-conscious process such as chiseling out the Ten Commandments or erecting a monument to your mate. In its simplest form, it happens when you create a nickname:

> *Weight—either too much of it or not enough—was a sensitive issue in Janet and Carl's relationship. Janet had always been "thin as a rail," as her mother never ceased to say, in a chiding tone, while Carl's battle was always to keep pounds from hitching a ride on his rotund form. Carl had long been a devotee of diet books, a constant searcher for a culinary Sermon on the Mount that could inspire him to the proper measure of asceticism. Even when they met, he had an entire bookshelf devoted to the subject, and he had added to it since. But to the same measure that no matter how hard Carl tried to keep weight off it never stayed off, so did it seem that Janet could eat any number of ice cream sundaes without gaining an inch.*
>
> *At times this created some friction between them, since Carl's diets usually ran counter to Janet's determination to eat rich foods. But as each of them found that neither was really unhappy with how the other looked, they were able to develop more of a sense of humor about the perverse fates that had cast such metabolic opposites together. Their nicknames for each other—Baby Huey and Olive Oyl—was one way they played with the problem.*

While we can see these nicknames as examples of playfulness, what I find most interesting is how this couple borrowed symbols from the broader culture—in this case, comic book characters—to create their own "couple culture." As a relationship matures, nicknames and other types of private language change, but those that endure have special meaning.

Ritualization

The culture of two is also made up of rituals. For example, in Chapter 5, I introduced two animal lovers—Rick and Carol:

> *In addition to including nicknames for each other —Bear and Tiger Woman—Rick and Carol's play often incorporated their two cats. Both of their animals were very affectionate and would invariably jump into their laps or sleep with them in their bed if given the chance. When Rick and Carol cuddled together on the floor in front of the fireplace, their two cats would pile on top of them and purr contentedly in a manner that reminded Carol of the way that kittens will snuggle together for warmth. Thus was born their term for snuggling together—"A Cat Pile." When either of them wanted some affection, they would say, "Let's make a cat pile."*

The best couple relationships manage to cherish tradition yet welcome growth. I use the term "ritualization" to refer to such recurring interplay in a couple. It celebrates the couple's past and repeats it in similar form at regular intervals, yet it remains unique and capable of change. There are important differences between such healthy rituals that contribute to a mature relationship and those that are limiting. We can learn something about these differences by looking first at rituals in other contexts.

Non-intimate Ritualization

Animals have their own ritualizations, with some of the most dramatic ones seen in courtship. For example, Desmond Morris describes the dance and display postures of pheasants:

The male runs up alongside the female and as she moves off he circles round in front of her and blocks her path. If she is to flee now, she has to turn away first, but, before she can do so, he starts to assume his display posture. If she is receptive and stays still when he displays he has only to complete his circle around her to mount and mate with her.

But this rarely happens at the beginning of a display bout. Invariably the female turns away and moves off. The male now makes his master move. He could, of course, simply follow and catch up with her, circle round to the front and display again. But this he does not do. Instead he makes a sharp turn *away* from her as if he is leaving her and then, in one extremely rapid movement, runs round in a tight circle which brings him quickly back into his vital position in front of her. The great advantage of this manoeuvre is that he does not give the female a sense of being pursued and thus he does not stimulate her to flee at speed. If he chased straight after her each time, she would start to panic and perhaps flee from the arena altogether, to be lost in the undergrowth.

Each time the female moves away after one of his displays, he swings away from her and then runs quickly back round in a circle to confront her again until, after a long period of this repeated displaying, the female begins to move away less and less. Eventually the male changes his tactics and instead of turning away after a display, turns *towards* the slowly moving or stationary female and places one foot on her back. If she then moves off, he starts all over again, but, if she stays still, he mounts her and mating takes place.

. . . In the case of the Amherst pheasant, the male always displays broadside to the female. The tail is spread and twisted round so that the upper surfaces of the feathers are shown off to the best advantage,

and the extremely elaborate neck-ruff is fanned out
and then swung round to the side on which the female is standing. At the moment of the display the
male hisses violently at the female.[30]

In some ways, our own courtship rituals are not all that
different. The folk wisdom that it's best to "play hard to
get" suggests a deep link to our aviary ancestors. As birds
use behaviors to send messages about their amatory intentions, couple rituals, whether verbal or nonverbal, similarly convey emotional states and each person's need for
closeness or distance. A reciprocal signal serves to create a
closer connection. As one couple put it:

> "Our moments of spontaneity are reminders or
> signs of the happiness we have and can create for
> each other. It's an indication that we're not getting
> tired of one another, a reaffirmation of our basic
> feelings for each other."

But the most important difference between us and pheasants is that although their tail-feather displays visually
dwarf our coiffures and new designer fashions, our repertoire is unlimited. What we lack in erectile face wattles and
ocellated feathers we make up for in unpredictability. The
pheasant is like an artist who has great technique but who
is capable only of endless repetition of one work of art.

Our own individual rituals can become nearly as stereotyped and repetitive as those ordained by evolution. Our
neighbor who walks his dog at exactly seven o'clock each
morning, buys a newspaper, and then reads the baseball
scores over an eternal bowl of corn flakes is said to be
"doing his morning ritual." Sometimes, these solitary rituals are so repetitive and invested with personal significance that psychiatrists label them as pathologic. The child
who must never step on a crack and who then taps himself
three times if he slips, the man who must wash his hands in

a specially prescribed manner every time he has a sexual thought, are prisoners of ritual. In contrast to the shared culture of a couple's nicknames or idiosyncratic ways of being intimate, these rituals are rigid, intensely private, and may often cut a person off from friendly contact.

There are, of course, public rituals, as in religious services or holidays. They can also be secular: for some reason that I will never understand, my New Year's Eve is never complete unless I watch that silly ball descend in Times Square as I drink champagne. One of the things that forever attracts me to sporting events, like baseball, are the rituals—the playing of the Star-Spangled Banner; peanuts, hot dogs, Crackerjacks; the seventh-inning stretch; the trip to the mound with the bases loaded as the knuckleball relief pitcher warms up in the bull pen; the pinchhitter stepping into the batter's box and taking his practice swings. I will never grow tired of these rituals, in part because they are a link to my childhood and my father—I remember, for instance, when he first taught me how to keep a box score. What keeps these rituals forever young is their capacity to renew themselves: spring training is a time for every team mired in last place for the past nine years to be reincarnated as rising young stars; opening day's charged with possibility, since everyone is batting .000 and there are no runs, hits, or errors. Each game, in fact, is like starting anew.

The threads in common between such public rituals and intimate play is that, at their best, they join people in an inseparable fellowship of tradition at the same time as they renew. Intimate play rituals are not totally private as in pathologic rituals, but they are not totally public, either. They may be just as personal and idiosyncratic as an individual's cherished secret routines, but, in order to serve the relationship, they must be a blending of *both* people's meanings and needs. The reason it is so important that you take a look at the rituals that have developed in your own intimate relationship is that, while over time the development of routines and habits is inevitable, they do not always serve the relationship. The "culture of two" is an achievement that, like vintage wine, takes time to mature and careful attention.

Intimate Ritualization

I remember in college when my fraternity brother told me he wanted to "lavaliere" his girl friend. Having never heard of the term, I thought he meant to practice some kind of French perversion. It definitely sounded like something I should experience. I never did get to lavaliere anyone in college or since, but later when I found out what it was, I felt less deprived. Like "pinning," it's a quaint way of formalizing a commitment; it refers to an ornament hung from a chain about the neck and is named after a mistress of Louis XIV, La Duchesse de la Vallière. Contrary to my perverse fantasies, it turned out that this lady became a nun and subjected herself to all sorts of fierce penances for her earlier indiscretions. Whether the lavaliere is meant to commemorate her lustier days or her subsequent asceticism is not known, but the practice of the custom endures. Dating, engagement, and marriage are highly ritualized processes, with each culture prescribing specific behaviors and roles appropriate to each stage of intimate affiliation. The anthropologist Arnold van Gennep described how primitive societies have very similar rites of incorporation that serve to unite partners together:

> Among the rites of incorporation it is possible to isolate those which have an individual meaning and which unite the two young peole to each other: giving or exchanging belts, bracelets, rings, or clothes which are worn; binding one to the other with a single cord; tying part of each other's clothing together, touching each other reciprocally in some way; using objects belonging to the other . . . ; being wrapped in a simple piece of clothing or a veil; sitting on the

same seat; drinking each other's blood; eating from the same food or dish; drinking from the same liquid or container; massaging, rubbing, anointing (with blood or clay); washing each other; entering the new house; and so forth. These are essentially rites of union. . . .

Furthermore, although the exchange of blood may be coarser or more cruel than that of a piece of clothing, a ring, or a kiss, it is no more primitive.[31]

In this society, although betrothal and marriage are rarely sealed in blood, similar so-called primitive practices still survive in many couples and may serve to bring you closer together:

> *"I remember the first time that I knew Craig and I were really serious about each other," said Gail. "It wasn't when we first slept together or when he introduced me to his folks or when he gave me an engraved bracelet for my birthday. It was when we started using the same toothbrush. Don't get me wrong—this wasn't anything kinky. We still prefer to have our own toothbrushes. But, sometimes when one of us stayed overnight at the other's place and didn't have a toothbrush, we used the only one available. It's a little thing, but I had never done that with anyone before.*
>
> *"Now that we live together, we have other ways of being intimate. Sometimes we shower together and wash each other's hair. I'm always the one that cuts Craig's hair. These simple and elemental things are more than they seem. It may be old-fashioned nowadays to think in these terms, but I need to know he's my man and I'm his woman."*

Van Gennep also described how such rituals are "rites of passage" that facilitate an individual's or a couple's movement through important developmental stages. Specifically, he felt that betrothal rituals serve to *separate* the couple from the outside world, including old ties, enable them to make the *transition* to being a couple, and help to *unite* them. As I provide more examples of couple rituals and you reflect on your own couple rituals, it may be interesting for you to look at the extent to which they perform one or more of these functions. My feeling is that culturally prescribed rituals, such as exchanging rings, the vanishing practice of getting down on one knee to ask for your lady's hand, and carrying her over the threshold of your heavily mortgaged condo, are necessary to define the couple but not sufficient. You need to create your own rituals that carry forward separation, transition, and union.

You and your partner need to modify old rituals and create new ones at different stages of your relationship. In the first few years, you're likely to experiment with a lot of new nicknames, private language, and rituals. It's a time when both of you are not yet sure of your commitment, and play is used to build bridges to each other. Each playful ritual is a reassuring sign that you are in sync with each other and share something unique. Later, when your relationship feels more secure and you are spending less time together, your play may become less prominent, but those rituals that endure tend to have special significance. In a mature relationship they provide a reassuring sense of stability while still being flexible enough to adapt to the changing needs of the two individuals. While symbols may be borrowed from other cultural contexts, the most meaningful rituals are deeply rooted in both partners' unconscious lives.

The Play Community

The danger in couples who have been together for a long time is that play and playfulness can get crowded out of the relationship. At times one of you may have to make a more conscious effort to bring back a bit of playfulness, but a little can sometimes go a long way. As Johan Huizinga observed,

> A play-community tends to become permanent even after the game is over. . . . The feeling of being "apart together" in an exceptional situation, of sharing something important, of mutually withdrawing from the rest of the world and rejecting the usual norms, retains its magic beyond the duration of the individual game.[32]

One of my favorite examples of intimate play helps illustrate this point:

> *Dan is an obstetrician who has an active practice, while Charlotte is a nurse. Recently, they put a new addition on their house to better accommodate their third child.*
> *"Going through the construction was the hardest time," says Charlotte. "Dan is usually exhausted after work, and he usually gets home late. I'm pretty done in, too, what with the kids and my part-time nursing job. We had no idea how disruptive the construction would be—we had to live with plaster dust all over the place and one working bathroom. One of those weekday evenings in January, when I was struggling to come up with something special but simple to eat for dinner, I had an inspiration. 'Let's have a picnic!' I said. Dan looked at me as if I was crazy. After all, there was snow outside and it was twenty-five degrees. But when he caught on, he really got into the idea. We spread a blanket on the living room floor and took out our picnic basket with the plastic utensils. Then we feasted on an assortment of cold cuts, sardines, bread, cheese, fruit, and*

*a bottle of wine. Some classical music helped com-
plete the mood.*

*"Our construction work is long finished, thank
God, but our feeling overwrought and overwhelmed
at times goes on. At those moments one of us will
say, 'Let's have a picnic!' It's a quick way for us to
escape from the doldrums without even leaving
home."*

Playful rituals can provide a safe harbor to which you
can return at difficult times. They provide a form of security that is different than habit and preserves a bit of
whimsy. A reassuring sense of continuity with the past is
evoked without either of you being constrained to enact
rigid roles—there is a mixture of repetition and spontaneity.

*On one of their vacations, Samuel and Jane had
gone to England, where they had come to enjoy formal high teas. In their relaxed moments at home, one
of them will sometimes invite the other to have tea.
At such times they will usually call each other Lady
Agatha and Sir Alistair, and they adopt aristocratic
British accents. They enjoy discovering exotic new
blends of tea and imported biscuits, all of which
helps them enter a fantasyland of another class and
culture.*

Couples who have been together for a long time may
retain rituals that began early in their relationship, but they
embroider them over the years:

*The Caldwells first bought a small sailboat when
they went on a summer vacation to the Eastern Shore
of Maryland—it was little more than a Sunfish, but
over the years, as they became more affluent and*

more confident sailors, they purchased a twenty-one-foot Soling and then a Pearson, which slept four. On weekends and for a month each summer they would take it out, and while on the boat they felt as if they were in a separate world. For a couple of years John had the nickname "Captain Bligh" and Sally was "Mrs. Mate." The latter metamorphosed into "Ms. Mate" after women's liberation came to Baltimore, and eventually "Captain Bligh" was dropped as John's dictatorial personality mellowed.

Part of the fun of being on the boat was making up fantasies about the boats around them, sometimes based on the boats' actual names and sometimes improvised. Thus, a tall-master schooner just visible on the horizon might become the Star of India, just in from Bombay with a cargo of hemp and incense. A central fantasy that endured through the years was that they would retire and sail around the world.

The "culture of two" that develops in mature relationships differs from the intimate play described in the earlier stages of a relationship primarily in its degree of elaboration and the couple's emotional involvement in it. It has a lasting quality, and some of these couples are very much aware of and seek to cultivate playfulness in their relationships. Thus, for example, many couples may experiment once or twice with wearing costumes, but some, who love to pretend and who have a flair for the dramatic, may take this further. I know of one couple who has an old trunk in which they keep interesting old clothes, costumes they have saved from Halloween parties, and odd things they have picked up at garage sales or antique stores. Every so often they'll dress up in some of these outfits and assume fantasy identities, some of which they have dreamed up before and some of them completely new.

In interviewing couples I have come to think that, while

many couples become less playful after the first few years together, there is a small number whose play improves. The myth that sex inevitably declines precipitously with advancing age has gradually been debunked. Play, like sex, is too important to be left solely to novices.

Personalizing Daily Events

A couple can turn mundane, daily events, such as bathing and eating, into intimate rituals. Instead of being merely a task to perform, such events become personalized and contribute to the culture of two. I'm not advocating that *every* bodily function become a shared event, and I suppose that's what The Prophet had in mind when he said there should be spaces in your togetherness. There is a legitimate place for privacy in your relationship, and if every corned-beef sandwich had to be consecrated by an intimate ritual, intimacy would soon degenerate into maudlin sentimentality. Years spent with the same person, though, can imprison both of you in numbing routine, so that you are sleepwalking through much of your time together. You can use play to transform small occurrences into intimate events. The trick is to focus your attention on the present moment, in which opportunities for sharing will often present themselves.

> *A young professional couple developed a morning ritual of rising about an hour and a half before work and going jogging together. It's often just about dawn when they head out during winter, their breath clouding the air and their golden retriever in tow. Afterward they shower and sit down in the kitchen for a light breakfast. There they can look out at the bird feeder and share their dreams from the night before. They don't try to interpret them, but they talk about what the dreams make them think of. Some-*

times they find meanings in their dreams, but at others they are content just to share them. It's an intimate time that helps them begin their day feeling taken care of.

You can start your day racing around, wolfing down a solitary Egg McMuffin or crabbing at each other, or you can make a choice to begin *together*. Such morning rituals can set the tone for the entire day and help to arrest the impersonal momentum that often takes over during a busy week.

Kathy and Ray usually begin each day by meditating together. During the sixties, when they were in college, they had been part of the counterculture in the San Francisco Bay area. While Ray has since become a successful businessman and Kathy a criminal lawyer, they joke sometimes about how they wished that instead of being "co-opted," they were selling leather on Telegraph Avenue in Berkeley or running a "head shop." They're not especially religious, nor do they have a guru, but meditating is one thing that survives from their college days. It relaxes them and is a way of spending some peaceful time together before the day's activities close in.

The end of your day is another good time to personalize with an intimate ritual, which may then lead into sexual intimacy. Here is another idea:

Joe and Harriet were always avid readers and they developed a ritual of almost always reading to each other at night before going to bed. They would explore new books, but they also had certain favorites, such as The Scarlet Letter, *that they had first read when they had gotten married and which every few years they would pick up again. They also liked*

> *to listen to radio broadcasts, such as Garrison Keil-*
> *lor's monologues on "A Prairie Home Companion"*
> *and recordings of old radio programs. Harriet would*
> *often do some knitting, and Joe would tinker with his*
> *stamps as they listened.*
>
> *"I suppose we're a little old-fashioned," said Joe,*
> *"'cause we hardly ever watch TV and rarely go to*
> *the movies. We like the simple pleasures that remind*
> *us of times gone by."*

There's something about participating in your entertainment, such as reading to someone and creating your own pictures in your mind rather than having them channel-fed by TV, that opens up more possibilities for intimacy. Every so often I come across some appalling statistic that the average American watches five hours of TV every day. I, for one, am quite attached to my television set, but I also see it as a menace. Beyond a certain number of hours I develop symptoms indistinguishable from an alcoholic hangover, and I am severely impaired in my ability to relate meaningfully to another human being. Unfortunately, if you and your partner are *both* watching five hours of TV, neither of you will notice that the other is staring at you through reddened, slit eyes as if *you* were the next program. As long as you have to watch that much TV, it's really not possible to get serious about being more playful in your relationship. In moderation, however, even television can provide some creative possibilities:

> *A couple who love watching old movies together*
> *on TV have come to know certain films so well that*
> *they know many of the lines by heart. During roman-*
> *tic scenes, such as with Lauren Bacall and*
> *Humphrey Bogart, they speak the lines before the*
> *actors. Another version of this play is turning down*
> *the sound and making up lines to suit their moods.*

Another couple, both of whom are into gourmet food, will often cook together on Friday or Saturday nights, with each of them preparing a special dish. Sometimes they'll invite some friends over to share the feast, but there is always the feeling of intimate collaboration between the two of them, with a lot of teasing and joking.

Commemoration Rituals

One of the things that contributes to the comforting stability of a relationship is the sense of a good past. To paraphrase an ancient Sioux proverb, a couple without history is like wind on the buffalo grass. Scrapbooks, trip mementos, and photograph albums are such tangible reminders. Holidays perform a similar function, each ritual rich with associations from past years. While intimate play rituals may be stimulated by such annual occasions, they are elaborated in personal ways by the couple rather than being prescribed by some external authority or tradition.

Linda and Richard have a ritual of making several homemade Christmas tree decorations every year. At this point their collection numbers over a hundred, and they practically have to buy a larger tree each year to accommodate all of them.

"The decorations have evolved, in a way, as our marriage has," says Linda. "We can tell you the year each one of them was made, because they all have very specific associations and meanings. Every year we try to make decorations that are symbolic of important events or new people we've met or milestones we have reached. We have one ornament that's a replica of our first house, carved in Balsam wood and painted with oil paints. The family dog is enshrined in papier-mâché. One year Richard made *a Scrooge-like figure who's a caricature of a boss that at the time he disliked. There's an olive tree that represents a big vacation we took one year to Greece. We have a whole series of ornaments that are quite awkward and clumsy but very beautiful to us, because our children made them when they were young. There's another collection of pottery ornaments, which I made at a time when I was doing a lot of pottery.*

"We begin planning ornaments some time after Thanksgiving. Some of them are quite elaborate and require sketches and even a model before the final one is done. Then there are always a few spontaneous ones, which are made in the few days before Christmas. Each year on the weekend before Christmas we invite some relatives and best friends over for tree-trimming, at which time we also have egg shells to paint and other materials that people can make ornaments from. Our children are all grown now, but they still carry on the tradition and bring home a decoration or make one here most every year.

"Each year it's a treat just to take the old decorations out and go through them all. They're like a family album or a treasure chest of memories."

Traditions that originated in your family while you were growing up or that go back several generations can be carried on in your current relationship. In addition to linking you to your own past and being a rite of passage to your new family, they may also initiate your partner into your original family's culture:

Caroline grew up in England and moved to the United States when she married her husband, Mark. She has carried on a family tradition of making mar-

malade and preserving it during the winter months.
"I couldn't do it for the first few years," she says,
"because I couldn't find the right oranges in the
States. You have cooking apples here to make pies
but no cooking oranges. You need tart oranges to
make marmalade. Then I found out from my mother
that the best oranges are Seville oranges, and ever
since I have had crates of them sent from Spain each
year.

"Making marmalade is a very elaborate project,
which I loved being involved in as a kid. Now Mark
and I do it in January and February in those long,
dark winter evenings. It's sort of an extension of the
winter holidays.

"There are so many steps to it—you have to peel
the oranges, mince the rind, and remove the seeds
from the fruit itself. Then you set up large pots on the
stove, where you boil the fruit, sugar, rind, and cit-
ric acid, which acts as a preservative. Each pot has
to be boiled over five or six hours. When it's ready,
you ladle the marmalade into jam jars. It may sound
like work, but it's very festive, and since initially I
had never done it on my own before and Mark was a
total novice, it was a real adventure!

"When I was a kid we used to seal the jars with
melted wax, which was another elaborate step. But
nowadays jam jars come with their own covers. The
best part is labeling the batch. For example, we'll
put Orange Marmalade, Caroline and Mark, and the
year, on top. Mark is quite artistic and draws a picture on the label, too.

"Mark and I often make a gift of the marmalade to
our friends. I think that for me, as someone who's
moved countries, that maintaining a family tradition
is one of the ways that I keep my sense of home. It's
something I also want to share with our children
when we start to have them."

Many couples start their own traditions and don't restrict them to the holiday season:

> After fifteen years of marriage, one Boston couple has a traditional activity that they do practically every month. It hasn't been by design—rather, over the years they've found things that they love and wouldn't want to miss.
>
> "Both of us grew up in this area, which is imbued with tradition. You can't go anywhere without running into the Boston Tea Party, Old North Church, the bridge in Concord. I think it's also the fact that you can't help but be aware of the changing seasons —each one is so different from another and has its special qualities that we love. We were 'doing' the outdoors before L. L. Bean—every October we reserve a room in an inn in Vermont and see the foliage, and there's raspberry picking at a local farm in September and blueberries in August. In March we try to get up north for the maple syrup gathering. We're also both avid sports fans, so in November we rarely miss the Harvard-Yale game, and in February there's the Beanpot (a hockey tournament of the Boston area colleges). We're kind of down on the Red Sox right now, but we still go to a game early in April, if possible Opening Day."

Just as recurring activities and places can acquire intimate associations that gain meaning through the years, so, too, can specific possessions. Jewelry, such as a wedding or engagement ring, or other gifts you give each other are common examples. In intimate play, all kinds of things can take on special significance:

> "When we were married we were living in Austin, Texas, where Steve was doing graduate work and we were quite removed from most of our friends. We

couldn't afford the time or the money to go back East for our wedding, so just our parents and a few friends came for the ceremony.

"One of my best friends from college, Janis, was unable to make the wedding. Janis was a real flower child, always on the move, living in the most 'in' places—the Village, Haight-Ashbury, Big Sur, you name it. We are both extremely fond of her.

"One day, a couple of months after we were married, we arrived home from shopping to find a beautiful plant—a purple passion plant in our doorway with a note from Janis. It was so typical of her. She was going out with a guy whose father owned a big nursery in Louisiana, just outside of New Orleans. They had hit upon the idea of renting a truck and driving it, loaded full of houseplants, from New Orleans to the West Coast, where they would sell them. They were driving straight through except for an impromptu detour to try to see us. Of course that was just like Janis not to call or anything. She said in the note that they had waited around for an hour or two and then had to go.

"Anyway, we still have this plant fifteen years later, and we're still very good friends with Janis, although through the years the plant has survived some pretty bad decimations. Once it was reduced to a single shoot and we were afraid it wasn't going to make it. We became very solicitous of it and fertilized it and watered it carefully and moved it around from window to window to follow the sunlight. We have always called it the Janis plant, and somehow it's very symbolic for us of our youthful, more restless days. It's survived all our moves and occasional neglect. The plant is the only perishable wedding gift we got, and we're glad to report that for a long time now it's been thriving."

It's not only history that holds a couple together, but it can sustain you through lean times. There are legacies from the past that we all would like to do without, but there are also parts of your two individual and combined pasts that are worth commemorating. It is the living continuation of your past in the present that gives both substance.

Renewal Rituals

I have always loved fall in New England—the yellows and reds and oranges, the cool air and the sun just warm enough to heat my insides but not the tip of my nose, football. I love nostalgia, and each falling leaf is full of it. It's comforting to remember that the trees aren't really dying; they're just molting. To stretch a metaphor, relationships also need to molt. Unfortunately, it's not as natural an act for us as it is for the trees. Nature gives us metaphors, but it is up to us to express them. We need to commemorate our past, but we also need to renew our relationships. Sometimes a couple's rituals do a bit of both:

> Rob and Sarah were married during the sixties when people were very much into experimenting with alternative wedding ceremonies. In addition, Rob is Protestant, Sarah is Jewish, and they wanted a non-denominational service that combined aspects of both of their religious backgrounds in an improvisational way. Perhaps the most important aspect of their creative wedding ceremony was that they were married outdoors, by the sea. Says Rob, "We were married on a rocky promontory overlooking Penobscot Bay in Maine. We had met in Maine, where we both spent the summers in our childhoods, and we are very attached to its rugged coastline."
> Sarah describes the beautiful fall day on which they were married. "Our wedding was on the second

weekend in October, and the New England leaves were all changing color. So for a backdrop we had the cliffs and the ocean on one side and the blazing red and yellow trees on the other. It was a very soft, Indian summer kind of day, and the sun had that clear, cool intensity of the last gasp of summer. Everyone was asked to bring flowers—I don't think there was anyone there who wasn't carrying flowers —and it gave a sensual air to the whole occasion. At the very end it had been agreed that everyone would throw their flowers off the cliffs. It was such a beautiful sight, this kaleidoscope of leafy colors falling into the ocean spray. We all stood around for the longest time feeling very dreamy, watching the flowers float out to sea. I thought of Molly's monologue at the end of Ulysses."

Throughout their marriage, Rob and Sarah have had a yearly ritual of returning in October to Maine. Says Rob, "We go for a weekend, usually as close to our actual wedding anniversary as possible. The weekend has been like a second and third and tenth honeymoon. But the most important part is that we always take a couple of bouquets of flowers and return to the site of our wedding and throw them into the sea. It's a very private rite of passage for us. It marks the end of one year and the beginning of another. It's a kind of renewal of commitment to our marriage. And it brings back all the memories of that special day many years ago."

Renewal rituals often require some willingness to pretend or at least to suspend your belief that you have any past together at all. In this way, you can recapture some of the feeling of beginning a new relationship.

"Sometimes we pretend we're meeting for the first time (not the same way we actually met). It will be a

Friday night and we'll have made a date to get to-
gether at Jack's place, although we haven't said
what we'll do. I'll be walking down the street and
Jack will see me. He walks up to me and asks me
where I'm going on such a cold night and I tell him I
just got into town and have no money and no place to
stay and I'm just looking for some place to get warm
(I don't have a coat on). He says I can spend the
night at his place, so we go to his apartment. While
I'm taking a shower and washing my hair he's put-
ting on some music and making some drinks. I come
out with just a towel around me, as he's put my
clothes in his washer. He hands me a drink and we
sit on the sofa. We both remember that we haven't
even introduced ourselves and we laugh as we do so.
We talk a while and just seem to be getting closer to
each other and he kisses me and we make love."

Every marital therapist has seen couples who report that
they were in love and everything was fine until they got
married. While we should allow for some retrospective idealization of the premarital state, for many couples marriage
changes the way they experience their relationship. For one
thing, if the wife takes on her husband's last name, she now
carries the same name as his mother. You don't have to be a
psychoanalyst to know that, however dearly a man may love
his mom, it puts a damper on his sex life to feel that, like
Oedipus, he's unwittingly married her. But it's not something you can avoid just by keeping your own names. Renewal rituals are a playful way of gaining back some of this
freedom that existed before either of them had a husband or
wife. It is a way for couples to recognize the marital roles that
they had been playing and get beyond them.

Another way for you to renew your relationship is to use
seasonal changes as reminders of the need to do periodic
emotional housecleaning. Spring is a favorite time for
many kinds of renewal rituals:

"On the first day of spring each year or as close to that date as we can get on a weekend, we try to go to an outdoors place that we love, such as an Audubon sanctuary. We talk about the past year together and our hopes for the year ahead and then join hands across a running stream in the manner of an Indian ceremony. It's less formal than making vows, but we like to think of the occasion as one of choosing each other again. We both believe that we need to affirm that we're together not just out of habit or because it's easy, but because we want to be."

New Year's is another traditional time for taking stock. One couple I interviewed keeps a little book in which they record their resolutions each year. At the end of the year they not only make new resolutions but they also include commendations—that is, even if they haven't accomplished what they had resolved to do, they give themselves and each other credit in whatever ways they can. It's a nice way of keeping a balance between acceptance of who they are while still trying to improve their relationship. They usually manage to introduce some humor into the occasion so it doesn't seem so deadly serious. Thus, one of them was given a commendation one year for walking the dog twice, and her partner, who had a tendency toward perfectionism, made a resolution to "try as hard as I can, not to be perfect." Commendations were made contingent on his having actually *tried* not to be perfect—inadvertent blunders didn't count.

Another renewal ritual is a day of silence. Not to be confused with "the silent treatment," this is an agreed-upon time of silence in which both partners take time to be alone together, to reflect, and have some peace. Television and work are strictly prohibited, and the telephone is disconnected. It can be a way of setting aside the usual distractions and can lead into some useful discussion afterward.

Growing Young

When your children have all left home, you may feel some relief. At last you can reclaim the basement for your own projects, assuming you've found somewhere to store *their* old junk, and you can each have your own bathroom, whenever you want it. On Friday nights you can blissfully go away for the weekend without worrying whether your teen-agers are drinking all of your wine before its time, or whether you'll return to find your newly painted Dutch colonial a boarded-up, charred shell.

On the other hand, your no longer fingerprint-smudged wall may also seem to echo now, and when it's just you and your mate face-to-face the disappointments in your marriage are much harder to ignore. Even the best of marriages must accommodate your new-found privacy. One couple, recognizing that over the years they had drifted into a polite but distant way of relating, decided that they had to begin "dating" each other: new circumstances call for a new start. Although you may be out of practice, a bit of courtship is a good antidote to taking each other for granted. Some couples also need to develop new interests that they can share:

> *Richard and Elizabeth were happy to see the younger of their two daughters move off to college, but they rapidly found themselves suffering from a version of the empty-nest syndrome.*
>
> *"It's amazing how much time you give to raising children when they're growing up," says Elizabeth. "When they're gone you suddenly find yourself with all this time on your hands."*
>
> *To fill their new-found time together, Richard and Elizabeth set about a new pastime: "We had always been museum goers," says Richard, "but it was mostly to the big shows that everybody went to. We*

*decided to get to know the museum a lot better, to
become really familiar with its permanent collection.
We began to make weekly visits to the museum, often
combining this with dinner out. We also bought cata-
logs and books about the major artists whose works
the museum featured.*

*"As we became familiar with our local collection,
we started visiting other museums. We began to make
weekend trips to other cities and spent much of the
time going to museum and university collections.
Last year we went to France to visit the Louvre,
Monet's house at Giverny, and a number of other
museums.*

*"Aside from all the enjoyment we both get from art
and learning about it, it's a great feeling that after
all these years we can still discover new things together and play off each other's enthusiasm. When
we wander through the halls of a museum, I sometimes feel like we're just like college students again."*

As people reach retirement age, there is often more leisure time, but they may have realistic worries about their
health and whether there will be enough money to sustain
their former life-style. If they haven't developed mutual
interests, having more time together can make both
partners feel terribly isolated. The next couple developed a
playful solution to some of these problems.

*"Jerry was an executive in a telecommunications
firm that was taken over by another company. Unfortunately, he found himself at age sixty out of work
and without prospects. We had just moved to the West
Coast. Our kids are all grown and married and scat-
tered about the country, so it's just the two of us now.
We looked at each other and said, 'What are we
going to do?' It seemed too late to start over but too
soon to retire. Neither of us were ever big on playing*

golf and taking it easy, so we weren't thrilled at the idea of being among the permanently unemployed. Besides, we hadn't put enough money away to keep us going that long. So we took stock and realized that one thing we had plenty of was antique furniture. Enough of it, in fact, to fill a house. Jerry is very handy and I like to do interior design, so we decided, why not open an inn?

"Well, it took some time to find the right place, but we've fixed up this mansion in New Hampshire that was a rundown historic building. It's been great fun furnishing the place in the original Victorian style, complete with balloon curtains and metal ceilings. We finished just in time for the fall foliage season. Every evening at six o'clock, we have our guests come into the parlor to have a glass of wine and to swap stories.

"Next spring we plan to convert the barn into an antiques store. We both love going to auctions and Jerry's good at restoration. I guess you could say that we both have found a second career, but this time we're in it together."

More people seem to be living longer these days. Whether because of jogging, eating more bran and less bacon, or a declining belief in an afterlife, there are more old people around, which means more widows and widowers. While some may meet new partners that they choose to marry, many more do not seek or may not find a second spouse after a near-lifelong relationship. Just as a playful, flexible attitude may help young couples define their relationship in personal terms rather than feeling constrained by our culture's traditional forms, so, too, may such youthful thinking best serve older folks.

Both Frank and Isabel had lost spouses many years before. They were now in their seventies, with grown children and growing numbers of grandchildren. They had known each other as friends for many years, and although they enjoyed each other's company, neither of them exactly wanted a new spouse. So when they decided to live together they jokingly referred to their arrangement as living in sin. Each had their own bedroom and separate life, but they wanted each other for companionship.

"We thought that our families might be scandalized," said Frank, "but they actually were quite supportive. They didn't say so, but I think our kids were relieved that Isabel and I both had someone to be with and who could take care of us. It took the burden off them."

Over the five years that they had lived together, their affection for each other has deepened. One of the most sensitive issues to deal with has been their memories of their respective spouses. "Neither one of us wanted to deny or forget our earlier marriages," says Isabel. For each of them the anniversary dates of their former marriages and the deaths of their spouses were particularly important. Over the years they have created some rituals in which they share with each other their feelings at those times. For example, each year they go together to the graves of their spouses on the anniversaries of their deaths. "It's nice to have someone with you to talk about how you feel as time passes," says Isabel. "It's also helped us become more intimate, without feeling disloyal to our old relationships."

On their wedding anniversaries they usually take each other out to dinner and sometimes take out their picture albums and retell old stories. "I suppose," says Isabel, "that eventually we may dwell less on the past, and maybe we will even get married, but right now this is what feels right to us."

Such flexible thinking and arrangements emerge from playfulness. If you can meet the changing demands of each life stage with a capacity to see yourself in new ways, you will not fall prey to the lament of my grandmother: "Too soon old, too late *schmart.*"

Playful Language

The private culture that evolves through intimate play is the accretion of many experiences of the couple: moments that were deeply felt, styles of relating that have endured because in some way they respond to partners' needs. In a sense, the culture of two is a history of the relationship. It is not so much a chronological, orderly rendering as the layering of successive meanings and events, much as any language is a condensed history of the culture.

> *Over the years that they have lived together, Andy and Shelly have nicknamed much of their furniture and household appliances. For example, they have a sprawling red sofa, which they call Big Red. The nickname, in part, serves to capture their ambivalance about the couch. It is a comfortable, overstuffed piece that has sentimental value, but it is also an embarrassing eyesore. If they could afford to replace it they would, but both Andy and Shelly are graduate students living off stipends, so for now "it's Big Red or the floor."*
> *In their living room they also have a worn Oriental rug which is threadbare in several places, earning it the nickname "Treadia." Shelly says she apologizes to the rug when she vacuums it and "wears it down a bit more." The vacuum, too, has a nickname—"J. Edgar"—since it is a large, old, sputtering Hoover.*
> *Among their kitchen appliances are a Cuisinart*

called Oscar, an electric mixer called Lady Sun-
beam, and an iron called Miss Proctor.

"Of course," says Shelly, "we've nicknamed the
car. It's a dilapidated station wagon that my father
gave us years ago when he bought a new car. I keep
telling Andy that it once was a fancy family car, but
it now has all the signs of old age—a faded paint
job, rust, and tears in the upholstery, so we call it
Faded Glory."

Shelly and Andy's play suggests how private language
can embody a couple's shared history, as well as serve to
personalize their everyday surroundings. Their common
possessions take on intimate connotations.

A couple's personal lexicon changes as their relationship
changes. Early in their relationship some couples have
words that refer to people who intrude on their privacy: one
couple used the word "humanoids," implying that other
people might look like human beings, talk like human
beings, but in contrast to the two of them, actually were
not human. The term corresponded to their feeling of living
in an intensely intimate enclave that they felt was worlds
apart from how other people related. As their love affair
mellowed into a more quiet, profound commitment, "humanoids" dropped out of their speech.

Similarly, when couples are beginning to explore each
other's bodies, their private language is rich with idiosyncratic sexual references. For instance, one man gave names
to each of his lover's breasts—Sabina and Colette. Henry
VIII's ardor for Anne Boleyn's charms found similar expression in his letter when he hoped to be "in my Sweet-
hearts Armes whose pritty Duckys I trust shortly to kiss."
But in time, he became enamored with other Duckys and
lopped off Anne's head. Evidently, he found that part of
her anatomy less enchanting.

Once couples become more familiar with each other,
they use fewer poetic and oddball terms. Euphemisms give

way to the vernacular, a function perhaps of habit over-coming modesty and also, sadly, of a loss of that wonderment that so often departs along with newness. Even so, some terms tend to endure. For example, one married couple refers to their position of sleeping tightly clasped together, back to front, as "spoons"—a metaphor for the way two spoons fit together.

As couples develop their own dependable rhythms of being together—the ebb and flow of intimate moments and arguments, of joining and separating—nonverbal rituals take the place of private language. But nicknames and other terms of endearment are the most common variety of private language and may also endure the longest. To understand the culture of two, it's best to study couples' nicknames. Just as Freud found meaning in the psychopathology of everyday life, so may we find some truths about mature relationships in the love talk of everyday couples.

Nicknames as Metaphor

When Juliet asked Romeo, "What's in a name?" and told him to "doff thy name," because "that which we call a rose by any other name would smell as sweet," she was really complaining about his *last* name—Montague—which made him a *persona non grata* to her kinfolk, the Capulets. I wonder, however, whether she would have been so cavalier about his first name if instead of Romeo he was called Dick or Harpo. Romeo is inclined to make up new names for her, such as "bright angel," "fair saint," and "my soul," but this seems due to passionate adoration and not from any innate distaste for the name Juliet. In fact, I think both of them, and most lovers since, would rail against being limited to any one name, no matter how sweet. Anton Chekhov, for example, was constantly coming up with new appellations in his letters to his wife, Olga Knipper: "My dearest helpmate," "little angel," "my river perch," "my dear one, my own," "Kewpie," "my atressicle," and "Dearest Gramsie." At times he would write, "Greetings, sweet horsy, my darling" or "I want to pet my horsy," while at others Olga would metamorphose into "Darling, my kind affable little puppy," "my joy and my dog," and he would urge her to "keep well, mongrel pup." Perhaps most touching and enigmatic, however, is when he said, "I embrace my little cockroach and send her a million kisses."

In newly christening a lover you establish a unique relation that sets it apart from all others. You are implicitly saying, "I know you in a way that no one else does." While the first time you call your lover a new name you may be tentative and unpremeditating and the name may not stick, some nicknames are remarkably long-lived. Some couples' actual names fall into such disuse that on the rare occasion that they are used, the partners may seem startled and wonder what's wrong, as if they had suddenly used the address "Mrs. Smith" or "Sir." Nicknames stand in the same relation to our given names as the French *tu* to *vous* —if you feel intimate, you should speak intimately.

Many languages have diminutive word endings, such as the Irish *in*, *ita/ito* in Spanish, and *ya* in Russian. American lovers seem indiscriminate with endearing suffixes, as in sweet*kins*, snook*ums*, honey*poo*, and baby*ness*, through which presumably even a snarling psychopath can metamorphose into a cuddly playmate: "But it's Christmas, Scroogekins"; "Guess what, it's Friday the 13th, Jason-poo." The French like to call their lovers "little rabbit" or "my cabbage," while Germans use "little treasure." Some Spanish nicknames, such as *Mija* (my daughter) or *Madre* (mother) can be as appropriately amorous in Mexico City as they would be in San Juan. But other endearments, such as *Negrita* (little black one) would cause hearts to flutter only in Puerto Rico, while *Cuero* (leather) would be a compliment only in Mexico. Our British cousins likewise have a language bearing some resemblance to our own but with distinctly different love terms. Welsh Witch and Curly

Cockney Runt would be understandable if not aphrodisiacs here, while Chipbucket, Marmite Soldier, and Superbloke would require further explanation. It is said that the British are a more cold-blooded sort, whose amorous declarations maintain a high level of decorum. But each Valentine's Day in papers such as the *Times,* the British show themselves to be every bit as unabashedly sentimental as we are. True, some Valentines are restrained, as in:

> How can I interface with our coparticipant situation when my Squeaker wears striped jimjams?— Love, Dormouse

and

> Let's go a little tactile, my sweet hump.

But far common is:

> Petal loves Poppy Crimble Crump Plumbum trillions; and that's not just poppycock.

and

> To my Darling porker-snorker,
> Vivicuddles, love, and despicable rattiness, from
> Fat Pugsley, Nice bit of beef!

Then there's the cryptic but unabashed variety:

> *Jiggling Joo*—wiggly wiggle woggly woggle wiggly woggly wiggly woo I love you

A French or American lover couldn't translate it, but either would readily empathize with the sentiments expressed. Under ordinary circumstances the number of couples willing to divulge their private names to others is quite small. Three hundred sixty-four days a year, they chatter furtively in their secret subversive code under cover of their public roles. Many are happy to tell the world on Valentine's Day, but even then only under cover of anonymity in newspaper ads. Whether in London, Washington, D.C., or San Francisco, on this day the credo is "If you feel it, flaunt it." I have looked through these ads for several years and, added to the examples I know in depth from interviews with couples, I have begun to decipher these underground codes. What follows is not intended as a couple's counterpart to a baby-naming manual, but more as a guide to understand your own names. If, however, the examples inspire you to try something more daring than your usual Sweetheart, or Honey, so be it.

Nicknames are metaphors whose imagery can be truly poetic, suggesting nuances of perception and meaning that reveal what we didn't know we saw of felt. Sometimes, though, maladroit metaphor can make you stop short, like potholes or stubbing your toe in the dark. Fortunately, most people don't require that their partners be poets and are willing to tolerate more than a little mawkish sentimentality and cliché in the nicknames they will let pass. An intimate relationship is one of the few places we are encouraged to wax poetic, even if our creations are not the stuff that your high school English teacher, who would forever admonish you not to write long sentences or end them with prepositions, would be proud of. Thus, love's tolerance has given birth to:

> Soybean:
> You are my protein
> You keep me lean and mean.

> You're the triple fudge cake
> In my banquet of life.

> Slow and steady our love does grow
> Sure do love you my escargot.

In many respects our lovetalk names resemble the given names of nineteenth-century American Indians, which were also felt to be magical and should be kept secret. Their rich metaphors were often inspired by a physical peculiarity, such as Bowlegs, Big Ears, and Crying Boy (for an especially cranky papoose), while others were ceremoniously bestowed later in life after some unusual exploit: Save the Others, Stumped His Toe, and Gal Catcher. For instance, a great Sioux chief, known as a boy as Jumping Badger, became Four Horns after deftly hunting a buffalo bull, and then Sitting Bull when he sat at councils as chief. Many Indian names originated in dreams and visions, which helps explain their rich unconscious language—for women, Under You She Goes to War, She Tries But Can't, Woman They Fall Downward, She Stretches It Out, Several Going Inside, and She Droops; for men, Bear with a Big Voice, Angry He Pounds with Stick, Burrs in His Tail, and Trotting Wolf.

There are a few anemic echoes of Indian names in our own culture, such as Dawn and Pearl and Violet. But if nicknames are metaphors, what is being described? In part, the nickname you give your partner calls attention to something about him. Can the same be said of the parent who decides to call her baby Hope or Faith? Nicknames often reveal as much about the namer as they do about the name. They also may not be so much a metaphor for you or your partner as for the relationship. One of the functions of a nickname is a kind of advance guard, probing the nature of your relationship. They are tentative definitions of who each of you are and how you will relate:

> "Early in our relationship I began calling Bob Roberto. He seemed to like it, so I started getting used to it. Although Bob is Canadian, I like to think of him as a Latin lover type.
>
> "Then, one time he left a note for me and signed it

*Bobby B (Barnes is his last name). When I asked him
about it, he said 'That's my nickname.' I protested,
saying that I thought he was Roberto. I felt a little
hurt and also jealous, wondering if this were some
name an old girl friend had dreamed up. Well, it
turned out this was his grandmother's name for him
when he was a kid. She was kind of a surrogate
mother to him since his own mother was sick a lot."*

Like dreams, nicknames usually have more than one
meaning. In psychoanalytic terms, they are condensations,
the mechanism by which several unconscious wishes or
impulses are combined into a single image. If you can decipher their meaning, you may learn quite a bit about your
own culture of two. In the examples that follow, you may
recognize some similarities to your relationship. But bear
in mind that there is no universal meaning for any symbol
or nickname. The images and memories that you associate
with your own nicknames are the ones that have the most
meaning for you.

Partners as Inkblots

"We see through a glass darkly," our perceptions shaped
by our inner hopes and fears. Hermann Rorschach's inkblot test is based on this simple fact—that any person presented with ambiguous stimuli will organize them into
images that mirror their own inner world. A psychoanalytic
interpretation of Rorschach percepts will often reveal
shadows and footprints of powerful instinctual drives, as
well as the defensive formations that keep them from running amok. Whatever else your partner may appear to be,
he or she is a walking inkblot who can inspire all manner
of instinctual cravings. For example, one of the most popular things to call your loved one is a type of food. There are
Lambchop and Sugarlump, Honey and Scooterpie. Baked

goods are popular and anything that's sweet, but peas and beans are fine (Sweetpea, Peapod, Garbanzo Man) and many types of fruit (Peaches, Pineapple, Pippin, Sugarplum). You would think that lovers, like armies, travel on their stomachs. No class of food or recipe is left untasted by romantics who are never happier than when they can, metaphorically, eat their mates:

Lemon Drop	Chow Mein
Strawberry	Cinnamon
Applefritter	Buckwheat
Pickles	Mutton Chop
Sweet Potato	T-bone
Amaretto	Sugar Lump
Ms. Donut	Animal Cracker
Gumdrop	Pop'n Fresh
Poppin Dough	Bean Fluff
Noodle	Jell-O Pudding
Cookie Monster	Little Cabbage
Jellybean	French Fry
Muttonhead	Yumyum
Dishdelish	Cheesecake
Marshmallow	Peachplum
Buttery	Stolichnaya
Pie	Georgia Peach
Sherbet	Banana
Nachoman	Little Enchilada
Meatball	Grits
Pamplemousse	Shortcake
Apple Dumpling	Beets
Clam Chowder	Soybean
Fruit	Ginger
Pretzel	Gingerbread Man
Dumpling	Honeypuff
Cookie Crumble	Wiener Roast
Cupcake	Cornflake

Chocolate Lady
Popsicle
Ju-Ju Drops
Coconut
Truffles
Peanut Butter

Gorgeous Fritter
Lemon
Kiwi Fruit
Miss Lollipop
Currant

Freud would also see in nicknames much evidence for desires of an anal sort. There are Taterbutt, Big Rear, Cheeks, Round Cheeks, Puffy Cheeks, Snugglebutt, Fuzzybutt, Fartlebutt, and just plain Butt. There are Huggerbuns and Snugglebuns, Stinks, and Dirtball, Butterbuttocks, Big Bum, Smelly Bum, Sugarbum, and Furry Bum, Smart Bottom, Bottom, and Wobble-Bottom, and the irrepressible Poopledrawers.

The instinctual elevator also makes stops at all other erogenous zones. Thus, there are Hot lips, Sizzle Lips, Kitten Lips, Strawberry Lips, Lucky Lips, Sugar Lips, Thin Lips, Pussy Lips, Lips, The Lip, and, perhaps, for the kinkily inclined, Sharp Lips. Breasts and genitals inspire names as well—Spike, Honeypot, Luscious Lunchbox, LongJohn, Fanny Trimbush, Labia, Beaver, Bigboobs, and Titmouse. The bedroom inspires all kinds of libidinous monikers: Lustful Loins, Silkstockings, Gentle Lover, Mr. Juicy, Jiggles, Rubstick, McCrack, Miss Quickie, Chocolate Box, Backdoorman, and Bellybutton Blower. We seem to call our mates quite literally according to our desires.

Another common image seen on the Rorschach is any kind of animal. Psychologically, we need animals to carry our excess instinctual desires. That way we can keep our impulses at a distance and on a leash. Perhaps for the same reason, lovers, if they are not food or some sexual body part, become some member of the animal kingdom. Bears and eagles were especially popular with the American Indians, but our own list is a veritable passenger list for Noah's Ark:

Tweety	Owl
Bison	Chubby Dogie
Pelican	Lobster
Leopard Lady	Moosy
Piglet	Puppy
Piggy	Ducks
Turkey Tail	Papillon
Gator	Worm
Crab	Frog
Da Moose	Silver Fox
Praying Mantis	Bunny
Chickie	Moose
Love Rhino	Chicken
Gorilla	Red Fox
Goat Lady	Sandpiper
Fox	Tiger
Pekinese	Turtle
Bambi	Pooch
Reptile	Owl Baby
Turkey	Little Prairie Dog
Hornet Toad	Doodle Bug
Penguin Pal	Rabbit
Pup	Fish
Cougar	Little Beagle Face
Bulldog	Baby Snake
Fishman	Horse
Lamb	Squirrel
Mouse	Pig
Mothman	Little Pink Elephant
Newt	Kitten
Chipmunk	Beetle
Lamb Lover	Pup
Beached Whale	Aardvark
Roo	Porpoise
Armadillo	Flamingo
Pterodactyl	Bald Eagle
Anteater	Cuckoo

Peacock	Kingfisher
Badger	Condor
Dragonfly	Hamster Girl

Fuzzy Wuzzy Revisited

Although pussycats, pigs, dormice, toads, rabbits, and rats have their devotees, the most popular animal in an intimate role is, by far, the bear:

Bearsy	Panda
Jambear	Grizzly
Pandabear	Poohbear
Buddhabear	Honbear
Dillydogie Bear	T-Bear
Booboo Bear	Tigger
Jellobear	Saffron Bear
Teddybear	Yogibear
Paddington	Snugglebear
Sugarbear	Little Bear
Boobear	Big Bear
Poodlebear	Huggybear
Little Brown Bear	Personal Bear
Puggybear	Toozbear
Polarbear	Naughtical Bear

One of the most universal functions of nicknames is to express warm and cuddly feelings. We are not so much dealing with Freud's erogenous zones as the kind of love a child has for his teddy bear. That worn-out stuffed animal with one button eye missing was so hard to part with because it was a stand-in when Mom wasn't around—our first baby-sitter.

It's no accident that "baby" is one of the commonest endearments. Many nicknames are throwbacks to our childhood, when language was a toy, and babbling and nonsense words were our way of communicating with loved ones. Thus, many couples' nicknames sound like baby talk, too. There are cozy, cuddly names: Cuddle Bumps, Snugums, Huggies, Huglette, Snuggle Bunny, Cuddles, Snuggleton, Snuggle Bunny Boop, Snuggle-ugams, and Snuggleupagus. There are rhyming names: Rooster Pooster, Goosey Poosey, Honey Bunny, Nitterpitter, Chickywicky, Razzmatazz, Pookielookie, Honey Bunny, Scoobiedoo, and Sweety Petey. One couple had his and her rhymes: Snooterbalooter and Noserbegoser. Babbling lovers are fond of assonance (FaceAche, Wattle Bottle, Big Popperwacker), and especially alliteration: Big Bopper, Chunky Chick, Dimple Dopper, Lovable Lump, Noodle Nose, Desert Dweller, and Warm Worm. Lest anyone think their own infantile names an aberration, you have a lot of company in the crib:

Dimples	Baby
Beeper	Baboo
Wuzzy	Boobie
Poopers	Buggy Poopoo
Snookie-pie	Pooder-pie
Pinkydinks	Tootie
Mamoo	Sweetieskins
Pooky	Boodiehead
Buggle	Weetums
Pookie	Poohkins
Biparoo	Wooly Punkeen
Thunda Piepie	Tinkerbell
Babycakes	Wabbit
Babe	Munchkin
Sweetsie	Tee-wee
Sweetypie	Boo
Dooties	Tootie
Tootsie	Toddles
Weezie	Toots
Wiffin	Hubbin

Beanerootie	Binx
Zizzie	Marky-moo
Babyness	Bobkins
Snowflake	Babyhead
Meansie	Bubs
Bubbles	Bootie
Wascally Wabbit	Booper
Bubu	Kissikins
Googsie	Snookie
Puddies	Smoot
Snoozie	Snukums
Squirky	Kittypoo
Pookie	Doobie
Boobalou	Doogie

Yet another way that nicknames evoke childhood is by emphasizing littleness. Your partner might be Peanut, Shorty, Halfpint, Squirt, Shrimp, Dwarf, Teeny Tiny, Pee-wee, or Itsy Bitsy. No matter what you call your partner, it seems that as long as you make it small, it's endearing; hence, Little Itch, Little Learner, Little Torment. On the other hand, your partner might be something huge, such as Big Un, Tank, Tree, or Hulk. The intent is to make yourself feel small *by comparison*. In fact, many couples have nickname pairs that emphasize size discrepancy, such as Rodent and Hippo, or Big Fat Ape and Wisp, as if one were big and grown up and the other very little.

Fables

Nicknames, like the burrow through which Alice fell into Wonderland, provide access to the magical world of childhood fantasy. For example, one of the most ubiquitous nicknames is some character from *Winnie the Pooh*—Tigger, Piglet, and Poohbear. Toads also get a lot of play, and there are other blatant plagiarisms, such as Goldilocks, Sleeping Beauty, Peter Pan, and Prince Charming. Sometimes people make up their own children's story characters: Tufty Fluffytail, Mooey Monster, Rainbow Rabbit, Untidy Idle Flop Ears, and Carrot Cruncher.

In some couples the wish is not so much to evoke childhood as to mythologize your partner or the relationship. You are no longer Melvin and Beatrice Goldstein but Antony and Cleopatra, Portia and Brutus, or Delilah and Samson. I suppose if Roy Fitzgerald can change his name to Rock Hudson and Doris von Kappelhof to Doris Day, why can't anyone else transcend mediocrity by wishing upon a star?

But once having cut your tethers to reality, there's no telling where your fantasy balloon may take you. All sorts of strange hybrid names occur: Red Beret Limpet, Santapaws, Thunder Pumpkin, and Chimpanzee Chop. You don't have to be a psychologist to realize that lovers utterly lose their marbles. But if you're lucky enough to be "Mr. and Mrs. Happy" or "Neanderthal Woman and Earth Mover," you won't really care that you're not with the program.

Twinning

Like animals in Noah's Ark, nicknames frequently come in pairs, such as Big Boy and Big Girl, Penguin and Penguina. Sometimes they have the same name, which is less often due to a lack of imagination than to a couple's wish for togetherness. As we described before:

> *Michael and Ann are avid skiers. Much of their free time is spent cross-country skiing, and on weekends they often make the trip north to go downhill skiing. Neither one can remember when they first used their shared nickname, but they are sure it must have occurred while on a ski trip. They spend a lot of time in their cabin wrapped up in blankets sitting in front of a warm fire. They often wrap themselves to-*

gether in one big blanket and talk or just watch the fire. At some point one of them began using the expression "snug as a bug in a rug" for the warm feeling of closeness they had on these occasions. From this expression came their shared nickname, "Bug." For Michael and Ann, "Bug" now represents the feeling of a private, special world they share whenever they are alone.

It's as if couples are trying to become emotional twins, their nicknames an umbilical cord that joins their inner worlds:

Pussycat and Meow
Redman and Redwoman
Honeydew and Melonhead
Wifeypoo and Hubbybin
Snoog and Snooger
Gnootz and Wootz
Pooter and Pooterette
Chocolate Chip and Brown Sugar
Dr. Snooz and Ms. Snooz
Poop and Boop
RugalachFace and Homentaschen
Unicorn and Phoenix
Pinkie and Binky
PizzaBoy and PizzaGirl
Binky #1 and #2
Sheepwoman and Midnight Shepherd
Duck and Duckette
Green Hippo and Blue Hippo
Slob and Slobbit
Banjoman and Ms. Rock'n'Roll
Boxer Shorts and Lacey Tights
Printout and Abacus
Coochicoo and Boogdoo
Running Wet Clothed and Chief Passing Cloud

Schmucker and Schmuckette
Superman and Superperson
Fungus and Mildew
Russian Princess and The Czar
LoveBags and ScruffBags
Plastic Chicken and Rubber Duck

Angels and Witches

Some endearments are starry-eyed idealizations. Ludwig van Beethoven addressed his letters to Giulietta Guicciardi "My angel, my all, my very self" and "My immortal beloved," and Theodore Roosevelt called his first wife "my bewitching moonbeam." Modern-day equivalents include Precious, Hunk, Angelface, Champ, Apollo, Lancelot, Buddha, and Bronze God. Admiring lovers are also free with royal titles: Prince, Serbian Princess, Aztec Priestess, Duke, and Queenie. One couple kept a certain sense of humor about their royal pedigree, calling each other Princess Stinkweed and Prince Hornytoad.

A step down from such encomiums are nicknames that pay tribute to a realistic physical or psychological attribute of your mate: Erotic Dynamo, Beautiful Legs, Ms. Goodbody, Hot Stuff, Sweet Knees, Muscles, or Thunderthighs, and, most likely coined by a bargain lover, Durable Woman.

Some nicknames merely acknowledge an attribute without implied praise or criticism: Texas Girl, Brown Eyes, Curlygirly, Orangutan Arms, LongLegs, Glitzy, and Shy Guy. One couple called each other Fluff Head and Forest Face, references to her perm and his full beard. Yet a step further removed from the company of angels and dukes are nicknames that call attention to undesirable traits: Bones, Rough One, Red Neck, Mousey, Teeth Grinder, Pinhead, Lumpy, Scruffy, Runny Nose, and Giraffe Breath. Much of the time such nicknames are good-natured ways of kidding your mate. For example, Chekhov, throughout his relationship with Olga Knipper, called her "Knippschütz." The nickname derived from the Russian equivalent of German opera titles such as *Der Freischütz* and *Der Wildschütz* and was a humorous reference to her German origins. Ethnic nicknames are still popular, such as Italian Stallion and Matzoh Maiden. But such kidding about each other's attributes, ethnic or otherwise, requires a sensitivity to your mate's attitude toward themselves:

> *Carl has never really been fat but he has to struggle sometimes to keep his weight down. His wife, Penny, describes her understanding of her name for him: Fatboy.*
>
> *"During one of our vacations when Carl was talking about his need to go on a diet but actually eating up a storm, I created this mythical character called Fatboy. I like to sketch on our vacations, and this time I did some humorous caricatures of Fatboy. In one of them, Fatboy was admiring himself in a mirror, in another he was balancing on a tightrope, and in a third he was 'Fatboy the Windsurfer.' In addition to the sketches, I'd kid Carl sometimes by saying, 'So, what would Fatboy like to have to eat today?' I'd say it as if I was eager to find out what Fatboy's next exploit would be. I think the name both recognized the fact that Carl has a weight problem that he wants to do something about, but also it gratified his wish to eat anything and everything, at least in fantasy. The name wouldn't have worked if Carl felt I really was pushing him to diet. I care because he cares about his weight, but I'm not invested in him being any different than he is."*

Sometimes nicknames are convenient outlets for irritation with your mate, as when Napoleon reproached Josephine for not writing to him, "You're a naughty, gawky, foolish Cinderella." Such is the fate of all idealizations when gilded coaches turn into pumpkins. Idealization and insult can alternate, depending on mood and how you're getting along:

> "Most of the time I'm the Sugar Plum Fairy. Jim will call me that when I've baked something nice for him or surprised him with some other treat. But when he's annoyed with me, I'll change into the Sugar Bum Fairy. He's usually Diamond Jim, but when he's acting or looking raunchy, I'll call him Moldy Oldy."

Some nicknames display their double-edged nature for all to see: Icky Friend, Lamb Shark, Attila the Honey, and Sweetie Dunce, while others are more subtle: Antique, Slow Hands, and OpusFace (as in "Your face is a work of art" or "O pus face"). President Warren Harding called his wife "Duchess," perhaps a compliment to her breeding but also a commentary on her domineering nature.

Some couples don't seem to mind much what they're called, as long as it's humorous or shows some creativity:

Evershrew	Ugly Baby
Dumbo	Joker
Goofball	Balderdash
Camelspit	Goof
Dirtball	Mrs. Dopey
Creepo	Bimbo
Bozo	Ratbag
Goon	Little Retarded Polish Boy
Sneaky	Mess
Battle Ax	Fishface
Stooge	Tramp
Rat Features	Old Hag
Face Monster	Beriberi
Big Oaf	Toadface
Nerdman	Bamboohead

Trojan Horse   Dummy
Nebbish   Yodaface

I'm reminded of Cyrano de Bergerac's speech, after someone has insulted his prominent nose:

You are too simple. Why, you might have said—
Oh, a great many things! *Mon dieu*, why waste
Your opportunity? For example, thus:
Aggressive: I, sir, if that nose were mine,
I'd have it amputated—on the spot!
Friendly: How do you drink with such a nose?
You ought to have a cup made specially.
Descriptive: 'Tis a rock—a crag—a cape—
A cape? say rather, a peninsula!
Inquisitive: What is that receptacle—
A razor-case or a portfolio?
Kindly: Ah, do you love the little birds
So much that when they come and sing to you,
You give them this to perch on? *Insolent:*
Sir, when you smoke the neighbors must suppose
Your chimney is on fire. *Cautious:* Take care—
A weight like that might make you topheavy.
Thoughtful: Somebody fetch my parasol—
Those delicate colors fade so in the sun!
Pedantic: Does not Aristophanes
Mention a mythologic monster called
Hippochampelepantocamelos?
Surely we have here the original!
Familiar: Well, old torchlight! Hang your hat
Over that chandelier—it hurts my eyes.
Eloquent: When it blows, the typhoon howls,
And the clouds darken. *Dramatic:* When it bleeds
The Red Sea! *Enterprising:* What a sign
For some perfumer! *Lyric:* Hark—the horn
Of Roland calls to summon Charlemagne!

Simple: When do they unveil the monument?
Respectful: Sir, I recognize in you
A man of parts, a man of prominence
Rustic: Hey? What? Call that a nose? Na na—
I be no fool like what you think I be—
That there's a blue cucumber!

In other words, if you're going to insult me, at least do it with style. Nicknames can be demeaning, and at times you need to take a hard look at whether your fun has turned into meanness:

> *For many years, one man had referred to his wife as Little Lady, in part an allusion to her small stature. But after she got her medical degree she became Dr. Jill, which increasingly began to irritate her, especially when he did it sarcastically or in front of their friends. Finally she confronted him on how put down she felt by these names. It was only after he could recognize his own insecurity about her career success that he could see her point of view.*

One of the morals here is that a nickname that may suit both partners' needs at one stage of the relationship may no longer fit comfortably as people change. Nicknames help define a relationship, and as it changes so must nicknames. Although it may be painful, you'll have to relinquish a cherished nickname at times or at least allow room for others. For instance, it's okay to be childlike some of the time, but you need to support each other's maturity as well. There's a Yiddish story that captures this best:

> A Jewish mother sent her son off to his first day in school with the customary pride and precautionary advice: "So, *bubeleh,* you'll be a good boy and obey the teacher? And you won't make noise, *bubeleh,*

and you'll be very polite and play with the other children. And when it's time to come home, you'll button up warm, and you won't catch cold, *bubeleh*, and you'll be careful crossing the street and come right home."

Off went the little boy.

When he returned that afternoon, his mother hugged him and kissed him and exclaimed, "So did you like school, *bubeleh*? You've made new friends? You *learned* something?"

"Yeah," said the boy. "I learned that my name is Irving."[33]

Blueblobs and Elephant Washers

In my search for couples' nicknames I sometimes feel like a beachcomber, watching for treasures tossed up on the shore. Most of the time there's nothing too remarkable— Honey and Bear and so on—but every so often something really odd shows up that fills me with wonderment. Trouser Worm and Tiny Sword are certainly evocative but hardly conducive to passion. What does it mean if you call your mate Blueblob or Elephant Washer: does Floor Tile love Sputnik any less than when he was named Pig Squeeze and will Butter Duck and Mr. Hooh-hah live happily ever after? I'm not sure that when Juliet said that a rose could be "any other name" that she reckoned on this. It may be that it's not what you say but how you say it, and while you or I might not appreciate being called Ugly Baby or Meat, who are we to judge?

American Indian names sometimes arose from some circumstance that stuck in the mother's mind at the child's birth, such as Mist on the River, Pale Moon, Owl Overhead, and the probably ill-starred Kettle Fallingover. Love names are now a kind of rechristening that can befall you as an adult if your partner is impressed with some event. I

have interviewed enough couples to learn that every nickname has a story:

*"It may sound awful, but one of John's nicknames
is Shithead. Naturally, I don't use it in public. I'm a
natural optimist—John kids me that I should have
been a cheerleader. But he's the kind of person who
if his glass were half-full he would think of it as
being half-empty. Anyway, here's how I remember
the name starting. He had had a streak of real bad
luck recently and was strolling peacefully with me
around the Illinois campus telling me about his mis-
fortunes. Just as we were passing beneath some
maple trees, a bird dropping fell upon his head.*

*"Thereafter, I would call him Shithead, especially
at times when he has or thinks he has been a victim
of some bad luck. It's always affectionate and teasing. I never do it when I'm really angry at him, only
when I'm a little exasperated perhaps."*

*Ramon and Elena are both college professors who
originally came from Brazil. They are a handsome
couple—Elena a petite, dark-haired beauty, Ramon
dark and aristocratic-looking.*

*"You might have thought that my names for Elena
would all be Portuguese and romantic," laughed
Ramon. "We both have endearments like that. But I
also sometimes call her Mrs. T., after the TV star,
Mr. T. It comes from a time when Elena was very ill
and needed to have a pulmonary angiogram. To do
this, they pass something up an artery in your groin
and they had to shave her pubic hair somewhat. We
were both feeling very tense before the procedure,
when she playfully said, 'Look, see what they do to
me!' I looked and her partly shaved pubic hair reminded me of a Mohawk-style haircut. I called her*

> *Mrs. T., and we both laughed. She insisted I buy her*
> *some gold chains if she was to live up to the name. I*
> *did, and she has."*

It frustrates me that Valentine's Day ads' anonymity
guarantee that I will never learn what some of these names
really mean. Greek Angel Bunny may seem confusing, but
if we knew Sally (or Jim?) like someone knows Sally, we
might realize how perfect a name it really is. It's not too
difficult to imagine how the couple Toe Crusher and Nine
Toes must have arisen, and Neck Ache and Back Ache as
well as Odd Socks seem clear-cut. But what about Window
Woman? Is this an exhibitionist, a comment on a lover's
pedestrian vocation, or merely the namer's perverse pen-
chant for alliteration? I lie awake at night sometimes wondering who Sheep Woman and Midnight Shepherd really
are and whether they live in Wyoming or Greenwich Village. Perhaps, some things are better not to know.

The magic of the culture of two is a spell cast in fragile
secrecy. Like seductive dress, romantic valentines reveal
only enough to make you curious about what they conceal.
As Georg Simmel has observed:

> The secret offers, so to speak, the possibility of a
> second world alongside the manifest world. . . .
> Human collective life requires a certain measure of
> secrecy which merely changes its topics: while leav-
> ing one of them, social life seizes upon another and
> in this alternation it preserves an unchanged quantity
> of secrecy.[34]

So it is that the most important feature of nicknames is
not their specific content but that they enclose an enigmatic, private meaning.

As couples age together, mystery may recede in importance, and companionship and loyalty become what matter
most in their culture of two. I remember well one elderly

couple, whom I interviewed one blustery winter's day as we sat drinking tea before a fire. They had been married for more than forty years and, though they had been through rough times and readjustments, they still enjoyed each other. At one point, the wife turned to her husband and asked, "Why don't you put another log on the scuttle, Old Shoe." I sensed a lifetime of respect in that name, and, humble as it was, I'm sure her husband would exchange it for no other. The nickname, like their relationship, had been grown into, had become well worn, but had served them both well. It's a good reminder that if your own favorite pet names are homely or more pedestrian than the exotica described here, you need not have an inferiority complex. Let others whisper in the night, "O Vortex, O Knockerberries, O my Bermuda Triangle!" "Darling," said with feeling, is more than good enough.

CHAPTER NINE

Play and Parenting

Whatever else children may mean to a couple, they represent hope. While they provide no guarantee of a secure future, they stand on the horizon of the relationship, drawing our sights toward tomorrows that may be. Our fond wish is that they will balance the scale weighted down with our past. But if more prospective parents read the professional literature on the relation of having children to marital satisfaction, we would soon be headed for negative population growth. Most studies have shown that becoming a parent is typically associated with a decline in happiness. For those who seek to repair their marriage by having children or who romanticize the effect of having little bundles of joy plopped into their cozy twosome, reality can be a harsh discovery.

Fortunately for the future youth of America, nobody reads the professional literature. Practically everyone wants kids, perhaps not as many as they used to, which may suggest that people learn more from experience than in the past. Those who can't have them will take fertility drugs, undergo *in vitro* fertilization, artificial insemination, induce sisters and friends to have one to give to them, and go to the ends of the earth to adopt one. Those who have them are as nervous as the owners of the Hope diamond, in constant fear of having them snatched away.

The heartache of involuntary childlessness is real, and I would not want to make light of it. But the perils of parent-

296

hood are often underestimated. A child represents the nearest extent to which the two of you can become one, yet he can also separate you. Many couples find that they become absorbed less in each other and increasingly in caretaking, and that intimacy with each other dwindles to stolen moments. This trend is not inevitable, but if there were ever a time that couples need to cultivate playfulness, it is when becoming and being parents. Strictly speaking, much of the play described in this chapter is different from the "intimate play" that adults create in their private relationship. But just as play can enhance a couple's intimacy, so can it make for good family relationships.

The Transition to Parenthood

The decision to have children is unlike any other decision people have made before, in part because, unlike with purchasing a car that may turn out to be a lemon or marrying someone who, you may discover, hates poetry, kids are relatively permanent. They give new meaning to the notion of commitment. I think this no-return policy that nature has decreed and society reinforces accounts for the need of parents to mold their kids in their own image (even when they don't like their own image); it helps explain why parenthood is so difficult and sheds light on the tragedy of child abuse. For better or worse, you and your kids are stuck with each other—some make the best of it, some the worst. But can anyone be prepared for it?

I'm reminded of two stories. The first involves my sister, a mother of three children. I was asking her what made her decide to have children and how she felt about it. She had been talking about various problems with them, and my question made her stop and think. "I don't know if I can really explain it," she said. "It's sort of the ultimate ambivalent experience."

The second story comes from one of my friends:

"My mother and I have always had a hard time with each other. I'm an only child and I suppose my mother never knew how to relate to me. She certainly tries hard, but she invariably winds up making me angry. It's definitely a love-hate sort of relationship.

"We were having a talk about having children. At the time I wasn't involved with a man, and I said that I didn't think I ever wanted to have kids. My mother said she hoped that someday I would.

" 'Why?' I challenged her, 'So I'll know how wonderful it is after all to be a mother?' (I was really sarcastic.)

" 'No,' she said.

" 'Oh, so I'll know how hard it is to be a parent?'

" 'No,' she said.

" 'Well why?'

" 'Just so you'll know.' "

These two stories say a lot about why people become parents as well as why it's not something that you can ever really be prepared for. In many ways, parenting is a unique experience. Despite this, it is still possible for people to have a more realistic sense of what is involved. Through play you can anticipate what lies ahead:

One husband wanted to have children, while his wife felt it would not be a good idea because of the commitment of both to their careers. In order to make her point in the face of his insistence, she dubbed a small children's teddy bear "baby" and began to refer to the baby's needs. In the middle of a romantic, candlelit dinner at home, she would say, "Baby's crying and needs to be fed. I have to go." When they were about to go out to a movie she said, "You have to find a baby-sitter first." And when they were going away for a weekend skiing holiday, she asked, "Will we bring baby, or should we leave him

*with someone for the weekend?" Gradually, faced
with the practical aspects of child rearing, her
partner began to appreciate that their lives were not
at an appropriate stage for having children and that
he was, in fact, ambivalent about having a child.*

There are other playful ways of "rehearsing" for parenthood. In another couple, one man gave his partner a sub-
scription to a parents' magazine. Each month an issue
would arrive. At times the articles were informative or
touched off a discussion between them. Sometimes the
magazine went unread. But its periodic return helped this
couple continue to talk about the real issues involved in
having a child.

Another couple tried a different approach:

*Barbara and Allen were unsure about whether or
not they really wanted to have children. "Both of us
were the youngest child in our families," says Barbara, "so we had no experience of helping to raise
younger brothers and sisters. We had no idea of what
was involved." Since both Barbara and Allen had
careers, they realized that they couldn't afford to be
unrealistic about the impact children would have.*

*"We bought every book you could buy on the sub-
ject," says Allen. "I'm an academic, so when I'm
anxious about something I try to read about it as
much as I can. But Barbara pointed out to me that
this wasn't sufficient. We needed 'hands on' experience."*

*When their best friends had a baby, they seized
upon the opportunity. "We knew they were reluctant
to leave their baby with a stranger, so we volunteered our services." Their friends were delighted
with the idea, and for six months Barbara and Allen
baby-sat most Friday nights.*

"It was a terrific idea for them and for us," says

Barbara. "We learned how to change diapers, mix formula, and even gave the baby a bath. At times we found it exhausting and on the way home we'd say, 'Thank God we're only the baby-sitters!' But then we got really hooked and didn't want to leave at the end of the evening. Even Allen, who had been afraid he wouldn't like babies, found that he was less concerned about the hard work involved."

At the end of six months, Barbara was pregnant and they were looking forward to their first child.

Even if you've decided you want a child, it isn't always easy for many couples. Older couples, who have waited till their thirties or even forties to have their first child, often find that while the spirit might still be willing, getting pregnant isn't quite so automatic as it might have been when they were younger. The more protracted the period of trying, the more tensions can develop, which can overshadow your sex life.

"When we decided to have a baby we thought it would be something that would just happen right away. We had been so used to using contraception. Without it, we felt unprotected, vulnerable. As time went on and Ginny still was not pregnant, we became more aware of her time of ovulation and making sure we had sex at the 'right' times. Sex became less fun and spontaneous and more of an obligation.

"It helped us to joke about our 'mandatory sexual encounters.' We also would joke about having to be 'in training'—eating virility- and fertility-promoting food, pumping iron, and so on. In order to hold onto a sense of sex as play we made sure that we also had what we called recreational sex. We didn't exactly use contraception but we made no concessions to procreation. We had oral sex and anal sex and fon-

dling each other—all the stuff we used to do when
we *didn't* want to get *pregnant."*

Pregnancy brings other new concerns. For many women
there is a fear of losing their attractiveness:

> *"Being slim and attractive has always been an im-*
> *portant part of my identity," says Allison. "I had a*
> *lot of fears about the weight one puts on during*
> *pregnancy and how I would feel about myself." Her*
> *partner, Rick, was sensitive to this and tried to reas-*
> *sure her as her profile grew. "He used a lot of corny*
> *language like 'bearing fruit,' and 'the glow of preg-*
> *nancy,' but I was feeling very sentimental and lapped*
> *it up."*
>
> *Rick does photography and very early in the preg-*
> *nancy began taking photographs of Allison in the*
> *nude, which also helped celebrate her growing pro-*
> *file. "We had done a series of nude photographs at*
> *the beach the summer before, so I had gotten quite*
> *comfortable in front of the camera," says Allison.*
> *"Rick decided to take pictures of me once a month. I*
> *now have a whole album showing my body changing.*
> *They're not exactly the kind of pictures my mother*
> *has in her family album! But what helped me feel*
> *good about them was that Rick said I was taking on a*
> *new kind of beauty. My favorite is one toward the end*
> *of pregnancy. I'm sitting in a Buddha-like position*
> *with this enormous belly and huge engorged breasts.*
> *I look the picture of contentment. Rick's attention to*
> *taking the pictures, developing them, and printing*
> *them really made me feel appreciated and helped me*
> *feel good about myself throughout my pregnancy."*

Becoming a parent requires that each of you take on new
roles and be able to support each other in unaccustomed

ways. You will often have to feel your way into what is right for you, and playful flexibility will serve you better than traditionally defined guidelines.

When Ellen became pregnant, she decided she wanted to have her baby by natural childbirth. Her husband, John, balked and said there was "no way he could go through it" with her. John has always had a low tolerance for pain and the sight of blood, and felt he couldn't coach Ellen through labor.

Ellen was worried that John's reluctance was part of a larger issue having to do with things he didn't want to do as a father. On the one hand, she wanted to have him with her during her labor. On the other, she didn't want him to feel trapped. Ellen discussed her dilemma with a number of her friends, one of whom volunteered to be her coach if John couldn't do it.

Ellen and John had several lengthy discussions about the problem, and she became convinced that he simply couldn't do it. She also didn't want him to feel shut out by having her best girl friend be her coach. So she named her friend her "hospital coach," and her husband her "home coach." This gave him a clear-cut role to support her around the house with all her needs as the pregnancy progressed. For instance, in the early weeks, when she was nauseous a lot, she asked John to prepare all the food and wash up after, so she wouldn't have to smell it any more than she had to.

The two coaches' solution allowed both partners to feel John was part of the pregnancy without his having to be present for the delivery.

No matter how much you rehearse for becoming a parent, your life suddenly changes. Whatever schedule you had before must bend to accommodate the unscheduled needs of a baby.

> *Sharon and Willard are both physicians. They waited until after they had both finished their long training before starting a family. When they brought their first baby home, having to get up all night to feed and change her reminded them of "being on call" in the hospital. In order to be equitable about the work load, they drew up monthly "call schedules," similar to those they had during internship and residency. "Then we would trade 'on-call' nights if for one reason or another one of us needed to have the night off for a conference or case the next day," says Sharon. "Drawing up a schedule reminded us that although this was a labor of love, it still was work, and we needed to plan ahead and have some flexibility if we were to keep our work lives going."*

No matter how eagerly a couple might anticipate their baby's arrival, it's natural that they will have mixed feelings about the need for so much unselfish devotion. Play can help you express such ambivalence in a way that keeps you and your partner together:

> *When Bob and Cheryl brought their first child, Edward, home, they were surprised by how demanding he was. "It seemed like every waking moment he needed something to be done—either feed him, change his diaper, do his laundry, change the crib linen, soothe him, entertain him. We were pretty good at not resenting it, but it did take us a while to adjust to it."*
>
> *During these early weeks and months Bob and Cheryl found themselves calling the baby Prince Edward. "We weren't aware of it at the time, but I think*

that nickname captured our complex feelings about the situation. We thought of him as very special—hence, the royal title. But we also felt like we were his subjects! We had to be at his beck and call, and when we weren't doing something for him we were usually anticipating his needs."

Another couple, with very similar feelings, coined nicknames for themselves. They would refer to themselves as their daughter's butler and nursemaid.

Some of the couples I interviewed commented that having a baby isn't all work, that in fact, it has helped them become *more* playful:

"Being exhausted sometimes makes us cross but more often makes us nicely loony; all aspects of parenthood seem to do this. Watch us flap our wings and play diaper fairy. Listen to us talk snurfle talk during the four thirty-seven A.M. feeding.

"Realizing that we both adore that baby, approving of each other as parents (more, perhaps, than we previously approved of each other as people), has brought us to a new high of affection, and a new intimacy, hence a new playfulness.

Playful Problem Solving

Anyone watching family sitcoms on television might think that any family problem could be solved by a clever line or outrageous prank. If this were the case, troubled parents would be better served by going to comedian school rather than seeing a psychotherapist. What most kids need is not more clever parents but more human parents—that is, for parents to be open and honest about what they feel, to respect and show interest in their children's feelings, and to be flexible in their approach to solving family conflicts.

Many of the playful strategies illustrated in other chapters may prove useful in family relationships, and there's no need to spell all of them out again. Instead, I'll illustrate a few playful approaches to stimulate your own thinking. Whatever the specific problem being addressed, keep in mind that the content is often less important than the process. At its best, problem solving enhances flexibility, open communication, and family members feeling close to each other while still having their need for privacy respected.

Changing the Context

Many problems with kids can be solved by changing the context, that is, by restructuring their environment. If you don't like what your child is doing, try to think about what needs to be changed in his play space in order for something more constructive to occur.

> "Our six-year-old, Joshua, is a little hyper. Most of the time we can deal with it, but he can get pretty aggravating, especially at dinnertime, when Dick and I really want to have a peaceful dinner.
>
> "We had noticed that Joshua would get easily set off by the hubbub of preparing dinner so we decided to make a rule that a half hour before dinner he had to choose one 'quiet' toy, like drawing or playing with a puzzle. Alternately, he could watch a television program if he wanted to. As a result, our dinner times have become much more relaxing."

Brainstorming

Whenever a problem exists with your child or between you and your child, you may be tempted to impose a solution. Often, you may have a good idea as to what's wrong and what to do about it. But remember you're not running a business in which productivity is the bottom line. There are also no rewards for being right all the time. Each family member needs to be a partner in problem solving, so that kids can feel that their thoughts and feelings are valued, and so that they can develop the confidence to rely on their own resources.

"I grew up in a minister's family, and whenever there was a problem with one of the kids we used to have family round-table discussions. Actually, they weren't discussions so much as lectures. We would be told what we had done wrong and why it was wrong and what we should do instead. It was pretty cut and dried. My parents were good people, but they thought they had all the answers.

"Now that I'm a parent myself, I do some things that my parents did with me, but we don't have round-table discussions. We call it brainstorming. Whenever there's a family problem, my husband and I get together with our kids and throw out ideas. We encourage everyone to participate and to be creative. Sometimes it winds up being funny, and sometimes these ideas lead to a good solution. There are times when as parents we have to make an unpopular decision, but more often we can eventually agree.

Learning about Yourself

A good many people shrink from having children indefinitely. "I'm not ready" is their lament. It's true that, just as with baking a cake, there are some essential ingredients. But some people feel that they have to have mastered all their hang-ups, all their ambivalence about procreation, in order to be "ready." The truth is that few people are already mature adults before they have children; it is in having children that many individuals *become* adults. This growth spurt is not an automatic dividend that comes like a free gift for opening a new account. It's a product of your making use of the opportunities that become available for learning about yourself. As has often been observed, you have to break a few eggs in order to make an omelet.

*When Don's son, Robert, got his driving license,
he began to use the family car for dates on weekends.
This became a sore point because Don was quite
strict, insisting that Robert pay for the gas and
scheduling when Robert could take the car, far in
advance. This tension increased over the course of
the school year and came to a head when summer
began and Robert wanted to use the car more frequently.*

*After one heated argument between father and
son, Don complained to his wife, Marie, about the
situation. She had attempted to stay clear but had felt
that Don was locked into a struggle similar to the
one he had had with his own father. After listening to
Don's concerns, Marie tried to bring this to his attention by a gentle, playful approach. Although she
herself wasn't Jewish, she had learned a few Yiddish
expressions from Don and from Don's family. "You
know," she said, "I think Robert is a chip off the old
block. Do you ever get the feeling that you're being
somewhat of a chozzer?" The Yiddish term chozzer,
which means stingy or unfair, had been Don's way of
referring to his father. Don and Marie had often caricatured his father's penurious, controlling ways in
the past.*

*As Don related, "If she had said I was being
stingy straight out, I'm sure I would have been annoyed. But here was this shiksa talking Yiddish. She
actually pronounced it strangely, like 'hoser,' which
made it all the more funny, but I knew what she
meant."*

Some people in Don's situation might have become
more defensive when their own contribution to a problem
was pointed out to them by their wives. When an insight is
offered without criticism and with an appreciation for how
both father and son share a problem (both "cut from the

same block"), it's less likely to be dismissed. Further, the fact that Don and Marie had already played around the issue of Don's father suggested to Marie that he might be accessible to a playful approach.

There is no fail-safe approach to handling such delicate situations, but play is one more tool that may help you learn about yourself. Just as couples can't help using their partners to reenact old conflicts from their own childhoods, so the shadows of the past fall upon our children. There's a lovely Yiddish word, *mishegoss,* that captures the best spirit in which to approach this. Literally, *mishegoss* means "insanity," but it is less often used to refer to mental illness than as a benevolent label for all sorts of irrational ideas. We are never "ready" enough to spare our own family from our *mishegoss*—the best we can do as parents is to be open to seeing our craziness. The worst sins of parents usually come from a blind reenacting of the past, coupled with an inability to recognize it for what it is. If you can approach your own and your partner's blind spots as so much *mishegoss,* you'll be well on your way to becoming something else Yiddish—a *mensch.*

Tuning In

If adults aren't always in touch with the emotional baggage they're dragging around, we can't expect kids to be always aware of their feelings or what they're really upset about, either. It's not fair to expect them to tell you their concerns straight out; but they are sending you messages all the time, even if the deepest truths are detectable only in fragmentary clues. Theodor Reik, one of Sigmund Freud's disciples, used the phrase "listening with the third ear" to express the free-floating attention necessary to tune in to such indirect, unconscious communication.[35] Not to be confused with the third eye, there's nothing mystical involved here. You don't have to practice yoga, whisper mantras as your kids desecrate the flower bed, or approach anything like an enlightened state. But you do have to be a careful observer and a good listener, and look for metaphors in children's play. Here is how one child expressed her concern about her mom being less available to her.

> After a period when her mother had been in the hospital for a month recovering from surgery, Jane, who was six, began doing some repetitive play. She would take her two "dollies" and put them in a drawer, carefully tucking them in with large amounts of tissue "to keep them safe and warm." They would be placed close together, facing each other. Her other doll play consisted of intense preoccupation with feeding them. She would take some Play-Doh and "prepare" it into food, and there was a lot of ritual involved. If it wasn't done just right, the food was "bad" and had to be thrown away. She would then take the good food and put it up to the dolls' mouths, making a lot of fuss over them, asking them if they had had enough food. If one of her dolls was "bad," however, she would send her to bed without her dinner.
>
> At the same time as Jane began playing like this, her parents noticed that she also began acting much younger: she would suck her thumb, constantly want to sit in her parents' laps, and would often have tantrums when it was time for bed.

You don't have to remain just a passive observer, waiting silently for truths to emerge from the mouths of babes. One way to be active is to help foster the conditions in which your kids can best express themselves. The most expensive toys are not always the most expressive media —some crayons and paper, Play-Doh, toy soldiers, a dollhouse, can be inexpensive yet ideal for fantasy play. The best media depend, of course, on the age of your child.

You don't need a degree in child-play therapy, nor do I

recommend that you try making deep interpretations, such as "You'd really like to kill Daddy so you can sleep with Mommy." Play itself can be healing and restorative. An accepting, encouraging attitude on your part may be enough.

Boundaries

In the same way that couples need to have a protected, private space in which to play, kids need to have a clearly defined, safe, and dependable environment where they have permission to play. I mean this both in a concrete sense—of a good play area—as well as psychologically, in the sense that adults are available but unintrusive, accepting, but also setting limits where appropriate. Kids need freedom within limits, and, if only for their own sanity, parents need to set those limits:

> *"We have a special 'mess' area near the kitchen sink where the kids can fingerpaint or set up an easel or mess around with clay. It makes for easy cleanup and less worry about furniture and rugs getting wrecked. Before we did that we were always having to tell our four-year-old not to do this or that. He really needed a place where he could be messy and we needed for the mess not to be all over the house."*

A good rule of thumb is that it's often preferable to try to shift or contain problematic behavior rather than entirely eliminate it. When a child is repetitively doing something, he usually has a strong need to continue. If your child has a "need" to trip old ladies, limiting the behavior to just once a week won't be satisfactory, but very often a playful limit is helpful. For example, one parent, who was tired of reprimanding her three youngsters for their poor table manners, decided to establish one meal a week that she called "Planet of the Apes." At this one meal everyone could eat with their hands, make grunting and slurping noises, and make a mess. No silverware was provided, and she used a plastic tablecloth and provided them all with large napkins. At other meals, when one of the kids misbehaved, she'd say, "Save that for Planet of the Apes." She quickly found that their table manners improved.

Another example comes from a children's story that I read when I was a kid. The story was about a young boy who was driving his parents crazy because he insisted on collecting tin cans. Initially, when his collection was small, his parents could overlook his idiosyncrasy, but when the cans filled his room and spilled over into the rest of the house, they panicked. The solution came from a relative—a kindly great uncle, I believe—who realized in talking to the boy that he was most attracted to the cans because of their colorful labels. He suggested that instead of collecting cans he merely save their labels so that he could have an even bigger collection. The boy was quite pleased with this arrangement, in part because this man understood and appreciated his hobby. Some time later, the uncle bought him a stamp album, and before long the boy had shifted his devotion from cans to stamps.

Many parents have trouble setting a limit. Quite aside from the fact that kids need to be able to test some limits in order to feel safe and also to help learn about themselves, the couple can't survive without setting them, either. Even when you realistically have to put aside many of your needs to accommodate those of a newborn, you need to take care of yourselves as well. Although free time, sex, and sleep may not be as abundant as in your preparental state, some pleasurable and playful moments must be preserved. It'll get easier as your kids become more self-sufficient, but it is a continual challenge to balance your own needs against theirs.

Like many professional couples with young children, the Flemings are hard-pressed to find time to be alone together. One of them often has to work late, while the other picks up their two children from day care or from the baby-sitter and then starts dinner. Most weekdays it's not until after ten that they can relax and read a book, watch some TV, or just "veg out."

One way this couple has devised to make sure they have a chance to talk to each other is to establish "the eleven o'clock news." Sometimes it's actually at ten, sometimes later, but they try to set aside a half hour to catch up on what's happened during their day. Giving it a name made it seem like a more inviolate time, a ritual that had to be kept or the day wasn't quite complete.

Another couple developed a different playful ritual:

Jonathan and Caroline both have to work at home a lot in the evenings—one has manuscript editing with tight deadlines to meet, the other is an accountant, who, particularly at tax time, is under a lot of pressure. They need a certain amount of peace despite having three pre-teenagers. They accomplished this goal without engendering an oppressive atmosphere by establishing "tiptoe time." After dinner, for two hours everyone has to walk on tiptoes and talk only in whispers.

Playing with Your Child

The nineteenth-century American author and journalist George William Curtis made an observation that may help explain the estrangement between parents and their kids: "It is a great pity that men and women forget that they have been children. Parents are apt to be foreigners to their sons and daughters." Quite simply, some adults forget how to play. Some are too embarrassed to remember—it's okay for kids to play, they say, but I'm too dignified, too busy, too old to get down on the floor and play with dolls or soldiers. Since for young kids play is their primary means of having fun and of relating to others, parents can't expect to meet them on other terms. You can talk the talk, but it won't help if you don't walk the walk. Play is the only native language in this culture. At the risk, then, of reminding some parents of what they already know, here are a few thoughts about playing with your kids. Although facilitating your children's play is different from the intimate play that you do with your adult partner, you may learn some things that can be applied to couples, too.

Follow the Leader

One way of trying to relate to kids is the Boy Scout troop leader approach. The parent thinks up and organizes an activity, and the child need merely follow directions. Such initiative is commendable, for kids need stimulation. I remember many a rainy day as a child when I would go to my mother or grandmother and say, "I'm bored. What can I do?" Maybe it was because I was never in the Boy Scouts.

It's also important to let the child be the leader, to follow his or her initiative. This doesn't mean that you have to be passive, but that you tune in first to where the child wants to go:

> *Tom and Karen noticed that their daughter Sally was very responsive to music at a young age. "When she was about a year old we noticed her spontaneously rocking and kind of dancing to music when we played our stereo," says Karen. "In fact, the stereo was one of the few things that would distract her from her other play. She would go and hold onto one*

of the speakers, listen intently, and dance beside it."

Because of the interest Sally was showing in music, Tom and Karen decided to provide her with a number of musical toys. "We bought her everything from a toy piano to a children's cassette tape player. We put a lot of time into choosing things that represented a wide range of music."

Now four years old, Sally continues to show a special interest in music that her parents support. "Who knows where it will go?" says Karen. "Maybe she'll end up a violinist, or maybe she'll be a lab scientist who listens to classical music in her spare time. Whatever, we're enjoying her enjoyment now."

Young kids will usually get into role-playing (doctor, mother, superman) or pretend play using dolls and action figures. With some encouragement, they'll tell you what their fantasy is, and you can join in, adding your own ideas, which the child can accept or discard. Let your imagination go and see what happens.

The only caution to your encouraging and joining in fantasy play is that sometimes kids get scared by things that you or they think up. Monsters that eat everybody up and are out of control need to have limits set on them so kids can feel safe. This doesn't mean that the play has to be stopped, but you might suggest that the monster needs to have a special park where he can live, so he won't hurt anyone, or that he needs to have a friend who can help guard him and other people. Occasionally, parents can also get carried away. For example, one mother started wearing a witch's hat to liven up a fantasy. When her child had a nightmare that evening, she realized that he had really been scared.

One of the keys to following your child's lead is to be *curious* about their inner lives. A Boston psychiatrist, Edward Shapiro, has observed that in troubled families people show a lack of curiosity about each other—they behave as if they already know everything there is to know about each other, and react on the basis of preformed, rigid notions instead of with true empathy. Be curious.

Finding Points of Contact

Parents who just can't get excited about joining their children's fantasy play may need to start with their own interests and see whether any of them could be translated into an activity their child might like. For example, a father who enjoys sports would most naturally start throwing a ball around with his son and could put up a Nerf ball basket in his son's room that they could play with. The trick is to recognize what you do best and see what you can do with it. Thus, while highly intellectual, bookish parents might be uncomfortable with rough and tumble play and hanging loose with their kids, they still have things to offer. The goal is to increase the amount of time you spend playing with your child by matching interests with needs.

> "Our six-year-old, Kenny, has a learning problem," Betty and Ted related. "It took a long time for him to learn his colors and the alphabet, and now he's struggling with math. He's gotten some special help in school, and we've also tried to help him at home. We were told not to put a lot of pressure on him, although we are worried. So we've managed to think up some fun ways for us to interact with him and give him some practice at math.
>
> "We try to use everyday situations. For example, we have a pile of pennies that accumulates from emptying out pockets and change purses. John will sit down with Kenny and ask him to help him put them in piles of ten and help him to count them. I'll try to make arithmetic games out of kitchen tasks like how many pieces of silverware we have, and so on.

*In addition to helping Kenny it has made us more
alert to finding ways to play."*

Another way to try to connect with your child is to get
back in touch with your own childhood playthings by going
to a toy store or museums.

*Going to the toy store together was a way that
Gene and Shirley have found things they and their
eight- and nine-year-old sons could enjoy doing together. There was one toy store that had a large collection of hand-painted toy soldiers, and Gene was
reminded of how much he enjoyed playing with soldiers as a kid. Now he and his kids have a biannual
ritual of going there to buy one for each of them for
their special collection. Gene has set up a woodshop
in the basement and is helping them build a fort.*

*"Sometimes kids get overstimulated in toy stores,"
says Shirley. "They want so many things, and of
course we can't buy them all. So we find other ways
to come up with new ideas. Going to museums has
been great—the Museum of Natural History, the
Science Museum, the Egyptian exhibit. These are
places that Gene and I loved to go as children and
we remember how it was. We're like four kids on an
outing. It's a lot of fun, and the experience carries
over. The kids want to learn about dinosaurs or
mummies, for instance, so we get some books out of
the library and read them together. One time Gene
bought some models of knights in armor, replicas of
the ones we saw at the museum, and we all helped
put them together."*

Making a Special Time

Some of my favorite childhood memories are of my parents reading to me and me to them. I was a New York

Yankee fan in the days of the legendary and unbeatable Mickey Mantle, Yogi Berra, Whitey Ford, and Moose Skowron. At the time, Red Smith was a sportswriter for *The New York Times,* and on summer mornings on Long Island, just after breakfast, my father and I would sit in the backyard under a shady tree next to the raspberry bushes and the lilacs. There I would read the account of the game from the day before, my father helping me with any words I couldn't make out. This is how I learned to read, enjoying baseball and Red Smith's columns with my father, the smell of lilacs in the air. When I was younger, my mother would usually read me a story before I went to sleep— *Curious George, Bartholomew and the Oobleck, How the Rhinoceros Got His Skin.* These were special times, too. Such regularly recurring times alone with a parent were things I could look forward to and count on. All children need such dependable play times, which can be ritualized in many different ways.

> *Robert and Selma have two children, a six-year-old boy and a one-year-old daughter. Soon after their second child was born, their older child began throwing tantrums and was constantly demanding attention. Both parents could sense that he was jealous of the time they were spending with the baby. Selma wanted to be more available to him, but sometimes she just didn't have the time or energy. It also seemed important to get Robert more involved with his son.*
>
> *"Selma suggested that I set aside twenty to thirty minutes every evening to spend only with Kenny,"* says Robert. *"Once he realized that I was serious about doing this, he got real excited. I wasn't sure I could think of enough things we could do, but it hasn't been a problem. We build models and play games and when he gets a bit older I plan to get him a chemistry set. I loved doing that myself as a kid—*

*making rotten-egg smell by heating sulfur—good
stuff like that. I can hardly wait!*

*"We've made a special play shelf in Kenny's room,
where he keeps the toys we play with, such as the
model we're working on. Kenny's stopped throwing
tantrums and, what's more, I'm enjoying him a lot
more."*

The play shelf can be a way of concretizing a commitment to play, a reminder to both parent and child of the
"contract" you've made to be together to play at a dependable time and place. This structure gives a child confidence
that he will have your undivided attention, so he won't
have to demand it constantly or ask for it in ways that are
off-putting.

Creative Play

There's so much more that families can do together than
renting movies for the VCR, playing video games, or
watching television. Leisure time has become a passive experience, and we are the lesser for it. In the days before
television it may be that there was less time for play, but at
least families had to be more actively inventive. On weekend nights they might have held a family reading circle,
passing a book from hand to hand for each to read aloud.
They could have baked bread or cookies or made homemade candy. They might have sat together listening to
radio programs. Without pictures to go with the story, people were left to conjure up images from their own imaginations. Simpler ages may be gone, if they ever existed, but
you can occasionally pretend that televisions and VCRs no
longer exist, without even leaving home.

*"During the blizzard of '78, we had a long stretch
together with not that much to do," says Carl, a father of three young kids. "We were sitting around the*

breakfast table in the kitchen and our nine-year-old, Robbie, was tapping a few of the partly filled glasses with a spoon to see what kind of sound they made. We all thought it sounded kind of good—you could almost make out a tune. Our five-year-old picked up a wooden spoon and tapped out a rhythm on the metal syrup container. So I suggested we put together a band. I remembered that you could make a 'wind' instrument by humming on a comb covered with wax paper, my wife found an old ukulele in the attic, and we gave our three-year-old some bells. After a little while we could do a passable 'Star-Spangled Banner' and 'Rudolph the Red-Nosed Reindeer.' But our 'Jingle Bells' was the hit."

You can make many of the things you need for creative play: the process itself is fun. For example, you can make your own finger paints by mixing one pint of creamy boiled laundry starch to half a cup of soapflakes (not detergent) and adding food coloring. (Alternatively, you can mix together flour, water, soapflakes, and food coloring.) Some families build their own kites and then go on outings on breezy days to fly them. You can make homemade clay by making a smooth paste of one and a half cups of flour and one and a quarter cups of water, then heating two and a half cups of salt in a frying pan and stirring the salt into the paste. Again, you can use food coloring, and after you've made something you can harden it by baking it briefly in a hot oven. Once you've made a head out of clay, you could cover it with papier-mâché and make a puppet's head; old rags can become the puppet's body—and don't forget the puppet show.

Carolyn, who is a secondary-school teacher, tries to use some of the activities at home that she's seen work well in her class at school. "Making collages has been a good family activity," she says. "Every-

one can be involved—either cutting out things from the newspaper or thinking of ideas. We start with a theme, like Halloween or 'my favorite thing' and see what happens. For one of my birthdays, my husband and kids surprised me by presenting me with a collage they had made in secret called 'The Greatest Mom.' Another thing I do at home with my kids that I do at school is making cards, for Valentine's Day or Christmas. I buy a lot of colored papers, sparkles, doilies, and such, and we have fun with it.

"Sometimes I can do things at home that I can't do at school, and that's more fun for me. One time we made life masks, using cold cream and plaster of Paris. A couple of them are still hanging on the wall in the den—we call it our Rogue's Gallery."

Another couple started a project that became a focus of their family play for many years:

When the Bradleys' daughter turned five they decided to give her a special dollhouse. They got the idea while they were up in Vermont on a ski weekend. They found a store that carried kits of all kinds of dollhouses, and they ordered a large Victorian replica. It had gingerbread trimming and a tower and windows with moving panes.

"At first we just bought the basic kit," said Mark. "Our daughter just loved it as it was, but my wife and I had so much fun putting it together that we went back to Vermont to get some additional touches, like a real slate roof and shingles for the side. The next step was to put in electricity and then to fix up the inside—with real wallpaper and flooring.

"It's turned out that the house is never really finished. I've gotten into making little doll furniture and my wife is completing the house decorating. She also makes doll clothes. It's been a wonderful hobby for

both of us and much more fun than fixing up a real house ever was. I hear that you can even get a kit to put in doll house plumbing, but I don't think we'll go that far!"

Some families develop nature hobbies. For example, one couple put up several birdhouses on their property and got their kids interested in studying bird behavior. They often visit Audubon sanctuaries and go on early morning "bird walks" together. There are many variations on this theme, including making an autumn leaf collection, drying flowers, or collecting interesting shells.

"When our family goes to the beach we travel light. Just a few beach chairs, cooler, crossword puzzle, cards, books, and Frisbee. In spite of all this stuff, we invariably go looking for something else— we love to go beachcombing. We take long walks and collect things. Not just pretty shells but odd things. We have categories like ugliest thing on the beach, most valuable, most interesting, and the like. At home we have a large glass jar where we keep some of these treasures."

Your family's latent dramatic talents can be mobilized by informal skits, such as "paper bag theater." This consists of dividing up into teams and providing each side with a few items in a paper bag, out of which you have to devise a skit. For more active play there are families that hold Olympics, in winter time involving snow play, in summer a sack race and egg balancing. Others enjoy a scavenger or treasure hunt, complete with a pirate map the parents have made. Making up clues for treasure hunts can be a lot of fun—one couple used tape-recorded messages in which they spoke in disguised voices intended to sound like ghosts. They also had clues that required looking up a specific passage in a novel, and "invisible writing" made with lemon juice that "magically" appeared when heated.

Many of these ideas are classics that have endured not only because they are fun, but because they enable family members of many different ages to share in different ways, to be creative, and to be intimate.

When Play Isn't Fun

Playing with a seven-year-old, or any child, can sometimes be a drag—such as when he insists on playing Candyland for the twelfth time in a row, or when she seems interested only in endlessly dressing and undressing Barbie in her seven different outfits. Such golden moments may feel like an eternity. Although it's not fun for you to sit through, kids sometimes need such repetitive play. They're trying to master something, whether it's eye-hand coordination in a video game or a psychological issue in repetitive dollhouse play.

Kids, particularly boys, may insist on playing competitive games, and further, may insist on winning. A lot of kids have trouble with losing. A lot of adults also have trouble with losing. Especially with losing to kids. Especially to kids who gloat about it afterward.

All children need to express hostility through their play, but you may not be comfortable with buying war toys or with your son's pointing the toy Rambo machine gun directly at you.

It's times like these that make parenting work. Everyone has to define their own limits and how much play that's not fun they're able to tolerate. But some amount of play that feels like work comes with the territory.

Family Rituals

Just as a couple has its own culture of two, a family evolves its own culture, too—its special connotations of words, its traditions and rituals, its rhythms of intimacy.

Young children, while they are active absorbers of the culture around them—for instance, by learning to talk—also contribute to this family culture. Every family has idiosyncratic words that come from a child's early speech. For example, one family forever called fish "shush," which was their eldest son's best approximation of the word at the age of two. Similarly, his blanket was "my bankalee." In another family, nipples were called "brellies," a word coined by a five-year-old and whose derivations remain obscure. Many of these new words become extinct, just as in any culture's language some terms are born and disappear quickly. But other words persist, a tangible evocation of the family's shared past.

Holiday Traditions

Special occasions, such as birthdays and religious holidays, have rituals prescribed by the ethnic group to which families belong. But families can elaborate and transform such rituals to better serve their needs. They become family traditions, a personalized version of a cultural event, with a unique character. Sharing such special rituals makes people feel that they belong to a group that has its own identity, a cultural counterpart to genetic kinship.

One family makes a Christmas candle each year, made up of the candle stubs saved from birthdays and other celebrations throughout the year. They also use the remnant of the previous year's Christmas candle. The new candle is burned at the dinner table during the Christmas season and at New Year's, and at these times they reminisce about things that have happened during the year.

Another family has a similar ritual of cutting their Christmas tree into pieces sometime after the holiday is over and the wood is very dry. They make a fire in their fireplace, and then each family member places a piece of the old tree in the fire after making a wish. Many families with young children have Santa Claus rituals, but some families add their own distinctive touches:

The Simmons family has a Christmas Room in which their Christmas tree is kept, and which they close off the day before Christmas. On Christmas morning, their four children line up outside the door, where they overhear their father having a "conversation" with Santa Claus, who often brings greetings from their relatives in Europe and California. (These greetings are actually letters written for this purpose by their relatives.)

As years passed and the children grew up, they would kid their father that "Santa Claus's voice sounds a lot like yours," but the tradition was maintained until they were in their teens and revived when they had their own children.

New Year's is another favorite time for rituals. One family has a ritual of "letting the New Year in": a little before midnight the family gathers at home and opens up all the doors and windows. Silent, they stand together for a time.

The Carlton family has a "fortune telling" ritual on New Year's Eve that has been handed down through several family generations. They take pieces of lead, such as small fishing sinkers, and melt them carefully over the stove. They open several windows for good ventilation of any lead fumes. Each family member (the youngest have help to make sure they don't get burned) then casts his fortune by dropping the melted lead into water. The cooled metal assumes all kinds of strange shapes which the family then "reads." There's a lot of playful fantasy and imagination, but some characteristic patterns of lead also have time-honored interpretations—a mossy appearance, for instance, means money.

In some families a seasonal occurrence, such as the winter solstice, is used to devise their own ritual:

"Some people think Maine winters are colder than they are long, others say they're longer than they are cold," says Ron. "Any way you look at it up here, spring can sure seem awful far away, like it's never going to come."

Ron and his family have a ritual for each winter solstice. They get up before dawn and, sleepy-eyed, crunch across the snow to their car. They bring lots of blankets and some thermos bottles of hot cider and coffee. There's a favorite place they drive to—a secluded beach that's part of a peninsula jutting out into the ocean.

"We go out there to welcome the sun when it comes up. Solstice is a turning point, a reminder that spring is coming because the days will be getting longer. That place reminds us of summer days at the beach and of solstices we've shared together. It's also a religious experience—we usually read a psalm or say a prayer—nothing formal, but it makes the occasion all the more meaningful."

Rites of Passage

Families go through many transitions: the couple's relationship changes, grandparents grow infirm and die, and each child passes through developmental stages. Rituals help mark such significant events. They provide psychological punctuation—ways of underlining meaning—so families can recognize their importance and better adapt to the changes they require. Like other cultural rites of passage, family rituals may facilitate transitions.

> *Having their first child had been more difficult for David and Corita than they had ever expected. Corita's first pregnancy had been uneventful until the twentieth week when she had a miscarriage and lost the baby. They had been advised to wait a bit before trying again, but they so wanted a child that they decided that the best thing was to go right ahead. This time, the baby was fine. But in other ways, life was difficult—Corita's father was very ill for a time, and David was under a lot of pressure at work.*
>
> *Shortly after the baby was born, they were lying in bed talking about their new family and David had the idea of tape-recording their conversation so that years later they would remember how they felt. Corita thought it was a great idea and they made a tape describing the events and feelings surrounding the birth, as well as some of their hopes and dreams. They then decided to make a kind of "time capsule" —an envelope made up of the tape, pictures of the baby and the house they lived in, newspaper clippings from the birth day, and a few whimsical things, like a lucky penny. The time capsule was then placed in their bank vault, to be opened by the family when their first child turned eighteen.*

The "time capsule" is a lovely memento to leave to a child. For David and Corita the making of it was also important. At a time when so much was going on in their lives, it helped them focus on the significance of having a child. It was a gift for the future, but it also was a celebration in the present.

Rituals can also help families deal with sad occasions:

"When our youngest child, Lisa, died several January ago, we had a very rough time. The following spring I was out planting an apple tree to replace an old one that had fallen down during a storm and our ten-year-old said, 'This is Lisa's tree.' It happened to be around the time of Lisa's birthday.

"Since then each year at this time the four of us plant another tree. It's a good feeling seeing the trees we've planted flourishing, and somehow I think it's helped us as a family."

With so many couples getting divorced and then remarrying, there are a lot of "second families," with children often feeling mixed loyalties. It is not uncommon, for instance, for there to be children from each of the spouse's previous marriages as well as children that they've had together. Working out these relationships so a new family can be created without ignoring the complex past requires a lot of sensitivity. Family rituals can sometimes assist in this transition.

Both Miriam and Zack were previously married— Miriam's boys are four and eight, while Zack has a seven-year-old daughter and a twelve-year-old son. Each parent had been divorced for about two years before they got married to each other and they have now been together for about a year and a half.

"It hasn't been easy joining two families," says Miriam. "Neither of our ex's had been that involved with the kids, but after Zack and I got together, suddenly they got more involved. I guess they saw it as a threat. The kids feel a lot of pulls, and for a while we went to see a family therapist. We've tried hard not to make them feel bad about spending time with their 'other' parents, but it's hard for us, too, especially at Christmas time when you want to have the family together."

Miriam and Zack suggested that their new family put together a booklet of their favorite family stories —like the time Miriam overcooked the Thanksgiving turkey, and when Zack's kids had built an igloo and they tried to have a picnic. They also put some old photographs and some drawings with the stories.

"It was a way that the kids could get to know each other's 'other side,'" said Zack, "a way of sharing that I think made them feel that the past was something no one had to be ashamed of or hide."

Commemoration

Carla and Allan have a family ritual which has been passed on from one generation to the next in Carla's family: children's clothes are carefully saved and handed down. For example, Carla has a number of antique-lace dresses, which were originally her great-grandmother's. She also has several miniature herringbone suits for little boys. A few pieces of furniture have been included in this tradition—an antique cradle, rocking horse, and four-poster bed.

"When I was an adolescent, I wasn't very much interested in the idea," says Carla. "I remember my mother dividing the stuff up between myself and my sisters and thinking, What will I do with this? But now that I have my own children I'm very into it. Allan and I often go rummaging through antique stores looking for nice things to add to our collection."

All families have photographs, motion pictures, or video recordings of their kids. In some cases, no milestone is left undocumented, no cute moment lost to posterity. This can sometimes prove a mixed blessing. I remember at age five feeling humiliated when guests were shown our family movies, which displayed my unexpurgated one-year-old bottom. More often, however, such mementos are cherished and though they may be dusted off for viewing only infrequently they form an important part of the family culture. One family had a whimsical approach to their photograph collection:

> Even in this age of "idiot-proof" cameras, on which you only have to press one button, and of guaranteed satisfaction printing or your money back, there are still a few klunkers in every roll of film. Aunt Sadie always seems to close her eyes at the critical moment, and your youngest son smirks instead of smiles. The Cooper family is no more photogenic than the average and has had its share of reject photographs. Instead of throwing them away, however, they decided to make another album, which they called the Stroke Book. The title came from the likeness to a stroke that many of these pictures suggested—one had one eye closed, one had a palsied grimace, another's head tilted awkwardly to the side. Looked at from this perspective and assembled in one album, they made for a hilarious collection.

Another family devised a lovely memento made up of another kind of throwaway:

> "I'm a packrat at heart. I rarely throw anything away. My husband kids me about this but he knows I'll never change. One of the things that I wound up collecting over the years are notes from our kitchen table. It started with my holding onto telephone numbers which one of us had written down next to the phone. I'd just stick them in the drawer in case someone needed them later. But it got so I put all our little notes to each other and to the kids in the drawer. Every year or so I'd go through them, and invariably I'd find some that were worth saving—not

*just the phone numbers, you understand. There'd be
memories in those scraps of paper: the small details
of our lives together, like 'Gone on a date with Sally.
Don't wait up' (of course, we did); and times of
worry, like 'visiting Mom in the hospital; dinner's in
the oven.' I put some of them in a scrapbook and
called it Notes from the Kitchen Table."*

What I love about the Stroke Book and Notes from the
Kitchen Table is that they are playful rituals that emerge
from a family's everyday life. They make the ordinary
memorable, intimate, and full of fun. This is what love and
play are basically about—not the extraordinary, but a
unique appreciation for the ordinary. Great novels, more
often than not, are stories about common people as seen
through an uncommon eye. Each family's story, including
your own, is waiting to be told.

CHAPTER TEN

Learning to Play

It's not clear that everyone can learn how to play or even that playfulness is a skill that can be taught. While it isn't as immutable a property as eye color or favorite ice cream flavor, our propensity for play is very much bound up in our personality. Nurture has played a role in its development as much as or more than nature, but by the time we're supposed to have become adults, our potential to become more or less playful is limited. Perhaps, learning to play is like picking up a second language—easiest when you're young but possible for most people even as adults. As with languages, almost everyone has the requisite neurophysiological equipment to play. It takes more than reading a book to become fluent in either area, and it helps to live with someone who already knows how.

Although our style of play is related to our personality make-up, this doesn't mean it can't change. Psychologists have long debated whether personality is a state or a trait. For example, does the fact that I'm being obnoxious to my wife today have to do with the fact that I am inherently an insensitive boor, or is it a function of the situation? My wife might argue that it is the former, while I would attempt to make a good case for the latter. The truth is that my obnoxiousness is both a state and a trait: some features are very much a part of me, independent of the situation, while others are sensitive to my environment.

I believe that playfulness has similar properties. It may appear that you have been unlucky enough to marry one of

331

the small minority of the terminally serious. Your mate may seem to be a humorless black hole, who is capable of swallowing up any attempt you make to be playful—your best jokes suddenly just disappear, your laughter gone into a void. Even enduring characteristics manifest themselves differently in different situations. The problem we are all faced with is not so much learning how to play as how to identify aspects of our relationships that can encourage or hinder playfulness.

The whole field of marital enrichment, which seeks to help couples improve their relationships by short courses in communication skills and other self-help procedures, is an enterprise I view with mixed emotions. Some couples undoubtedly benefit from such practical help, but much that goes under the name of marital enrichment is a superficial attempt to patch up marriages by suppressing or repressing their seamier sides. In a real sense, marital enrichment should begin with the infant-mother relationship, that is, with the earliest roots of how we handle intimacy. It's not that the only viable approach to improving a marriage is for both people to enter psychoanalysis—even those of us who have spent years on the couch have to settle for partial solutions—but it's important to take care that partial solutions don't preclude more thoroughgoing investigations.

One of the fundamental truths that I learned in my personality-theory course in graduate school is that there are two kinds of people—those who divide people into two kinds and those who don't. By extrapolation I conclude that there are two other kinds of people—those who make lists and tables to help guide them, such as the Ten Commandments, the seven Deadly Sins, the five steps to a better golf swing, and those who don't. I have always fancied myself as one of those who don't. But as I near the end of this book I find that I am overcome by an irresistible urge to make lists. (Evidently, making lists is a state-dependent characteristic, after all.) One way to become clearer about what constitutes healthy adult play is by contrast with the characteristics of destructive game playing.

INTIMATE PLAY VS.
DESTRUCTIVE GAMES

Mutuality	vs.	Self-centeredness
Ambivalence	vs.	Hostility
Flexibility	vs	Rigidity
Freedom within limits	vs.	Overly restrictive or permissive
Clarification	vs.	Confusion
Adaptive compromise	vs.	Defensive avoidance

Intimate Play vs. Destructive Games

The ancient Greeks were well aware of the potentially disruptive effects of play on intimate relationships—Eros is frequently represented as a perverse mischief-maker, inciting passion at the most inopportune moments with his invisible magic arrows. Many people still look upon play as more vice than virtue. Playfulness has only itself to blame for its unsavory reputation because it has kept company with sloth, idleness, capriciousness, immaturity, seductiveness, regression, and a host of other modern sins. Play can be an asset or a liability; there are some reliable ways to differentiate between play that contributes to intimacy and games that are destructive to your relationship. In many of the examples that are destructive games there will be more than one characteristic that will help you distinguish it from healthy play. My categories are meant only to help highlight common features of destructive games so that you will be better able to recognize them. There may be times when you will have only a vague or intuitive sense that your own or your partner's play doesn't feel right. Trust your feelings. You will probably learn something about your relationship by talking it out.

Mutuality vs. Self-centeredness

The game playing that Eric Berne's book *Games People Play* made famous is characterized by manipulativeness. Both partners may be involved in the game, but there is no joint enterprise. Each person uses indirect and covert strategies, many of which are not fully conscious, to protect his own interests and to maneuver the other into the position he finds personally most advantageous.

Healthy play can also be indirect, but it is not a tricky way to gain power over your mate or to get what you want. Neither is it a covert attempt to do therapy on your partner. Instead, play is based on an appreciation that your partner has distinctive needs and hang-ups that you may not like but with which you can empathize. Couples seek solutions that are fair, that benefit both partners, and that are based on a balance between opposing needs and psychological forces. Partners may use each other at times for their own purposes; but such use is reciprocal, acknowledged, and a limited feature of the relationship. For example:

> Ed and Maryanne are good dancers who enjoy a variety of styles. They like disco but they especially love ballroom dancing. The tango is Ed's favorite:
> "It's sensual and dramatic, but I also like it because in the tango you really get to throw your woman around. Maryanne won't let me manipulate her in other ways, but in the tango I'm boss."

When couples play out each other's sexual fantasies, they are often "using" each other in healthy ways. For example:

*"One of our frequent sexual fantasies is where one
of us is the seductive aggressor while the other is the
naive innocent who falls prey to irresistible charms.
Jonathan started it—he enjoyed being the aggressor
and I fell in with his play since I could see he really
got off on 'seducing' me. But sometimes we change
roles and I get to be the dominant one. We each have
other fantasies that are real turn-ons for only one of
us. I like to imagine that we're secretly making love
in a public place, such as in a train compartment or
in our car at a drive-in movie. We've actually made
love at the beach and in a closet at a party, but Jonathan doesn't get off on this as much as I do. He'll
help me fantasize, though. One time we had some
opera music on at home while we were making love.
He whispered to me that we were actually in a box at
the Metropolitan Opera. As the audience was watching the climactic victory march in* Aïda, *we reached
our own climax."*

In game playing, partners are excessively preoccupied
with their own needs or with pleasing their partners. For
example, some people appear to be very playful, but
they're actually entertainers. They're constantly on stage,
and although they give pleasure to others by making them
laugh, they are fundamentally seeking approval and admiration. In contrast, healthy play is collaborative. The difference is one person gets someone to laugh *at* them, the
other to laugh *with* them.

Much destructive play occurs because there is a lack of
empathy. I remember a flagrant example from my childhood, and although it concerns a children's game, it still
has implications for the intimate play of adults. In second
grade we used to play punchball. This was like baseball,
except that you used your closed fist instead of a bat, and a
rubber Spaldeen ball that when new was bright and had

some grainy white stuff on it that came off on your hands. The boys in my class were divided into two punchball teams. The sides were always the same, and what distinguished one team from the other was very simple: all the good players were on one side and all the inept, uncoordinated kids, who could barely catch or hit the ball, were on the other. I'm not sure how my friends and I (the "good" team) managed to pull this off, but we did. Every recess during the fall we went out onto the asphalt schoolyard, where we marked off the bases with chalk. Every time, we won, except once when recess ended early before we could finish the game (the loss was therefore disputed).

It was just as if we were the Harlem Globetrotters vs. the Washington Generals—the other kids were the pathetic foils for us to display our talents. Actually we had other names. Not only did I come up with a suitably vainglorious name for my own team—the "All Americans" (the "Ugly Americans" would have been more apt)—but I had the gall to name our poor opponents the "Mighty Oaks." I suppose that I thought they should be grateful for not being called something *really* bad. Actually, it was a masterpiece of damning with faint praise: what self-respecting second-grader wants to be an oak? Eventually, the Mighty Oaks revolted, and our teacher forced us to trade some of our players to the other team. Of course, no one agreed to go over to the other side unless they changed their nickname.

Such is the self-centered cruelty of youth. It wasn't really meanness on my part as much as a failure to empathize. I grew up in the fifties and sixties rooting for a baseball team—the New York Yankees—that rarely lost. It seemed to me that the order of the universe decreed that there be teams that won all the time and those who achieved the same perfect consistency by losing. My play mirrored what I had learned about how the world worked. Unfortunately, many adults have conceptions of play that are just as devoid of empathy, and that they try to impose on their partners. Adults can treat others as objects to be exploited, but this ceases to be play, and if it includes anything sexual, is called a perversion. The difference is that healthy sexual play is collaborative, not self-centered.

"Before I met Cory," says Rita, "I had been involved with a man whom I'll call Tex who liked to have 'rough sex.' He would pinch me, hard, and pull my hair and he wanted me to slap and bite him. I wasn't comfortable with it and told him so, but he said he was just playing around and why was I so uptight. Before too long we broke up, largely because I didn't feel he really cared about me—it wasn't just in bed that he insisted on doing things his way.

"With Cory I felt it was different. I knew he cared whether I enjoyed our sex. Sometimes we made slow, tender love and sometimes we had hard fucking. He'd grab me and push me up against the wall and fuck me hard with his hands cupping my ass. One time he came up behind me in the kitchen while I was preparing dinner and said, 'Don't turn around, I want you.' He started telling me things he knew would turn me on as he fondled my breasts and he had me right there as I leaned over the table. I had left the oven open and I remember looking at it and thinking my own oven was getting filled. At one point he picked up one of the carrots lying on the table and fucked me with that. Afterward, we had a good laugh about it and I told him 'This is the first time I've ever been laid by a vegetable.' We then fantasized about other kinds of food that would make good or bad lovers.

"In one of my fantasies, I had him be my slave who had to do anything I asked. I commanded him to give me an orgasm but without touching my genitals. He was so inventive and I got so turned on I finally gave him his 'freedom.'

*"We did a lot of crazy things, the crazier the better
we liked it. We wanted 'unspeakable intimacies.' "*

Ambivalence vs. Hostility

Another way to differentiate healthy from unhealthy play
is by the role of hostility. In both of Rita's sexual relationships there is an aggressive element. But in one situation
sadism masquerades as play, and inflicting pain becomes
the primary goal. In healthy relationships you can be rough
and tumble as long as limits are respected and the context
remains loving.

In many forms of play, as in much humor, there is a
hostile undercurrent. For example, when we surprise someone the pleasure we feel is in part due to the startled dismay of our victims—momentarily they are caught off
guard, undone, vulnerable. Here is a vignette drawn from
Herbert Otto's *More Joy in Your Marriage,* which describes a game called Escalated Taste Exploration. The
couple first makes an agreement to taste anything new that
their partner gives them.

Wife: He won the first turn and started off mild
with something that tasted very good. It turned out to
be smoked whale meat. . . . One time he had blindfolded me so I couldn't see what I was eating. It
tasted delicious and I thought it was some sort of
smoked vegetable. I told him it was very good and
had a second helping. When I removed the blindfold,
I found I had been eating smoked grasshopper. Was I
shocked! [Laughs.] But this taught me that we have a
lot of prejudices about food just like we have about
people. I believe I can taste anything now and not be
squeamish. At least I'll try. Before we played this, I
wouldn't try some things, because I felt maybe I
wouldn't like it. I have more fun now eating out and
trying new dishes.

Husband: I guess she is ahead of me in some ways. My big shock came one day when Joan brought some white meat in a round can. To understand what I am about to say, I have to tell you that I had a bad injury as a child from a snake. I ate the meat in the can and it tasted like chicken—very good. Had three helpings and noticed that Joan was looking at me in a peculiar way. After I had talked with her about how it tasted to me, she told me it was rattlesnake meat. I almost jumped out of my skin. Then I decided this was silly and made myself eat the rest of the can. It didn't taste as good as the first time around, but I figured he bit me, I'll bite him back. [Laughs.] Since then I feel a lot better about snakes.[36]

I can't help wondering if the next adventure in "escalated taste exploration" would be to feed each other hazardous waste material: "Guess what, dear, that thing you said was so tasty and looked like filet mignon was actually radioactive! And, silly boy, you thought fallout was something to be afraid of!" As this vignette makes clear, the victim of a hostile joke may often become a willing accomplice. They are bribed into going along by the humor, which camouflages the hostile intent, or fooled by the perpetrator's protestations of innocence: "I was only kidding," or "What's the matter, can't you take a joke?"

When John and Dory were engaged, John required that Dory go through a hazing exercise by his all-male club. John had been a member of the club for three years, and most of his best friends from high school were members. They chided him about getting "tied down" to a woman who would turn him into a "houseboy."

Each fall, new members entering the club had to go through an initiation. The men were blindfolded, taken for long drives, sleep-deprived for a night, and put through stress exercises.

"I wasn't keen to do it," says Dory, years later. "They told me fictitious stories of women who 'didn't have what it takes' to make it through hazing. I went along with it because I loved John. Looking back on it, it was sick. I was terrified by their stories and felt helpless. It turned out that the actual hazing wasn't that bad, but it was a bad beginning to our marriage. John never quite made as strong a commitment to me that he had to his friends."

While pretending can give couples license to be more adventuresome than is their wont, it can also be a cloak for daggers. I recall going to a Halloween costume party at which one couple came dressed as the current rivals for the district House of Representatives seat. The man in the couple "pretended" to lambast his opponent, calling her "a whore" and "an idiot." Her embarrassment left little doubt that her partner was no longer playing. In the same way, adult war games may be a dangerous perversion of play: under the white flag of the pretend they lull us into thinking that war really isn't such a serious matter, after all. In the unhealthy play of couples the consequences, while not generally lethal, can be destructive to the relationship.

A young couple frequently played a game in which one would hide in their apartment and then suddenly jump out to scare the other. Each time this happened, the stage was set for the other person to look for opportunities to retaliate. Eventually this practice was accompanied by a deterioration in their trust. As one of them put it, "When I return home to an empty apartment, I can't feel sure that I'm alone. It's difficult to relax."

In defense of aggressive games, it is said that they provide a safe outlet for dangerous impulses. Similarly, intimate play can be an outlet for ambivalence, a controlled and sublimated form in which to vent frustrations with your mate. But we should never ignore the potential for teasing to become hurtful putdowns, for clever nicknames to actually be insensitive epithets, and for humor to degenerate into biting sarcasm. For example, although one woman was sensitive about having some facial hair, her husband sometimes called her "Fuzzface."

In Edward Albee's play *Who's Afraid of Virginia Woolf?* a middle-aged couple indulges in sadistic pseudoplay in the presence of a younger couple. George, a professor in the history department of a small New England college, had married Martha, the daughter of the college president, and has never succeeded either in his own or in his wife's estimation. Childless and bitter, they engage in orgies of self-indulgent flagellation and goading of each other. In Act I, "Fun and Games," the following dialogue unfolds just after they have told the other couple (Honey and Nick) a story about George's reluctance to fight Martha's father, in which Martha "accidentally" knocked George off his feet with one punch:

Martha: It was awful, really. It was funny, but it was awful. . . . I think it's colored our whole life. Really I do! It's an excuse anyway. (George enters now, his hands behind his back. No one sees him.) It's what he uses for being bogged down, anyway . . . why he hasn't gone anywhere. (George advances. Honey sees him.) And it was an accident . . . a real, goddamn accident! (George takes from behind his back a short-barreled shotgun and calmly aims it at the back of Martha's head. Honey screams . . . rises. Nick rises, and simultaneously, Martha turns her head to face George. George pulls the trigger.)

George: Pow!!! (Pop! From the barrel of the gun blossoms a large red and yellow Chinese parasol. Honey screams again, this time less and mostly from relief and confusion.) You're dead! Pow! You're dead!

Martha later characterizes the couple's play: "You think I'm kidding? You think I'm joking? I never joke. . . . I don't have a sense of humor . . . I have a fine sense of the ridiculous, but no sense of humor." Her statement would serve as an apt differentiation of healthy from destructive play.

You need to know the limits of how much joking or teasing you can do on a sensitive topic before your partner will take offense. Even when you have good intentions, I don't think you can totally avoid bruised feelings and sharp edges in your play without imposing too many restrictions on your spontaneity. To be playful requires that you loosen up your self-controls. Sometimes what climbs out of the cauldron of your unconscious isn't so pretty. You can't inspect every bit of play before it happens, but if something goes wrong, don't hide behind your humor.

Flexibility vs. Rigidity

One of the tip-offs that distinguishes true play from destructive games is its creative unpredictability. The essence of play is flexibility, whereas game playing is often stereotyped and predictable. Play can sometimes masquerade as flexibility, such as when a person pretends to be loose and mellow. The person who always has to be the "life of the party" is actually acting from compulsive urgency. Play ceases to be play when it is the only way you can relate instead of being an option. True play coexists with other modes of relating, so you can shift back and forth from serious, or confrontative, or sad, to being playful as the spirit and situation warrant. It is the *having to* do something that unmasks it as a destructive game.

> *Shortly after Sam and Marie began living together, Marie became irritated over his bad habit of slurping. It seemed to her that whenever Sam drank anything warm, like soup or tea or coffee, he slurped, even when he was in public. "To get revenge and make him notice what he was doing," Marie says, "I made like a slob myself—dreadful slurping noises, for instance—whenever he did it. I thought it was funny, and even though Sam got very annoyed with me, I wouldn't stop doing it."*

In contrast to the situations in which a person might exaggerate an annoying behavior of a partner in a thoughtful and selective way, Sam experienced Marie's repetitive imitation as coercive.

Another way that rigidity may occur is in the ways that couples handle fantasy. Temporary flights of fancy that enrich your daily lives are characteristic of intimate play. With some couples, however, their inner lives are fragmented, so that fantasy is sealed off from reality, with neither able to influence the other. Such rigid segregation of a couple's private fantasy life from their public "real" life is characteristic of maladaptive play. For example, in Harold Pinter's play *The Lover:*

> Richard and Sarah maintain a double life in which they alternate between being spouses and being each other's lovers cheating on their respective partners. Far from being able to integrate this split, their marriage depends on continuation of a *folie à deux* in which they speak about each other's affairs and spouses without ever acknowledging that they are role playing. When Richard begins to merge into

Max (the lover), threatening to end their game, Sarah rescues them from the threat that it will only be the two of them alone together by pretending that she has other lovers besides Max. The play ends with Richard urging Sarah to change her clothes—that is, to change her identity once again.

In contrast, in the playful "illicit affair" of Richard and Laura (see page 3), a couple developed a similar fantasy while on vacation together; the boundary between their play and real identities was present but far less rigid—there was a healthy crossfertilization between fantasy and reality. To pretend without acknowledging that you are pretending is to mislead your partner or to deceive yourself. In a sense, you lock the doors between your "real" life and your fantasy life. It is as if you allow yourself to dream but not to understand your dreams, so that your unconscious life remains cut off from your conscious experience.

Freedom within Limits vs. Overly Restrictive or Permissive

Freedom is essential to play but so are limits, and where either is lacking in its proper measure play disappears. In intimate play, the freedom lies in the willingness of both of you to relax your usual inhibitions, to let what British marital theorist H. V. Dicks called your "little needy ego" to "peep out." Permissiveness and tolerance of each other's childlike sides are inherent in intimate play; their absence is destructive to a relationship.

"I once had a relationship with a man," recalls Joan, "who reprimanded me when I would get silly or loud. If I tickled him or jumped up and down he'd caution me that people might see. Actually, he was just uncomfortable with my acting like a kid. I felt like I was with a stern parent. It was stifling."

The next couple, a clinical case from Wilhelm Stekel's *Sexual Aberrations*, illustrates several features of destructive games—isolated rather than collaborative play, overly infantile play, as well as a partner's gross intolerance:

Mrs. G. J., a woman in her forties, has the impulse always to be playing the child. She talks baby-talk, prefers to wear children's or very short dresses.... Among other things, she has several old dolls with which she used to play years ago. She begins to pet the doll and imagines that she herself is the doll.... In the beginning of their marriage, her husband was very tender towards her, but lately he has been more and more indifferent. She still has, however, a tremendous need for being pampered and can still this desire only in her activity with the dolls.

At first, she satisfied herself by playing with the dolls behind the locked doors of her room. The hours passed in sheer delight, and she felt herself transported back to the days of her childhood. At the time, her husband had no notion of her habits. One day he came home unexpectedly and found his wife in the midst of her practices, a doll in her hand and surrounded by all kinds of dolls and childishness. With the lightning accuracy of the lover he had realized that these dolls were his rivals. Blind with rage and jealousy, he tore the dolls out of her hands, ripped them to pieces... and threw the lamentable remains into the great fire in the fireplace.... Formerly, she had frequently had an orgasm during coitus and was easily provoked to orgasm by irritation of the clitoris. Now she became anesthetic. She could not forgive her husband the murder of her dolls. She ceased to be a child. She felt old and often said that she had nothing more to live for.... The analysis showed that as a child she had suffered a

curious series of [sexual] traumata. . . . When she was
seven, her nine-year-old brother played with her and
carried out cunnilingus on her. Then, one day, he
brought three of his friends who also played with her.
Later she slept with her aunt in the same bed and was
always petted and stroked over the whole body. Her
aunt called her "my dolly" and said that she was as
pretty as a doll. . . . At thirteen, she became the mistress of her piano teacher.

She vowed she would be true to her husband and
also kept her promise. Her faithlessness was expressed only in her play with the dolls.[37]

Stekel's case is a sad contrast to the mutual revelation of
secrets and tolerance of each other's childlike sides that is
characteristic of intimate play.

Several types of limits are also important in healthy play.
Play needs a defined and protected space, such as the privacy of your home, and the assurance that neither of you
will share the private self that you have revealed to any
person outside the couple.

When Bob would come home from work upset and
complaining, Ellen would encourage him to "just
relax and be taken care of." She would offer to give
him a bath, towel him dry, feed him a good meal,
and then "put him to bed." On occasion, this soothing ritual would make Bob feel very childlike, and
his voice would even start to sound babyish.

Several years after they had started this ritual,
Bob and Ellen were out with another couple, Mark
and Sally. Sally was needling Mark about what a
"big baby" he was being because he refused to challenge his boss. Ellen took up the theme of "big
babies" and divulged her and Bob's ritual in detail.

"I was shocked and hurt," says Bob. "We had
never formally discussed it, but I thought we had a

tacit agreement that the ritual was a very personal one. I felt exposed and betrayed. Because Ellen was telling the story, it appeared to be all my doing, when in fact she had always had a large part in it."

The wife in another couple had the playful idea of giving her husband a photograph of herself posed in seductive attire. She hired a female photographer who knew how to use soft lighting that achieved a sensual feeling and that highlighted her best features. The photographer set her at ease so that by the end of the picture-taking session she felt relaxed in her garters and chemise. The pictures were tasteful but provocative. Her husband was delighted with the gift, but to his wife's dismay he wanted to show the pictures to some of his friends at the office.

Even when both partners agree to reveal their play to other people, it is often a sign of emotional immaturity.

At a small dinner party one couple began talking "baby talk" to each other. The other couples cringed as they billed and cooed to each other and addressed each other as "Snookums" and "Boogaloo." Although this couple seemed unabashed by this public display, the others wondered if they had had a little too much to drink.

Both partners of this couple have poorly developed boundaries between themselves and other people. Their openness is not a sign of health but suggests an inability to discriminate between intimate and public contexts. Similarly in *Who's Afraid of Virginia Woolf?* George and Martha perform their antics in front of another couple; in fact, they use their audience to deliberately humiliate each other.

Both of you must be able to call a halt to play. As Shakespeare suggests, "If all the year were playing holidays, To sport would be as tedious as to work." The risk in unbounded play is more than tedium, however, if either partner has a tenuous hold on their impulses or on reality. For example, the woman who got her partner's attention by taking off her panties (see page 95) was indulging in whimsical play. But if she *consistently* dealt with frustration by impulsive acts, she would be better off developing ways to be less "playful," that is to put her feelings into words rather than action. Other individuals are not impulsive, but their inner world is so chaotic that they can lose themselves in a fantasy; for them, indulgence in fantasy can be dangerous. For example, according to the National Coalition on Television Violence, between 1979 and 1985, there were thirteen known deaths attributable to the children's fantasy game Dungeons and Dragons. One fourteen-year-old who shot himself left a note saying, "I want to go to the world of elves and fantasy and leave the world of conflict." Another sixteen-year-old's suicide came about because "Dungeons and Dragons apparently became a reality . . . [he] thought he was not constrained to his life, but could leave and return because of the game."[38]

For most people, the risks of giving free rein to the imagination are much more tame. But just as basically healthful things like intimacy are not always helpful to all people at all times, so can fantasy play be a mixed blessing.

Clarification vs. Confusion

The true test of whether play is helpful to your relationship is whether it aids communication or makes it more difficult. Playful communication is often complex. For example, two messages may be expressed simultaneously, such as making fun of your partner's behavior, while reassuring him that you accept him, anyway. One theory of schizophrenia holds that people can be made crazy by mutually contradictory messages. For example, a mother may say to her child, "Why can't you understand how much

your Mommy loves you," while at the same time she
stiffens when he tries to embrace her. It can be very confusing to have someone who's very important to you seem
to accept and reject you at the same time. But it is dangerous if two other conditions are fulfilled: you can't get away
from the situation, and you aren't allowed to point out the
contradiction. In destructive games, couples communicate
all kinds of covert messages, and both partners conspire to
remain unaware of or at least avoid facing what they are
doing. Consistently vague or mixed messages do not serve
your relationship.

> When James first started going out with Marianne
> he found her hard to figure out. He'd ask her for a
> date and she'd say, "Are you sure you want to do
> this?" When he asked her what she meant, she
> laughed and said she was joking. When they'd go out
> she seemed to enjoy herself, but at the end of the
> evening she'd make sarcastic comments like, "I'd
> better treat next time, big spender," that made him
> think she wanted him to spend more money on her.
> However, when he asked her about this, she denied
> it.
> What eventually became more apparent was that
> Marianne had trouble being direct. She was an un-
> happy person who felt bad about herself and didn't
> know what she wanted.

Play, too, can be highly ambiguous and can misfire.
Spontaneity has its risks. But, distinct from destructive
games, obfuscation is not deliberate or sustained.

Adaptive Compromise vs. Defensive Avoidance

Although Sigmund Freud felt that humor represents the
covert gratification of a repressed impulse—whether sexual or aggressive—he also saw it as being a defense

against painful emotions: "The essence is one spares one-self the affects to which the situation would naturally give rise."[39] Humor helps us to triumph over unkind circumstance by asserting our invulnerability—a kind of whistling in the dark. This explains why a person's favorite joke is often revealing of their deepest concerns. We laugh at things that, if they lost their pleasant wrapper of humor, would make us anxious. But isn't this a contradiction—how can humor both gratify impulse, as well as act as a defense? This paradox runs deeply throughout psychoanalytic theory, and it is one that reflects the complex reality of our psychic lives.

Play is double-edged. On the negative side, you can use play to sidestep painful issues, to avoid feelings, or to skip away from closeness.

Jeremy had begun to drunk heavily during high school, but it had never seemed to be a problem. He had his own business, so if he got up with a hangover and went in to work late, it didn't matter. He got arrested once for driving under the influence, but his family passed it off as having one too many on a Saturday night. His wife, Sheara, liked her margaritas, too.

"Things started to unravel after Jeremy's father's death," says Sheara. "He began to drink every day and often wouldn't go in to work at all. Sometimes he'd come home at three in the morning. The thing was that he was such a pleasant drunk—he'd never swear at me or the kids or abuse us in any way. When I tried to confront him about his drinking, he'd laugh it off, like he had some kind of minor quirk instead of the serious problem that it had become. It was difficult for anyone not close to the situation to see the problem, because everyone feels Jeremy is such a great guy—he always has a good story to tell or a witty comment. It was only when I stopped

*drinking myself and threatened to leave him that he
agreed to get some help."*

In Tennessee Williams's play *The Glass Menagerie,*
Laura Wingfield, a young woman crippled by a childhood
illness, lives in a world of illusion, her fragility and separation from the real world represented by her collection of
glass animals. Laura's glass menagerie is like some couples' private world of play—a psychic refuge in which one
or both partners feels safe, but which shields them also
from love. They feel less pain but know less joy. You can
use play to get just the right distance from a problem so
that you and your partner can face it. Also, play often
provides creative ways for you to gradually deal with a
problem. For example, many couples who are unable to
have children develop playful substitutes—some have dog
menageries, and I know of one that raises ducks. In contrast, in *Who's Afraid of Virginia Woolf?* George and
Martha maintain a secret fantasy of the child that they have
never had. In this situation, play is used to avoid mourning
instead of helping the couple to work through their feelings; their emotional growth is stunted by a magical solution.

It is helpful to think of humor and healthy play in general as being a compromise between impulse and defense
or between fantasy and reality, a kind of truce between
inner psychic factions in which neither wins totally and
both achieve recognition. The next couple illustrates a subtle blend of wish fulfillment and acknowledgment of reality, or what Charlie Chaplin might have called "playful
pain."

*Karoline and Ralph had just bought their first
house—a 1920s stucco colonial in a fashionable
Boston suburb. The house, while not a ruin, had
crumbling walls and a brooding, cold dampness that
badly needed some replastering and a coat of paint.*

But grandeur lay beneath its faded grace, waiting to be brought back to life.

"We fell in love with it when we first saw it," says Ralph. "It had three chimneys, lovely hardwood floors, an inlaid wood pantry with a copper sink, and original glass fixtures everywhere. When we first bought it there was so much to do—rewiring, floors, plumbing. I took over most of the responsibility for hiring the workmen. Of course, there were some problems. We had turned down a bid from a group of women painters for a less expensive quote who turned out to employ only Rastafarians. Unfortunately, they probably had never painted a house like ours before. They painted over some bronze hardware and accidentally broke a couple of our beautiful glass fixtures. When I called this to their attention, they were very apologetic. 'So sorry, Mahn,' they'd say and shake their heads and scratch their dreadlocks. Karoline got very upset."

"It felt like our dream house was being destroyed," says Karoline, "and I felt so helpless, like there was nothing I could do to protect this precious thing. One evening Ralph and I were lying in bed and I was bemoaning what was happening. We talked about how to deal with our workmen in the future. Somehow Ralph started telling me a fairy tale, about this man who loved this woman so much that he bought her a wonderful house and he went on to describe our house, partly as it was and partly as we planned it to become. Occasionally he teased me, like saying that there would only be one fireplace in it, but when I pleaded with him, he'd change the story. The fairy tale soothed me and lifted me out of the distressing details of our current predicament back into the dream that we shared."

How, then, can you know whether your play ultimately benefits or harms your relationship? All you can do is reassess it as you go along. Your holidays from reality should be temporary ones, your stepping back from problems not so far that you lose sight of what is painful and unresolved between you. Fantasy should exist alongside of reality and not replace it. Magical solutions have no staying power, but we all need ways of leavening our reality "sandwiches." I am convinced that love, like play, is also a settlement between reality and desire, and you need not be ashamed of compromise.

TEN STEPPING STONES TO INTIMATE PLAY

Establish the conditions for a relationship

Think positive but small

Safeguard privacy

Think of play as rehearsal

Intimate play is the play of everyday life

Timing is everything

Play is only part of your repertoire

Let history be your guide

Take the team approach

Learn about yourself

Ten Stepping Stones to Intimate Play

Learning to play does not lend itself well to a step-by-step approach. I suppose any kind of play could be broken down into segments like a golf swing, and each component painfully and obsessively mastered. You could have slow-motion video tapes, like they have in New England at indoor driving ranges in the wintertime. During the first week, instead of learning the proper way to shake hands with your golf club, you'd learn the playface—"hold the corners of your mouth at a thirty-degree angle, tilt your head slightly, crinkle your eyes, relax, and let the laugh just come easily." Just as with golf, it would feel, at first, like the most unnatural thing in the world, but your play pro would reassure you that with practice it would all come together. I've had quite a few golf lessons, but I've never broken a hundred yet. The problem is that I've never been willing to approach the game as something that requires that much work. I think of play as a very important matter, but its spirit is fragile and it can be approached only in a fanciful manner. Still, I think it's fair to try to codify some guidelines, which I have called stepping stones, to intimate play. The mystics say, "Those who speak do not know, those who know do not speak." But there's already enough mystery in play and love without deliberate mystification on my part.

Establish the Conditions for a Relationship

Rather than strive to make your relationship more playful immediately, a better strategy is to try to foster the conditions conducive to playfulness. People need to feel safe before they can venture into new territory—you can't expect that either of you can act playful in a setting of acrimony or criticism. I have no thirty-minute workout to offer that can warm you up to be playful. There are no shortcuts to trust, mutual acceptance, and empathy; though working hard in these areas is bound to result in a greater willingness to play. Similarly, if your relationship used to be more playful than it is now, your first step should be to look for what may be going wrong. The state of play is a good weather vane for how the two of you are getting along.

When you try to induce a change in the couple system, you are asking your partner to relinquish a habitual response and at least implicitly to acknowledge that there may be a better way than what you're used to. No one likes to admit he's wrong, but if your partner really feels appreciated for who he is and for how truly difficult it is for him to change, he's more likely to accept your attempt at play in a good spirit. Play must be done lovingly. Further, if your attitude is that you want to make the relationship more playful as opposed to making your partner more playful, you are less likely to meet headstrong resistance.

Think Positive but Small

One of the biggest obstacles to achieving any kind of change in a relationship is having unrealistic expectations. Begin with trying to achieve a small change, such as setting aside more time for relaxation on a weekend or giving your partner a playful gift. Whatever requests you make of your partner should be phrased in positive terms, rather than as an attack on his character. Thus, instead of saying "You have no sense of humor," you might try "I'd really like you to surprise me sometime" and offer some ideas. The less playful your partner is, the more encouragement she's going to need. This includes not just thanking her for when she's done something playful that you like but also making her feel good about herself in areas unrelated to play.

How playful you are is partly a matter of gender identity, as well as personality style. For example, men tend to be more comfortable with competitive and aggressive play, while women are more at home with imaginative play. I don't know of any way to turn a frog into a prince— you've got to find ways to work with your partner's limitations:

> One wife was able to gradually overcome her husband's reluctance to play by being careful to choose the optimal moments—when they were alone on vacations or when he was feeling especially mellow and relaxed. She also used nicknames for him that called to mind characters with whom her husband could readily identify, such as Clint (for Clint Eastwood). Similarly, in their fantasy play, he would typically be a superhero—tall, dark, and handsome—who rescued the "damsel in distress."

You can encourage but not insist on change and try to find forms of play with which your partner can become comfortable.

Safeguard Privacy

One of the essential preconditions for intimate play is privacy. In Albee's *Who's Afraid of Virginia Woolf?* George and Martha engage in "fun and games" in front of another couple, and exploit their audience for each other's maximal humiliation. But most people's "little needy ego" won't peep out if others are around. At the very least, you need to set aside a time and a place for play. If your life is already so arranged that these conditions are frequently available, such further premeditation may be unnecessary. The majority of us, however, sometimes need the equivalent of a machete to clear out enough space in the ashphalt jungle so we can have some undisturbed peace and quiet. If you truly value play, you need to make it a priority.

When I speak of ensuring privacy, I also mean that you have to have respect for it. When either of you lets down your guard a bit and allows a hidden side of yourself to come out, you must have reciprocal confidence that your secrets will be held as closely as you would keep them yourself. The culture of two thrives only under conditions of secrecy—its betrayal to another precludes intimate play.

Think of Play as Rehearsal

The exciting thing about intimate play is that it is a tentative way of establishing a new kind of relation to something or someone. It is a probe into unexplored territory with your mate, through which you may learn something about you, something about them, or something about the atmosphere of the relationship. Play is a way of your experimenting, of trying things out. It's a way of saying, how about seeing things in a way we never thought of, or thinking of me in a way you never thought of before. Play brings "once upon a time" into the here and now.

To feel bored and stuck in your relationship and to resign yourself to the stance that "this is all there is" is to succumb to a failure of the imagination. The alternative is to take some risks. You don't have to go straight up to the high board, but at least take a jump in the pool. Playing won't license you to be a completely different person, but it can enable you to bring out parts of your personality that you usually don't express. I suggest that you think of play as a kind of rehearsal. You have to take responsibility for it, but you also don't have to be committed to it. Just as kids can try out all sorts of different identities in their play, you can give yourself the same permission.

Some places in your life may provide more room than others for this kind of experimental attitude. Once having begun to give yourself and your partner some leeway to play, you may find more and more opportunities.

Intimate Play Is the Play of Everyday Life

The first place to look for ideas and opportunities to play is exactly where you are. Intimate play is not some exotic hothouse flower or a pungent spice that must be imported from distant shores—it usually grows out of something that is already present in your lives. It depends less on your changing partners or circumstances than on being playful about who you are and making use of the day-to-day opportunities for playfulness that come your way. For some couples, their children can be a catalyst:

> *"Our children have been a great source of bringing out the child in us," say David and Valerie. "Both of us were on the reserved side before this. For example, we have this family game called playing socks. Whoever is around—two, three, or more people—will get down on the floor with their shoes off and match their feet up sole to sole, and push each other around in an affectionate way. It's like arm wrestling, only with your feet. When you have only two people, you lie opposite one another, like mirror images on the floor. When you have several people you form a triangle or circle. We feel like the biggest babies playing socks, but it's really a lot of fun."*

Some couples find that playing with a pet can provide a bridge to more playfulness in their relationship:

> *"Although Charley doesn't play with me too much, he plays with Clyde, our cat. His play with Clyde sometimes extends to me. I remember once, in particular, Charley and I were chasing Clyde around the house. I think he had some of my pantyhose in his mouth—the cat, that is. Somehow, it ended up with*

Charley chasing me around the house. I hadn't had so much fun since the time he chased me (both nude) around his parents' house before we were married. His Mom and Dad were gone, of course. (Boy, was that fun!)

"I'm not sure why, but it seems that we have a lot more fun together since we got Clyde. I think it has something to do with the fact that Charley needed to learn to play again. It's hard not to play with a kitten, and now he's gone from playing with Clyde to playing with me."

Some couples therapists at the outset of therapy recommend a game called I Spy to help couples become more observant of relationships and also to induce some playfulness. The instructions are to follow another couple around secretly wherever they go and just observe them. When I told a fellow therapist that I had some concern about following people around, he agreed there were some hazards. Years ago he and his wife had followed an older couple. They had tailed them to a department store and watched them grouse about a purchase. Then they had followed them to a travel agency and an art gallery. They tried to get close enough to have an idea of what was going on, but not so close that they would be noticed. Finally they wound up in a restaurant, both couples on line waiting for a table. The man in the other couple came back to them and said, "I don't want to make a big thing out of it, but are you following us?" It turned out that the other couple had played the same game themselves years ago and thus caught on more quickly to what was happening. They decided to have dinner together, and my friend tells me they still exchange Christmas cards.

I'm not confident that your being caught would always have so congenial an outcome. I mention this exercise only as an instance of tuning in to what is all around you, and making it into something playful. Intimate play is the unique appreciation for the ordinary. You have to start with the present moment and with familiar things, and let your imagination do the rest.

Timing Is Everything

One of the difficult aspects of trying to convey how to use play in a relationship is that it's not something that you can learn just by following directions, as in assembling a waterbed. It's more like learning music. The danger is that by trying to become more playful, couples may end up like someone who has learned to tell a joke that makes sense only in a foreign language—they can tell the joke, but it isn't funny.

It's like the story about the man who went to prison and on his first night heard his neighbor call out "Fifty-two" and several people laughed. Then somebody else said "One-oh-six" and everybody laughed their heads off. The series of numbers continued, each time bringing forth much amusement. Finally, he turned to his cellmate and asked what was going on. "Oh that," he replied, "the numbers refer to jokes. We've heard them so many times that we've memorized them by number." The new inmate jumped up and yelled "Thirty-six!" and waited for a response. Nothing. "What's wrong?" he asked. "You didn't tell it right."

Likewise, a little finesse and a fine sense of timing are critical to playfulness. You need to know when to dance around the edge of a problem and when to take a direct approach. Joking won't be well received while your partner is throwing a tantrum or feeling hurt, although play can provide a transition between separateness and sharing. You have to learn each other's rhythms for play just as well as you pick up on other moods. There is always the danger that when you joke about a sensitive issue, while your intent may be supportive, your partner may experience it as hurtful or devaluing.

Timing isn't something that can be taught. But I have faith that, as with a sense of rhythm and making love, at least a rudimentary sense of play is innate, and you can refine your own capacity for play by experience.

Play Is Only Part of Your Repertoire

Intimate play is effective in dealing with problems when there's already the beginning of a shared definition of the difficulty and an alliance for change. Put another way, play is more successful in dealing with attitudes and conflicts close to your awareness rather than with emotional labyrinths that you have never entered before. One implication is that play is not a replacement for serious discussion. You will have to continue to cultivate other communication skills in addition to play.

Play alone cannot guarantee intimacy or a relationship's longevity. In John Osborne's play *Look Back in Anger,* a couple has a favorite ritual of squirrels and bears:

Jimmy: [Staring at her anxious face] You're very beautiful. A beautiful, great-eyed squirrel. [She nods, brightly, relieved.] Hoarding, nut-munching squirrel. [She mimes this delightedly.] With highly polished, gleaming fur, and an ostrich feather of a tail.

Alison: Wheeee!

Jimmy: How I envy you. [He stands, her arms around his neck.]

Alison: Well, you're a jolly super bear, too. A really sooooooper, marvelous bear.

Jimmy: Bears and squirrels *are* marvelous.

Alison: Marvelous and beautiful. [She jumps up and down excitedly, making little "paw gestures."] Oooooh! Oooooh!

Jimmy: What the hell's that?

Alison: That's a dance squirrels do when they're happy. [They embrace again.]

Jimmy: What makes you think you're happy?
Alison: Everything just seems all right suddenly.

But everything really isn't all right. By the end of the play Alison has decided to leave Jimmy and reveals this poignant realization:

Even bears and squirrels seem to have gone their own ways now. . . . It was one way of escaping from everything—a sort of unholy priesthood of being animals to one another. We could become furry creatures with little furry brains. Full of dumb, uncomplicated affection for each other. Playful careless creatures in their own cozy zoo for two. A silly symphony for people who couldn't bear the pain of being human beings any longer. And now, even they are dead, poor little silly animals. They were all love, and no brains.

A similar conclusion was reached by a woman who tried to recapture the special feeling she had had with her old boyfriend:

"When I was in high school, Darrell and I were best friends. We were both misfits, but we had each other. We shared an offbeat sense of humor, a peculiar way of looking at the world. We'd go to the department stores in Manhattan and pretend we were getting married—we'd sign up at the bridal registry and act like we were picking out china and so on. Doing that sort of thing was the farthest thing from what we ever thought we'd really want to do. We had nicknames for each other—I was Priscilla Belleflower and Darrell was Boston Bergdorf the third.

"We'd lost touch after college, but I recently got a phone call from him. I didn't recognize his voice

*at first, but then he said 'Priscilla, this is Boston.'
I was so excited to hear from him.*

*"We had lunch the next day and reminisced about
the past—the zany things we used to do together. But
I felt that we were trying to make something happen
that just wasn't there. It wasn't just the passage of
time but the reason why we had drifted apart after
high school. I had gotten involved in politics and
decided to go to law school, and Darrell couldn't
take anything seriously.*

*"After all the time that had passed, we could still
laugh together but not the laughter that brings you
close to tears."*

Let History Be Your Guide

Your past history is an important determinant of how
playful your current relationship can be. For example, if
either you or your partner experienced a lot of teasing or
hurtful sarcasm in the past, similar kinds of play may stir
up negative associations, even though there is no longer
any ill intent. Such obstacles to the enjoyment of play must
be handled with much care and patience.

At the same time, the playful ways you related as a kid
are a valuable resource. Likewise, if in previous love relationships as an adult or early in your current relationship
you were more playful than now, you may be able to re-
kindle this spirit. It's generally easier to get back to something that's familiar than to try to graft something totally
alien onto your relationship. For example, try to remember
your most pleasant memories growing up or other times at
play. You might try visiting the house where you grew up
or places where you used to play—a playground, a field
—or browse in a toy store to stimulate your memories.
You can't simply repeat the past or try to return to what
seems now like a former state of bliss, but the good parts
of your past can provide a base on which to build.

Take the Team Approach

The best way to change your relationship is not to try to change your partner but to try to change the couple system. Most of us harbor fantasies that we can create a perfect mate, although my hunch is that if we were granted this wish the result would be closer to the bride of Frankenstein than to Pygmalion's Galatea or Eliza Doolittle. If it has taken two or three decades or more for our partner to get the way they are, our attempts at basic redesign are doomed to failure. I believe that a good love relationship can profoundly transform, though it is never through the intentional design of one partner acting on another but through their collaborative venture for the growth of both. No matter how well motivated you may be, your partner is likely to resist with obstinacy and vigilance any attempts to change him, even if it's clearly for his own good. Moves on your part to try to make him more playful are not likely to be cordially received.

One way to mitigate your partner's resistance to change is to demonstrate a willingness to acknowledge your own part in the situation and to try to change yourself.

Rachel's husband is an associate professor who is under a lot of pressure to publish in order to get tenure. He often works on weekends, either at the library or at home.

"I was tolerant for a long time of Jeff's needing to work," says Rachel, who is a pediatrician. "But I missed the times when we would go away for the weekend or spend a lazy Sunday morning in bed reading The New York Times. We were getting along okay, but we weren't having much fun. What particularly drove me wild was that Jeff would bring some of his work on our vacations. Often he'd deny it at first. For instance, after we had packed for a trip to

*Bermuda, I noticed an extra suitcase. 'What's that?'
I asked. 'Just a few things to read,' he replied. I
picked it up—the thing was so heavy it had to be
textbooks. I made him leave most of them at home,
but the fact that he even wanted to bring work along
bothered me.*

"But then I thought about the fact that I brought
work home a lot as well. At dinnertime, I'd talk
about what happened at the office in great detail.
Also, partly in response to Jeff's working all the time
I had gotten into a work mentality myself. So I an-
nounced that I was turning over a new leaf. I was
going to spend less of our dinnertime talking about
work. Further, I was going to make sure that at least
one weekend day was spent doing something that was
fun. I got back into reading novels, taking long, lux-
urious bubble baths, and listening to classical music.
Before too long Jeff started to join me."

Take a hard look at what you may be doing to keep
playfulness out of your relationship. Are there ways that
you could take risks with yourself to be more venturesome
and spontaneous? Are there some playful ways that you
could give to your partner that might then inspire him or
her to respond in kind? This needs to be more than a token
effort, a tit that demands an immediate tat. On the other
hand, you shouldn't have to do it all on your own.

*Charlene is a very creative interior decorator who
was always giving her boyfriend playful surprises.
Even when it wasn't Valentine's Day, she made an
elaborate card with doors that opened to reveal hidden messages. She often cooked him special desserts
and one time made him a "coupon book," with each
coupon to be redeemed for a special treat—a massage, breakfast in bed, a strip tease performance.
She really enjoyed doing all of these things for her*

man. But he never reciprocated. She was constantly thinking about him and what he might like and never made any demands on him. It never occurred to him that some of the things she did for him she would have loved him to do for her.

To have good teamwork you need to communicate with each other about what you like and don't like about your play. My assumption in writing this book is that many couples haven't recognized play as being an aspect of their relationship that needs such regular attention. Like a good sexual relationship, play needs to be cultivated and both partners have to be willing to be involved.

Learn about Yourself

I've tried to make clear that you don't have to have it all together in order to have a good relationship. You also don't have to be free of neurotic traits in order to play. What you and your partner do need is a willingness to continue to learn about yourselves. I don't believe that every fantasy need be analyzed, every playful remark dissected for its hidden meaning. But when you relax your guard and allow yourself to be spontaneous, there is always the chance that you or your partner will feel uncomfortable about what comes out. It's important that you can talk about what happened and what may be making you uptight.

Jim and Renata had originally gone into couples therapy for help with their "communication problem" and to clarify the nature of their commitment. Both of them had had emotionally difficult childhoods with alcoholic parents and as a result were deeply mistrustful of intimacy. After several months of treatment, at one of their sessions, Jim jokingly referred to Renata as looking like a "praying

*mantis," ostensibly because of the intent gaze she
directed at him. This comment reminded Renata of
an incident that had occurred on a Sunday afternoon
a few weeks before while they had been playfully wrestling on the grass. Jim had called her a
"spider." At the time, she had felt vaguely troubled
by this name but had put it out of her mind. During
their therapy session they were both able to associate
to these nicknames. Renata could identify with the
praying mantis insofar as she wanted revenge on her
father by emotionally injuring men, while Jim could
begin to see that his negative nicknames came out of
a deep fear of powerful women.*

The next couple illustrates what can occur if couples are
not open to learning from their play:

*After a lovely day having a picnic at Golden Gate
Park, Kate and Nick had come home and started to
make love. They were relaxed, loving, and passionate. As Nick nuzzled and sucked on her nipples, Kate
drifted into a fantasy. She felt very turned on and
aware that she was making love. At the same time,
she felt that she was nursing, giving to her man in a
way that she had never done before. "Drink," she
said softly. Nick hesitated a moment, then continued
making love. But there was a tension between them.*

*Later, Nick told her he didn't like the idea that he
was a baby sucking on her breasts. It made him feel
less manly. Kate was hurt but said she wouldn't say
something like that again. They never talked about it
after that, and their lovemaking was subdued for
some time.*

My sense is that Kate's fantasy was so intolerable to
Nick because of his own conflicts about dependency and
perhaps also because it seemed incestuous to him. Unfortu-

nately, this couple couldn't deal directly with Nick's discomfort, and their relationship suffered as a result. The more you can both adopt an attitude of learning from problems that arise during play, the more leeway you will have to play in the future. You are bound to come up against inhibitions at some point; what matters most is how you deal with them.

In addition to facing and learning from your mutual *mishegoss* when it inadvertently makes an appearance, you can also actively seek to become better acquainted with your inner lives. You might, for instance, keep a dream diary, or while alone with your partner in bed or at the beach try to fantasize. At first, you may need to have a structured game. For instance, instead of playing Twenty Questions, you can think of some person (including yourself) and then have your partner ask, "If you were a fruit (or an animal or a song) what would you be?" It's then up to you to think of the closest metaphor in that category. Through a series of questions of this type, your partner can gradually develop a feeling for who the mystery person might be. You and your partner can also develop a mutual fantasy in which you pretend to view the world as if you were an animal or an inanimate object. When with your partner around a lot of other people, you can share your fantasies about what their true relationships with each other might be, or while on a walk, imagine new uses for the objects you see around you. The purpose of all these exercises is to make your shared fantasy life more robust. With time, you may find that both of you are able to do this kind of sharing spontaneously.

A Modern Myth

Every culture has its own stories that explain its beliefs and practices and suggest a link between the experience of its most lowly citizen with the tragedies and heroic deeds of our ancestors. Some of these myths derive from actual events, but they are also much elaborated by creative imagination. Whether real or imagined, the myths endure because they provide a familiar way to see things that makes sense. While some myths enrich our experience of life, others may prevent us from grasping more complete truths. All couples have their own idiosyncratic myths, but many of them are the stereotyped legacy of earlier years, often embodied in parents' favorite sayings. Thus one woman told me that, despite herself, she continued to live by her martyred mother's motto, "You have to suffer to be beautiful." Similarly, many children of alcoholic parents and grandparents wind up marrying alcoholics whom they vainly seek to rescue, as if destined to live out or undo the sins of their ancestors. One woman related to me that her need to continue to live out this myth was captured by her grandmother's well-worn phrase "You made your bed, now lie in it."

It's important that you learn about such destructive myths, which may have all the more power because you're not aware of them. Couples also get into trouble when they lose touch with the richer meanings of even their mundane moments and fail to develop new myths and metaphors from their personal experience that could enrich their relationship. As Anaïs Nin so beautifully put it, "The personal life, deeply lived, always expands into truths beyond itself."

To no small degree we are stuck with our culture's myths about the love of men and women. We have myths about what happens when people fall in love, and how natural and easy it's supposed to be. We have an old myth about marriage being "until death do us part" as well as a new myth that's rapidly taking its place: that marriages inevitably end in disenchantment. There's also a myth that play disappears as couples mature, and that if it persists at all, it's a sign of neurotic conflict. But I wonder whether we've sold play too short. Perhaps, for instance, laughter is not just a flight from something else, another secondhand emotion, but a *final* emotion. Like anger or tears, or orgasm, it is an irreducible human need. If this be true, play, which after all is laughter's consort and midwife, may be too precious for us to give up at any age.

I suggest that as we reassess our beliefs about marriage and play, the Greek myth of Cupid and Psyche is worth a closer look.

Once upon a time there was a woman named Psyche, whose beauty was beyond words, or, as they said in those days, her face could have launched a lot of ships. In fact, she was such a knockout that the Goddess of Love, Aphrodite, became jealous and called upon her son, Eros (a.k.a., Cupid), to cause Psyche to fall in love with the most repulsive man he could find. Aphrodite thought that this was just the sort of mischief that Eros would enjoy—after all, he was an incorrigible prankster who took pleasure in fomenting adultery and ill-starred love affairs with his magic arrows. Unfortunately for Aphrodite, Eros's behavior was always unpredictable: he accidentally pricks himself with one of his arrows and falls in love with Psyche himself. Psyche is smitten too and becomes pregnant.

Not unlike modern couples, these lovers have to endure many trials, some caused by Psyche's family, some by their own faults of character. To make matters worse, Eros's mother, who can't tolerate that he has become a man, does everything she can to come between them. A meddlesome God, known for his interest in dreams and slips of the tongue, reproaches her about this:

"Some sex goddess! You're the one who's always saying 'Make love, not war!' But as soon as your son gets the hots for some luscious doll, you think it's abnormal and try to interfere. After all, from whom do you think he learned about the birds and the bees? I know some guy named Oedipus whose parents really messed him up by acting like this."

Aphrodite, who clearly has never been in psycho-analysis, rejects these insights into her unconscious and pursues Psyche with unrelenting wrath. She even considers having her arch enemy, Sobriety, knock the pricks off Eros's (sic) arrows and snuff out his (sic) torch. In desperation, Eros asks Zeus, the head of this motley celestial throng, to intervene on his be-half. After Eros promises to procure a heavenly groupie for him too, Zeus calls together the entire Divine Council and issues this proclamation:

"My fellow Gods and Goddesses. We all know Eros is an adorable but impossible brat. He's con-stantly creating romance in people's everyday lives. Couples are always falling in love instead of advanc-ing Western civilization. Well, I've decided that the only way to keep this romantic nonsense within bounds is to marry him off. He's seduced some girl named Psyche. Let him play around as much as he wants, so long as he does it with his wife."

In other words, from now on, son, you'll be playing for keeps.

It is said by one ancient authority that this tale was actu-ally made up by a half-demented and drunken old woman, but, if so, at least one half of her was very wise: there are truths in this ancient myth for modern times. Arranged marriages have since gone out of style. We no longer have the gods or our parents to blame for our marital choices and troubles. But although unrestrained, immature playful-ness can cause all manner of problem in adult relation-ships, Eros is still a god of love. There is also one last detail from the Greek myth that I should mention. Eros and Psyche have a big wedding and in time she bears a child—a daughter whose name is Pleasure. The Greeks incorpo-rated play into marriage, suggesting, perhaps, that each is enriched by the other.

Notes

References and Quotations

1. William Betcher, "Intimate Play and Marital Adaptation," *Psychiatry* 44 (1981): 13–33.

2. Konrad Lorenz, *King Solomon's Ring* (New York: Thomas Y. Crowell, 1981), pp. 128–29.

3. Caroline Loizos, "Play Behaviour in Higher Primates: A Review," in Desmond Morris, ed., *Primate Ethology* (Chicago: Aldine, 1967), p. 183.

4. Jerome Bruner, "Nature and Uses of Immaturity," *American Psychologist* 27 (1972).

5. Sigmund Freud, "Beyond the Pleasure Principle" (1920), in *Standard Edition,* Vol. 18 (London: Hogarth).

6. D. W. Winnicott, *Playing and Reality* (New York: Basic Books, 1971).

7. H. V. Dicks, "Object Relations Theory and Marital Studies," *British Journal of Medical Psychology* 35 (1963).

8. Verrier Elwin, *The Baiga* (London: John Murray, 1939).

9. *Ibid.*

10. Kuan Tao-Sheng, untitled poem quoted in Theodor Reik, *Of Love and Lust* (New York: Farrar, Straus, 1949), p. 73.

11. Stendhal (Marie-Henri Beyle), *On Love,* trans. C. K. Scott-Moncrieff (New York: Liveright, 1947).

12. James Miller, *The Wedded Life* (Philadelphia: Presbyterian Board of Education, 1886).

13. L. N. Fowler, *Marriage, Its History and Ceremonies* (New York: S. R. Wells, 1855).

14. O. S. Fowler, *Matrimony* (Boston, 1859).

15. T. M. Coan, "To Marry or Not to Marry," *The Galaxy* 7 (1869): 493–500.

16. John L. Brandt, *Marriage and the Home* (Chicago: Laird and Lee, 1892).

17. Harry Stack Sullivan, *The Interpersonal Theory of Psychiatry* (New York: W. W. Norton, 1953).

18. Henri Bergson, *Laughter: An Essay on the Meaning of the Comic*, trans. C. Bereton and F. Rothwell (London: Macmillan, 1911).

19. Clellan Ford and Frank Beach, *Patterns of Sexual Behavior* (New York: Harper and Bros., 1951).

20. Daniel Defoe, *The Use and Abuse of the Marriage Bed* (London: T. Warner, 1727).

21. Alice B. Stockham, *Karezza* (Chicago: Leonidas Publishing Company, 1896.)

22. T. H. Van de Velde, *Ideal Marriage: Its Physiology and Technique* (New York: Random House, 1961).

23. John E. Eichenlaub, *The Marriage Art* (New York: Dell, 1961).

24. Sigmund Freud, *Totem and Taboo* (1913), in *Standard Edition*, Vol. 13 (London: Hogarth, 1961).

25. Ivan Boszormenyi-Nagy, *Invisible Loyalties*.

26. *The Technique and Practice of Psychoanalysis*, Vol. 1 (New York: International Universities Press, 1967).

27. Sigmund Freud, "Humour" (1927), in *Standard Edition*, Vol. 21 (London: Hogarth, 1961).

28. *Redbook* (November 1982): 80.

29. Suzannah Lessard, *The New Yorker* (September 26, 1977): 27–28.

30. Desmond Morris, *Patterns of Reproductive Behavior* (New York: McGraw-Hill, 1970).

31. Arnold van Gennep, *The Rites of Passage* (Chicago: University of Chicago Press, 1960).

32. Johan Huizinga, *Homo Ludens: The Play Element in Culture* (London: Routledge, 1949).

33. Leo Rosten, *The Joys of Yiddish* (New York: Pocket Books, 1970), p. 54.

34. Georg Simmel, *The Sociology of Georg Simmel,* trans. Kurt Wolff (New York: Free Press, 1950).

35. Theodor Reik, *Listening with the Third Ear* (New York: Grove Press, 1948).

36. Herbert Otto, *More Joy in Your Marriage* (New York: Hawthorn Books, 1969).

37. Wilhelm Stekel, *Sexual Aberrations* (1930), Vol. 1 (New York: Liveright, 1971).

38. *National Coalition on Television Violence News* 6:1–2 (1985).

39. Sigmund Freud, "Humour" (1927), in *Standard Edition,* Vol. 21 (London: Hogarth, 1961).

375

376